FAULKNER
The House Divided

ERIC J. SUNDQUIST is associate professor of English at the University of California, Berkeley. He is the author of *Home as Found: Authority and Genealogy in Nineteenth-Century American Literature* and the editor of *American Realism: New Essays* (also published by Johns Hopkins).

FAULKNER

the house divided

ERIC J. SUNDQUIST

JOHNS HOPKINS UNIVERSITY PRESS
Baltimore and London

The Johns Hopkins University Press, Baltimore, Maryland 21218
The Johns Hopkins Press Ltd., London

Chapter two appears in slightly different form in William E. Cain, ed.,
Philosophical Approaches to Literature (Lewisburg, Pa.: Bucknell University Press, 1982).

Library of Congress Cataloging in Publication Data

Sundquist, Eric J.
  Faulkner: the house divided.

  Includes bibliographical references and index.
  1. Faulkner, William, 1897–1961 — Criticism and
interpretation. 2. Race relations in literature.
3. Miscegenation in literature. I. Title.
PS3511.A86Z9735 1983   813'.52   82–8923
ISBN 0-8018-2898-8   AACR2

to the memory of
LAURENCE B. HOLLAND

Contents

Preface

M Y TITLE, *Faulkner: The House Divided,* refers to the sectional conflict over slavery that grew into the Civil War and defines aspects of Faulkner's novels on racial conflict dealt with in the second part of the book. More immediately, it defines a division I have made, within the larger context of Faulkner's fiction, between the three major novels that preceded his discovery of a theme emblematic of the combined passion, fear, and promise of racial conflict — the problem of miscegenation — and the three great novels that discovery produced.

Faulkner did not, quite obviously, suddenly discover that the issue of race was at the center of the South's troubled history and its convulsive contemporary experience; at the least, it was implicit in much of his earlier work. What he discovered were the visionary powers the problem of race was capable of engaging as it became, over the course of his career, the definitive crisis of twentieth-century American social history and the violently explicit subject of his fiction. The risk in pursuing Faulkner's more sensational themes is that they may come to seem simply that — perverse distortions of historical actualities. Faulkner did not set out to be a historical novelist in the strictest of terms; yet it is only when we lose sight of the climate of social thought and legal proscription in which he wrote, a climate sometimes difficult to imagine so few years later, that his fiction seems out of proportion to the troubling realities of race relations in America. On the contrary, the least attention to that climate and to Faulkner's native traditions reveals that there is no dimension of American history more subject to — and whose essential reality is more constituted by — distortion, hallucination, and utter contradiction, as contemporary events and ideas continue to confirm all too frequently.

While Faulkner has, on the basis of his fiction and his public statements alike, been variously denounced as a racist and admired as a civil rights advocate, and while no one in his right mind has ignored Faulkner's treatment of difficult racial issues, there is surprisingly little in the critical literature about him that has suggested the complexity, in both emotional and social terms, of his imaginative commitment or examined it within the relevant historical contexts. Given the fiction he wrote and the violent, actual tensions it reflects, it is perhaps entirely appropriate that judgments about Faulkner should be hard to make. It is not my intention to make those judgments easier but to suggest ways to account for their abiding difficulty.

The methodology of this book, which often depends in part two on reconstructing a context for Faulkner's fiction out of historical experience, contemporary literature, or political and sociological documents, and which sometimes depends in part one on pointing out latent anticipations of later, more explicit treatments of racial conflict, may strike some readers as unwarranted or simply wrong. Of course I believe it is neither of these; not only that, I would rather think that it is the only way in which Faulkner's power and significance can be made to emerge. The predominant mode in Faulkner criticism has been formalistic — usually, given his subject matter, in the extreme. There are many factors involved in this tendency, to be sure, including Faulkner's modernist pronouncements about his art, his ready availability to endless explication, and his regional affinities with influential spokesmen for the New Criticism. But another factor (not by any means separate from these) would have to be ideological: simply put, that Faulkner's own recalcitrance about desegregation (for those who have agreed) or the embarrassment caused by his public remarks (for those who have not) has often discouraged his readers from speaking critically or even historically about questions of racial conflict in his fiction.

Light in August and *Absalom, Absalom!* are Faulkner's most important novels, while *Go Down, Moses* may be said to represent the extraordinary strain his moral vision and fictional design came under as he drove to the heart of the South's experience, at once casting back to its originating myths and confronting the increasingly intolerable burdens those myths had to bear nearly a century later. The strain is both formal and actual; that is, Faulkner's best work reflects a turbulent search for fictional forms in which to contain and express the ambivalent feelings and projected passions that were his as an author and as an American in the South. Faulkner's public statements on desegregation from the late 1940s forward are notorious, but his recalcitrance is everywhere tempered with a sympathetic understanding that, however unfortunately it represented itself on occasion, is not simply racist; in any event, the role of public spokesman, thrust upon Faulkner by the coincidence of his fame and his country's accelerating crisis before and after *Brown* v. *Board of Education* in 1954, is overshadowed by the prior achievements of his fiction. That fiction is extremely ambivalent as well, but there lies its importance as a measure of the nation's most fratricidal war as it became extended into more complex and frustrating forms.

Faulkner's earlier fiction afforded him the ways to take that measure by allowing the development of his authorial voice and difficult narrative forms. While one could, of course, trace that development from the start of his career and follow it to his death, I have restricted myself for the most part to his best works, with brief treatments of *Sartoris* and *Intruder in the Dust,* the two novels that significantly frame the others. Other patterns could be discerned and other arguments made; it is nevertheless true, however, that much of Faulkner's work is of interest only because he wrote it. (The exceptions of note here are *The Hamlet* and "Old Man," his best comic works, which are outside the scope of my interests.) My attention, then, is largely divided between the three novels in which he developed his characteristic fictional forms and the three in which he extended those forms into novels of major social and historical significance.

Because they deal with Faulkner's best writing on his most important subjects, the chapters of part two are relatively continuous; those of part one are somewhat more formalistic to the extent that, though they intend to create the context for Faulkner's dramatic explorations of racial conflict and to indicate his development of those themes, they concentrate on the distinctive features of each novel. In the cases of *As I Lay Dying,* Faulkner's most crafted and formally experimental novel, and *Sanctuary,* his foray into hard-boiled naturalism, this presents no significant difficulty. *The Sound and the Fury* offers rather a different problem, however, for the novel has assumed such a central place in estimations of Faulkner's career (including his own) that it can hardly be treated otherwise. My purpose is not to deny that importance but simply to suggest that it is indeed paradoxical — that while the novel is not his best, his whole fictional effort, even the great design he envisioned, must nevertheless be judged in relation to it for reasons both formal and thematic. *The Sound and the Fury* will always be there, like the sudden discovery it is; likewise, the entirety of Faulkner's work will never cease to be of interest, not least because he worked so hard to force it into a single imposing configuration. But the novels that demand our attention now, as they always will, are the ones in which the nation's most tragic and defining historical experience found its appropriately convulsive forms of expression and in which Faulkner became the great writer he has always been recognized to be.

Acknowledgments

T HE critical attention devoted to Faulkner has been immense and shows no signs of decreasing. Anyone who writes about him is indebted, as I am, to the scholarly and biographical work of Joseph Blotner, Cleanth Brooks, Malcolm Cowley, Michael Millgate, and David Minter. Beyond that, I should like to say that I have benefited especially from the critical studies of Faulkner by Irving Howe, John T. Irwin, Myra Jehlen, and Donald M. Kartiganer. Among the historical studies I have drawn on, the work of George Fredrickson, Winthrop Jordan, and C. Vann Woodward has been of particular value.

For their generous responses — in approval, caution, and dissent — to my entire manuscript, I am grateful to Richard Bridgman, William Cain, Norman Grabo, Carolyn Porter, and Michael Rogin; and for their equally generous suggestions about various portions of it, I want to thank Mitchell Breitwieser, Richard Brodhead, Sharon Cameron, Evan Carton, Robert Caserio, Eric Cheyfitz, Frederick Crews, Basil De Pinto, George Forgie, Robert Pinsky, Thomas Schaub, C. Vann Woodward, and David Wyatt. Marcy McGaugh deserves special thanks for her excellent typing. For support of the kind that is very special indeed, I thank Tania, who shared it all.

A fellowship from the American Council of Learned Societies, supported in part by funds from the National Endowment for the Humanities, as well as a research grant from the University of California, Berkeley, made possible the writing of this book.

My greatest debt, intangibly reflected but everywhere felt in these pages, is recorded in the dedication.

part 1

chapter 1

The Myth of
The Sound and the Fury

T HERE is some irony in the fact that Faulkner's deserved public recognition came at a time (the late 1940s and on to his death) when his best work was a decade old and he was writing some of the most disappointing fiction a major novelist could conceivably write. Little that he produced after *Go Down, Moses,* including *Intruder in the Dust,* the novel that guaranteed that recognition, merits sustained attention. The larger irony is that once we begin backtracking to see where he went wrong we must return to the novel often taken to be his masterpiece. With fanfare Faulkner surely would have relished, and did his best to facilitate, *The Sound and the Fury* (1929) has become a myth. No one would want to deny its importance, but it is worthwhile considering where, exactly, that importance lies. The novel has been so thoroughly explicated that it should prove more useful to read it with an eye to its place at the starting point of Faulkner's career and in the larger self-imposed design of his fiction, a design one may certainly admire without taking altogether seriously.

The Sound and the Fury is not, of course, the starting point of Faulkner's career. He had already written three novels: *Soldier's Pay* (1926), a good postwar novel, which unevenly rivals Dos Passos and Hemingway; *Mosquitoes* (1927), a dismal tract on aestheticism; and *Sartoris* (1929), a minor historical novel much improved by editorial revisions that Faulkner had little to do with. Beyond that, he had written two volumes worth of *fin de siècle* poetry and a handful of short stories, some of which were later incorporated into novels, or — in the case of *The Sound and the Fury* — blossomed into whole novels, or got added to others and then posed as novels. Without *The Sound and the Fury* and the work that followed, however, few of these earlier efforts would get more than a glance. And there is reason to believe that without Faulkner's work of the next ten years *The Sound and the Fury* would itself seem a literary curiosity, an eccentric masterpiece of experimental methods and "modernist" ideas. This states the worst case, as it were, and proposes the unknowable. But Faulkner's insistent announcements (to choose one of many examples) that the novel was "the most gallant, the most magnificent failure" of all his failed works,[1] and that he therefore loved it most, make inevitable its glamorous position at the dawn of his creation. This is not to say that *The Sound and the Fury* is not a superior novel but simply that it prefigures many problems in Faulkner's later fiction and is far too likely to appear the monumental work against which his other fiction must be judged.

Faulkner vigorously promoted this view (and apparently subscribed to it himself), and any reading of his career in whole or in part will necessarily depend on it. One may, nevertheless, accept the novel as his moment of discovered genius without concluding that it is the key to the treasure of Yoknapatawpha. It would not be apparent until 1945, when Faulkner wrote the appendix to the novel, or until after his death, when two versions of an introduction he wrote and discarded in 1933 were published, what a burden the novel would have to carry. The introduction says more eloquently what Faulkner had always said in public — that the novel was a wonderful failure, a story so great that it could not be put into words, and had produced in him an ecstasy he had never been able to recapture; but the appendix exposes something more unsettling — that the muse of Yoknapatawpha was in decline, that her author was struggling to extend his great design out of any odds and ends he could dream up. The appendix adds, in the ponderous, often absurd prose that is characteristic of Faulkner's late style, accounts of the Compson ancestors and brief surveys of the later lives of the novel's characters. Far from illuminating the novel, except in the interests of family chronicle and the retrospective purpose of Faulkner's design, it everywhere clashes with the novel, whose signal virtues create a world of timeless hallucination in which, when they are right, the words float lightly, silently through the novel's mysterious nets of consciousness, falling each into its ordered place.

The novel's appendix first appeared as a set piece in Malcolm Cowley's *The Portable Faulkner,* and Faulkner claimed then that, had he written it for the novel to begin with, "the whole thing would have fallen into pattern like a jigsaw puzzle when the magician's wand touched it." He also remarked, however, that it was "a piece without implications," and later, when challenged about its apparent contradictions to the novel, he replied that the inconsistencies prove "the book is still alive after 15 years, and being still alive is growing, changing." [2] These confusing claims are entirely relevant to the larger problem of Faulkner's fictional design, in which novels simultaneously stand alone, contradict one another, or (it is said) fall into magic patterns from which no one piece of the puzzle could possibly be removed. Faulkner insisted that the appendix, when added to the novel, should appear at the beginning rather than the end (it has been published both ways) and described it at once as "the key to the whole book" and "an obituary." [3] Analogously, the more he wrote — from *Absalom, Absalom!* on, say, after he had actually drawn a map of Yoknapatawpha — the more his fiction resembled new keys to the kingdom and a record of its creative decline toward death. Nowhere is this more apparent than in *Requiem for a Nun* (1951), where Faulkner attempts to extend the story of *Sanctuary's* main attraction in the form of a play and indulges in long, cascading prose accounts of early Yoknapatawpha in which the ancestors of many of the characters and events of his fictional career appear in a patently legendary story of The Creation. Like the appendix to *The Sound and the Fury,* these accounts intertwine fine anecdotes and exceptionally bad writing, and they indicate how fragile and disordered the vision had become. But they also present a special kind of problem to readers: If the very essence of Faulkner's design is that it will remain incomplete, if the design (like that of Thomas Sutpen or the South itself) is flawed to start with, and if its whole development expresses a falling away from that which can never be reliably or precisely articulated, how then are works that claim such failures as virtues to be rejected?

The problem, of course, is not an imposing one: bad writing is bad writing, and some of Faulkner's is very bad indeed. It can be recognized as such, just as his great design, which will continue to attract encomiums and explication, can be ignored novel by novel. Yet the risk in ignoring it altogether, a risk *The Sound and the Fury* with its drummed-up appendix perfectly represents, is that the problems inherent in the greater design so resemble the problems with individual novels, and so much become part of their avowed thematic material, that one is left incapable of exact judgment if they are dismissed. There is little need now for more detailed analyses of the Faulkner canon or further exposés of his philosophical vision. The chapters that compose the second part of this study will take up social and historical contexts that are in need of more consideration: ones in which, to be precise, Faulkner becomes a great novelist. His explorations of the issues of race conflict and miscegenation, while they are implicit in earlier works, only come to the fore in and after *Light in August,* and one may justly divide his career in two, as I have done, recognizing one period to be devoted to a study of novelistic forms and the other to carrying those developed forms into a domain of greatest resonance. Moreover, *The Sound and the Fury,* as my reading of it will suggest, assumes just such a position of divided sensibility when one begins to examine its place in Faulkner's career.

There was not, of course, and there did not need to be any such strict division in Faulkner's own mind, and the latter portion of his career is in certain respects an extended, romantically failed attempt to deny that there were any disjunctions whatsoever. These kinds of characterizations may in any event seem somewhat arbitrary; others could be made and justified, but it needs to be emphasized, for example, how different *The Sound and the Fury* appears after it is put in the context of *Absalom, Absalom!* The powerful and instructive cross-references the later novel makes possible are what Faulkner's whole design depends on in more demanding ways; but leaving aside *The Unvanquished,* an addendum to *Sartoris* primarily of veiled autobiographical interest, and the sequential Snopes trilogy, this is the only instance where anything decisive or productive gets accomplished by comparison. In *Sanctuary,* to take a striking example, Faulkner's own revisions demonstrate that the novel, far from being ruined, is vastly improved by his discarding those sections that most connect the character of Horace Benbow to *Sartoris* and particularly its original version, *Flags in the Dust;* whereas *Requiem for a Nun,* at the opposite extreme, depends on *Sanctuary* and fragments of other novels to such an extent as to be a vacuous charade by itself. In this case and others, Faulkner's experimentation simply runs wild, as though its very purpose were to devise insurmountable dangers and create a context in which the strained forms and rhetorical excesses of earlier novels would appear to have been marvelously checked at the point of utmost distention.

In this respect, the great design reproduces the structure of many individual novels, where characters and stories, however the plots may strive to entangle them, often seem to collide or to stand in taut juxtaposition; and while this method may produce superlative results at the contained, local level of the novel, its magnification through the span of a career makes the dubious virtues of disorder and conflict far too prominent. (What it also makes prominent is the apparent necessity of the design, for with the exception of *Soldier's Pay,* the novels having little or nothing to do with Yoknapatawpha — *Mosquitoes, Pylon, The Wild Palms,* and *A Fable* — are also the least successful.) At extremity, as in *Go Down, Moses,* stories are nearly crushed together on the assumption that recurring themes and names, and the forces of rhetoric, can be made to dramatize their connection; and it is surely no coincidence that this novel marks by its precariously extenuated form the end of Faulkner's major work, as though his creative powers, after a final, draining surge, had broken under the pressures of the envisioned design. Like Cooper and Hawthorne before him, Faulkner set out to create a native American tradition, in his case by creating a whole country and people, and proceeded to do so on the modernist grounds prepared by Eliot and Joyce where tradition was a fabrication, a false and broken pattern of ruins. As these intentions became superimposed on the lost dream of the South, the design fell apart — what else could it do? And what could Faulkner do but continue adding to it, all the while assuring readers and critics that it was supposed to fall apart — what else could it do?

Despite such caveats, however, and despite his own cunning complicity in the authorial game of romantic failure, Faulkner wrote great fiction — the greatest when he wrote of the South as an explicit topic (as distinct from using it for regional atmosphere, which he always did) and, perhaps paradoxically, when his own anxieties about the value of the fictional forms he had chosen were most apparent. There is no doubt, to borrow from Martin Green's irreverent attack, that Faulkner produced "engines of mental torture, crucifixions of literary sensibility" [4] — *The Sound and the Fury* is one of them — but he did so in a fashion that, at its better moments, created unseen worlds of unimagined words, and at its best perfectly accorded with the single most agonizing experience of his region and his nation: the crisis and long aftermath of American slavery. The formal explorations his finest early novels engaged in were preparation for things to follow, a search for a way to say things that had not been said but desperately needed saying, things that for good reason could barely be said. What he had to say is implicit in *The Sound and the Fury;* what is remarkable, and what constitutes the novel's central drama, is the difficulty he had in saying it at all.

F AULKNER'S achievement, as Robert Penn Warren has written, was foremost to articulate truths about the South and Southerners that had long been "lying speechless in their experience" and to confront turbulent issues that "would not have been available, been visible in fact, without the technique" he employed.[5] This is certainly true, though it would only become visible some years after *The Sound and the Fury*, where what is speechless in the Southern experience nearly remains so and what is made available by Faulkner's technique is not immediately clear. Faulkner, however, had already articulated one dimension of the Southern experience, its contemporary estrangement from the heroic drama of the Confederate past, in *Sartoris*. The earlier novel anticipates many of Faulkner's themes and creates a number of characters that would reappear throughout his fiction. In particular, it anticipates a problem Faulkner would never fully resolve but, rather, would make the implied subject of all his work: that the estrangement of present from past is absolutely central to the Southern experience and often creates the pressured situation in which the past becomes an ever more ghostly and gloriously imposing model to the same extent that — like the childhood of a doomed, beautiful girl — it cannot be recaptured, relived, or even clearly remembered.

It is worth remarking in this regard that *Sartoris*, though it is not a great novel, is nonetheless emblematic of Faulkner's larger design as it explores the dilemma that is offered as the best possible evidence of the disjointed mind of the South: its inability to involve the spent dreams of the past with the pale realities of the present in dramatically convincing ways. In *Go Down, Moses* and *Intruder in the Dust* such failures of dramatic coherence and moral vision are so close to being the very material of the novels that arguments against them entail a certain risk; in this case, as in others, one must simply recognize the point at which mimetic disorder, in either moral or structural terms, destroys the coherence of the fictional design. In the case of *Sartoris*, the risk is a more peculiar one, for the same feature that makes the novel appear inadequate in its development, the missing or weakly characterized generations of the Sartoris family, is precisely what reveals the painful gap between the Civil War and World War I, between the wasted heroics of the first Sartorises and the suicidal courage of their descendants, and even — as it would turn out — between Faulkner's own early modernism and his gradual turning toward the materials of classic American fiction.

Beyond that, the original version, *Flags in the Dust*, was marred by excessive attention to the character of Horace Benbow and his incestuous attachment to his sister (a problem that would recur in the original version of *Sanctuary*). Faulkner's editor, Ben Wasson, complained that *Flags in the Dust* was six books in one — a charge that might also be leveled, say, at *Light in August* or *Go Down,*

Moses — and set about the revisions that made *Sartoris* as good as it is. When Faulkner reflected on the novel and its revisions two years later, he began to speak of it in terms that only the work of the intervening years could have made possible:

> I realized for the first time that I had done better than I knew and the long work I had had to create opened before me and I felt myself surrounded by the limbo in which the shady visions, the host which stretched half formed, waiting each with its portion of that verisimilitude which is to bind into a whole the world which for some reason I believe should not pass utterly out of the memory of man, and I contemplated those shady but ingenious shapes by reason of whose labor I might reaffirm the impulses of my own ego in this actual world without stability, with a lot of humbleness, and I speculated on time and death and wondered if I had invented the world to which I should give life or if it had invented me, giving me an illusion of greatness.[6]

Aside from the botched prose and rather premature self-estimation, these remarks — almost mystically — allow a glimpse of the creative turmoil that did indeed seem to possess and invent Faulkner for over a decade after *Sartoris,* a period during which he worked off and on, as though "demon-driven," with the "insane fury" he would later say a writer requires.[7] Although *Sartoris* is his most autobiographical novel, the world of the South that had truly "invented" Faulkner would only be re-created in bits and pieces, novel by novel, as successive personae and their families appeared. Over that period Faulkner would probe more deeply the limbo of "shady visions" from which he and his contemporary South had sprung; in *The Sound and the Fury,* written in part in the insane fury of his dejection over the problems and reception of *Sartoris,* he drove straight to the heart of that limbo but revealed only a suggestion of the shady visions it contained.

Even though the essay is a barely revised sketch, Faulkner's remarks on *Sartoris* suggest his fundamental cloudiness as a philosophical thinker; such ideas, of course, are not where his importance as a writer lies, and the novels most given to intellectual argument (*Mosquitoes, Intruder in the Dust,* parts of the Snopes trilogy, and *A Fable*) are striking disasters. Because *Sartoris* contains more able thinking about the dilemma of the South than any of his first major novels, however, it presents a peculiar point of departure for the work of the next ten or twelve years. On turning from *Sartoris* to *The Sound and the Fury* one feels, in effect, that thought has been declared impossible and ideas irrelevant, that "the mind of the South," which W. J. Cash later set out to define as a romantic continuum in a book by that name, rests rather, as C. Vann Woodward has observed of Cash, "on the hypothesis that the South has no mind."[8] There is some danger in approaching Faulkner from the perspective of Southern intellectual history, and, as the allusions to Faulkner among historians suggest, there is only one issue about which he has much to tell us: the issue of race and its many implied or visibly actual dilemmas, whose precise nature is that they can seldom be thought about clearly but instead leap instantly into the realm of hallucination. Of course there is good reason in this case to suggest that the *one* issue is *the* issue that determines and defines all others; and it is surely no mistake that Cash's *The Mind of the South* is most stridently powerful on the subjects of race hysteria and the correlative myth of a fallen aristocratic dream, just as Faulkner's most important novels revolve around the same subjects, for Cash and Faulkner are both romantics *manqué* — that is to say, severe critics of the romantic consciousness they feel most defines the essence of the South, to which they are enchantingly drawn and from which they recoil in horror.

While there is no doubt that *The Sound and the Fury* is troubled by deep underlying issues, the most perplexing thing about the novel is the discrepancy between its merits and the burdensome interpretations it has inevitably had to support. It is read as an allegory of the South, an exposition of the Oedipal complex, an ironic enactment of Christ's agony, and a sustained philosophical meditation on Time. While it engages all of these issues, it illuminates none of them very exactly; rather — and here lies part of its strange magnificence — it engages these issues, allows them to invade the domain of the novel's arcane family drama, and disavows their capacity to bring the novel out of its own self-enclosing darkness. The "psychology" that is of most interest in the novel is not Benjy's or Quentin's or Jason's or Dilsey's, but the psychology of the novel as a form of containing consciousness, one that is self-contained and at the same time contains, by defining in subliminal projection, Faulkner's most significant accomplishments and their ultimate derangement. There is more to be said of this psychology, but we may note again that the "mind" the novel does not have — and will not have until Faulkner's career develops — the mind of "the South," is paradoxically the only one that fully explains Quentin's incestuous fascination with Caddy's purity and the novel's strange obsession with her.

T HE *Sound and the Fury* begins in the mind of an idiot. Faulkner's detractors have suggested that once he discovered this impossible world he never left it, that Benjy Compson is, ironically, his one great creation, or, at best, that the novel is a fine modernist experiment unrivaled by following novels, in which Faulkner became obsessed with white Negroes and the like. This is at least half wrong, for *The Sound and the Fury* is not Faulkner's best novel, but the paradox is this: its importance only appears in the larger context of novels to which it gives rise, and at that point it comes to seem indispensable. Here again the question is genetic, so to speak, for the novel is demonstrably about failed integrity — in the Compson family, the Southern dream, the novel as a conventional form, and the "mind" of the author. All of these issues, rightly enough, appear to converge in the mind of Benjy, and the rest of the novel is a slow extraction of attention from this originating abyss. Such a narrative development produces paradoxical effects that bear on, and reappear in, all of Faulkner's work, but their most salient feature in this case is a thorough devaluation of traditional novelistic plot or action.

Nearly everything that "happens" in the novel happens in the first section — and this is exactly what Faulkner, who largely created for readers the idolatrous admiration of Caddy Compson they have expressed, asks us to believe. The genetic myth of the novel — that "it began with the picture of the little girl's muddy drawers, climbing that tree to look in the parlor window" at her grandmother's funeral [9] — has so overwhelmed the novel itself that one no longer questions its relevance, even though there is good reason to do so. One might rather say that this scene stands in the same relation to Caddy as Caddy does to the entire novel, for we find out so little about her that we might conclude, on the basis of the action of the novel, either that she is a tender-hearted tramp or that, because she is surrounded by every conceivable form of mental and emotional instability, her own actions are justifiably inevitable. But since Caddy is not a character but an idea, an obsession in the minds of her brothers, we cannot rightly be said to find out much at all about her. Caddy is "lost" psychologically and aesthetically as well as morally: she is the very symbol of loss in Faulkner's world — the loss of innocence, integrity, chronology, personality, and dramatic unity, all the problematic virtues of his envisioned artistic design. To Benjy she smells like trees, to Quentin she is would-be lover, to Jason she is the whore mother of a whore daughter, and to Faulkner she is at once "the sister which I did not have and the daughter which I was to lose," and "a beautiful and tragic little girl" who later becomes, apparently, the mistress of a Nazi officer in occupied France.[10] There is probably no major character in literature about whom we know so little in proportion to the amount of attention she receives. This is surely no objection to the novel, but it is quite certainly a measure of its drama, which is submerged to the point of invisibility.

Because the entire intent of *The Sound and the Fury* is to sequester modes of consciousness and formally depict them as incapable of responsive interaction, however, there may be no dramaturgical objection that can stand up on the grounds the novel presents. Its avowed strategy is to divide our attention among discrete modes of narrative revelation from which the novel's plot must be drawn over the course of several readings; once that is done — or even quite aside from it — we may then pay attention, respectively, to Benjy's libidinal creativity, Quentin's psychosis, Jason's satiric viciousness, or Dilsey's humble endurance. Holding together these discrete modes of narrative experience is the figure of the doomed girl; she lives in the formal vacuum of the novel, and in doing so she represents the still point, the "innocence" of mute action the four sections break away from as they dissolve into increasingly logical and coherent forms of narration. One has only to record the scene that Faulkner maintained was the heart of the novel —

> "All right." Versh said. "You the one going to get whipped. I aint." He went and pushed Caddy up into the tree to the first limb. We watched the muddy bottom of her drawers. Then we couldn't see her. We could hear the tree thrashing.

— to see how invisible Caddy truly is.[11] Despite its marvelously elliptical portrayal of vanishing innocence and its vaguely erotic suggestion of something "dirty," this scene, without Faulkner's repeated insistence on its centrality, would itself vanish into the novel's larger pattern of glimmering memories.

If one were determined to choose any descriptive scene as central, surely either the muddying of those drawers or the wake of Caddy's deflowering or particularly her wedding (which formalizes those earlier events) would be more obvious:

> *In the mirror she was running before I knew what it was. That quick, her train caught up over her arm she ran out of the mirror like a cloud, her veil swirling in long glints her heels brittle and fast clutching her dress onto her shoulder with the other hand, running out of the mirror the smells roses roses the voice that breathed o'er Eden. Then she was across the porch I couldn't hear her heels then in the moonlight like a cloud, the floating shadow of the veil running across the grass, into the bellowing. She ran out of her dress, clutching her bridal, into the bellowing.* [12]

Here, in this lyrical passage, is the wondrous center of the book — Caddy vanishing from the mirror of Quentin's narcissism into the wrenching, mindless vacuum of Benjy's bellowing: the death of Eden, Jefferson, April 1910; and the resurrection of the Edenic myth, Faulkner, 1929. But resurrection is yet to come (April 8, 1928): there is no rising without a fall, no fall without genesis, and it is eminently just, perhaps, that the scene Faulkner grew enamoured of should appear, in the novel itself, no more consequential than others and vanish into the creative past of created loss. The genetic myth must remain mysterious, and its focal point must be projected as the one instant, the one spark that produces a whole world without necessarily resembling or defining it.

This peculiar and powerful dilemma goes to the heart of the novel, for the "loss" of Caddy (wherever one pinpoints it) represents the crucial generative event in the book — in fact, the event that forecloses generation. It is the moment of discovered grief that brings death, actual and metaphorical, into the psychological worlds of Benjy and Quentin; it is the moment of potential but elusive tragedy, envisioned deep within the novel's mind, from which the increasingly furious and distorted saga of the Compsons follows; and it is the catalytic moment of frightening disturbance that Faulkner would spend the better part of his career trying to recapture and define by transfiguring into ever more convulsive and historically searching dimensions. Each fragment of a scene devoted to the memory of Caddy is charged with a sure passion, at once moving and inadequate, that derives from the fragmentation of the narrative form itself, as though her figure were receding, reappearing, and receding again in the acts of remembrance that create her doomed, ethereal life. Those scenes together often constitute so fine and so troubling a memory, and so render in prose the poetry Faulkner had never found in verse, that we may forget that much of the novel — including many of the larger scenes in which those acts of memory are embedded — appears driven to madness in the further attempt to sustain their power in dramatic form and symbolic meditation. Caddy's story, as Faulkner leaves us to divine it (and, I will suggest, as his later fiction would reimagine it), is stunning. But it is also the novel's essential paradox that the small, certain beauties of Caddy's remembered fall should seem thoroughly at odds with the rhetorical fever and philosophical bewilderment that event produced in her family and her creator, while at the same time appearing to be their distant, irrevocable cause.

The last two sections of the novel may be said to suppress its greatest event altogether, for Caddy there becomes more and more marginal and eventually disappears altogether from the novel's conscious attention. Caddy is "the past" to the extent that she defines remembered moments that have been transfigured into disembodied hallucinations of lost love for Benjy and Quentin, and fierce hatred of his entire family for Jason; and as she is "past," so she is as dead as Mrs. Compson makes her by ordering that her name never be spoken in the house, and as dead as Jason treats her by embezzling her money and castigating her equally promiscuous daughter. With the possible exception of the bitterly peripheral Mrs. Compson, Jason is the novel's most brilliantly drawn character, and there is reason to feel that the same motives that later led Faulkner to put Caddy in the arms of a Nazi also led him to release his disgust with the family he had created in the restrained rage of Jason. Though he is conniving and corrupt, and though Faulkner and others have routinely spoken of him as a classic villain, Jason no doubt expresses every honest reader's response to the Compson family: "Blood, I says, governors and generals. It's a damn good thing we never had any kings and presidents; we'd all be down there at Jackson chasing butterflies." [13] Without the edge of intimate hatred his narrative affords the novel, it would drift even further into psychological chaos and dramatic incoherence.

Yet the importance of Jason's section appears not simply in his brutal characterizations of his family — not, that is, in his lucid antipathy to their variously repelling personalities — but in the implied antipathy to the modes of narrative consciousness in which those personalities get presented. While Jason's wit forever fixes each of the novel's characters with penetrating sarcasm, its real value lies rather in its ability to reveal the necessity of a narrative consciousness that is capable — at last, it seems — of clear thought. Although his obsessions grow as well out of childhood betrayal, Jason's memories of the past are scant, and in each instance they lacerate those idealizations of unconscious frenzy the first two sections of the novel afford. His compulsive "I says," simmering with rage and maintaining the drive of his narration at a pace and a pitch furiously, mercenarily intent on making up for the lost time of childhood, stands in complete opposition to the chaotic first-person effusions of Benjy and Quentin; and his moral fervor, however disingenuous, immediately implies a reactionary aversion on Faulkner's part to the mindless riches of his first two central characters and to the claustrophobic forms of their narratives.

As though we were in danger of forgetting, Jason's pragmatic energy reminds us, among other things, that *The Sound and the Fury* is a novel, a fictional fabrication, and that despite Faulkner's apparent intentions it offers few philosophical ideas of lasting concern. When it does — in Quentin's speculations on time or Dilsey's experience of enduring salvation — it veers off into eccentricity at best, and at worst blooms into a grotesque caricature of its elementary symbolic structure: the death and resurrection of Christ. The novel is not an Easter vigil except by extraordinary sleight of hand or by sheer coincidence of dates. The Compsons inhabit the wasteland of Christian modernism Eliot had recently invented, to be sure, but this is scaffolding, not a stage; it is part of the novel's defunct mythology and has, with Faulkner's encouragement, become part of the myth of the novel. It is difficult to take seriously Quentin's memory of his father's teaching "that Christ was not crucified: he was worn away by a minute clicking of little wheels," or that "all men are just accumulations dolls stuffed with sawdust swept up from the trash heaps where all previous dolls had been thrown away the sawdust flowing from what wound in what side that not for me died not." And surely readers have only accepted the revival sermon of the "monkey" preacher in Dilsey's section because they are taken in by its pose of cathartic naturalism:

> And the congregation seemed to watch with its own eyes while the voice consumed him, until he was nothing and they were nothing and there was not even a voice but instead their hearts were speaking to one another in haunting measures beyond the need for words, so that when he came to rest against the reading desk, his monkey face lifted and his whole attitude that of a serene, tortured crucifix . . . Dilsey sat bolt upright, her hand on Ben's knee. Two tears slid down her fallen cheeks, in and out of the myriad coruscations of immolation and abnegation and time.[14]

As the conclusion of this passage demonstrates, the problem here, as so often in Quentin's case, is not that the emotion of the scene is improbable but that its expressionistic contortions are made to bear an inconceivable burden, a symbolic weight far out of keeping with the novel's expressed inability to imagine and sustain such opaque philosophical ideas. The timelessness of Dilsey's experience, the eschatological sublime of *Uncle Tom's Cabin,* validates the Christological structure of the plot only by declaring that, Negroes and idiots aside, it is of no real value whatsoever. Like the bloated, decaying bodies of Dilsey and Benjy with which we are confronted in the opening pages of section four, the book's typological vision, as though physically contorted by pressures originating deep within the mythical innocence of the book and of western civilization, inflates and bursts into dramatic parody and philosophical nonsense.

The more intently one examines any of the novel's philosophical positions or symbolic structures — most notably their correlative appearance in the ludicrous masque of the Passion — the more they reduce to seemingly unintentional parody or dissolve into a chaos of fragments. It could be argued that this is precisely the case, that the novel's strategy, in both dramatic and formal terms, is to portray a shattering of belief and to depict the urgent failure of modern consciousness to sustain any useful moral or temporal structures. One might then focus attention on the various symbolic patterns — mirrors, clocks, pear trees,

Caddy, water, mud, fire, funerals, more clocks, the Easter apparatus — and declare the novel a vast prose poem, an interpretation of dreams, or an extended essay on *symbolisme*. As Hugh Kenner rightly points out, however, Faulkner's essential strategy (which he flamboyantly admitted on any number of occasions) "was not to symbolize (a condensing device) but to expand, expand," and his work characteristically "prolongs what it cannot find a way to state with concision, prolongs it until, ringed and riddled with nuance, it is virtually camouflaged by patterns of circumstance." [15] Certainly, this is one of the primary effects of *The Sound and the Fury*, especially to the extent that the novel moves with deliberation from the static image-making capacity of Benjy's "mind" to increasingly conscious and compulsive first-person modes of narration, dwelling as last in the comparatively hyperbolic omniscience of the fourth section, where the crucifixion of the Compsons and the novel (and the reader) becomes most agonized. But it is just as certainly one of the novel's most paradoxical effects that, as it moves progressively out of its first frozen moments of lucid astonishment, a movement required to "tell the story," it also betrays its own proclaimed ideal and acquires the traits of bulging prose and crude, idiosyncratic symbolism Faulkner would become famous for, as though it were enacting its own deterioration and failure in the very course of getting the story told.

Another way to put this is to note that, once the plot of the novel is untangled, the first two sections give way almost entirely to similar but disconnected psychological and aesthetic problems. Benjy's section is compelling for the simple reason that it reduces the fictional vocabulary to a spare set of images that project, with kaleidoscopic accuracy, the whole "action" of the novel. Above all, his section is a masterpiece of controlled monotone, and its peculiar array of speech can only be construed as *interior dialogue*, for Benjy not only "says" nothing but can barely be said to think anything. The voices that appear, recollected at near random from some dozen enlightened moments of his existence, drop suspended into an area of consciousness that hauntingly resembles the pages of a novel, each act of speech punctuated by a full stop and a "said" almost without variation. It would not be unreasonable to suggest that Benjy is Faulkner's ideal narrator, the disembodied mode of consciousness he had in mind when he later told Malcolm Cowley that his method of composition was simply to "listen to the voices" and put down what they said, and that his desire (to borrow from a different context) was to "blue pencil everything which even intimates that something breathing and moving sat behind the typewriter which produced the books." [16] The narrative consciousness of Benjy mosaically projects (in memory) the "action" of *The Sound and the Fury*, and in this respect it also forecasts Faulkner's most persistent stylistic trait — composition by analogy, one detail or phrase suggesting another that resembles it, the second suggesting a third, the three brought into fortuitous dramatic alignment and swelling from within as though a whirlwind of rhetorical implications had grown from each seeded image.

This process is most obvious and most successful in *As I Lay Dying*, whose entire narrative containment, its limits as fragile and exact as the invisible boundaries of Benjy's mind, is a vacuum in which one "I said" after another, as it were, hangs suspended. Because both narratives are extended meditations on grief, on the fracturing of self into lost, discrete moments of memory, the resemblance between the perfections of control in Benjy's section and *As I Lay Dying* is no coincidence. More generally, one may see each of Faulkner's extrapolated formal experiments — in *Light in August, Absalom, Absalom!,* or *Go Down, Moses,* for example — as developments of narrative as a form of containing "voices," in those later cases not simply voices as first-person utterances but rather as they expand under frenetic pressure into character, destiny, and obsession, whole stories hanging suspended in the perilous form of a novel as they recapitulate and refer to actions that are past, that are lost, that are dead, and have become the materials of prolonged elegy. In the cases of *Light in August* and *Absalom, Absalom!* and more particularly that of *Go Down, Moses,* the integrity of such form is tenuous in the extreme; stories not only arise by a method of analogical creation that virtually brings them into being at the moment they are required, but they also fuse with and "tell" one another's tales. As they are held at a point of merged and approximate conflict, the stories inhabit the form of the novel and absolutely determine it, in each instance complicating and extending the method Faulkner discovered in *The Sound and the Fury* of turning his novels into haunted chambers of consciousness, a discovery the anarchic arena of remembered voices in Benjy's section lucidly defines.

It is appropriate that Faulkner would later claim that in writing Benjy's section of the novel he had experienced an "emotion definite and physical and yet nebulous to describe . . . that ecstasy, that eager and joyous faith and anticipation of surprise which the yet unmarred sheets beneath my hand held inviolate and unfailing," for the disembodied narrative there accords speech by speech, syllable by syllable, with the strained but exacting forms of consciousness Faulkner's best work would require.[17] In the other version of the introduction he associated that ecstasy more generally with the luminous image of Caddy in the pear tree; and he often claimed, of course, that he wrote her story four times without getting it right and gave up, and that none of his following novels allowed him to recapture the thrill of *The Sound and the Fury.* This too is part of the novel's myth, and one need not take it entirely seriously — except to note that the second attempt to tell Caddy's story, Quentin's section, often seems an anxious, enraged rehearsal of this view. Quentin's story is overrun by a vapid philosophizing that has elicited from readers the most regrettable kinds of attention. Quentin is, of course, both the sum of his Compson past and the sum of more and less recent literary pasts: like Stephen Dedalus, he is trapped in the nightmare of history (which in his case has as yet virtually nothing to do with history); and like Hamlet, moreover, Quentin is trapped in an obsession with incest (which in his case has as yet no clear bearing on the problems of the South or the novel, even though it appears to be at the center of both). *Absalom, Absalom!* will clarify these predicaments by giving Quentin and his novel a historical dimension of disturbing power. For the time being, however, Jefferson is neither Dublin nor Denmark, and the theme of incest slips lifelessly into obscure aesthetic fantasy.

One can measure the dangers of maturing the idiot narrator by comparing two passages in Quentin's section:

> I was running in the grey darkness it smelled of rain and all flowers scents the damp warm air released and crickets sawing away in the grass pacing me with a small travelling island of silence Fancy watched me across the fence blotchy like a quilt on a line I thought damn that nigger he forgot to feed her again I ran down the hill in that vacuum of crickets like a breath travelling across a mirror she was lying in the water her head on the sand spit the water flowing about her hips there was a little more light in the water her skirt half saturated flopped along her flanks to the waters motion in heavy ripples going nowhere renewed themselves of their own movement I stood on the bank I could smell the honeysuckle on the water gap the air seemed to drizzle with honeysuckle and with the rasping of crickets a substance you could feel on the flesh.

> The draft in the door smelled of water, a damp steady breath. Sometimes I could put myself to sleep saying that over and over until after the honeysuckle got all mixed up in it the whole thing came to symbolise night and unrest I seemed to be lying neither asleep nor awake looking down a long corridor of grey halflight where all stable things had become shadowy paradoxical all I had done shadows all I had felt suffered taking visible form antic and perverse mocking without relevance inherent themselves with the denial of the significance they should have affirmed thinking I was I was not who was not was not who.[18]

The one passage concerns Quentin's remembered painful encounter with Caddy after she has lost her virginity; the other describes his — or rather, Faulkner's — extension of that trauma into the self-conscious domain of "ideas." The passages are entirely distinguishable, but they both move toward parodic inflation — in the first case introducing the erotic fantasy of murder and suicide with a knife Quentin proposes to Caddy, which leads in turn to the fantasy duel with Dalton Ames; and in the second hammering in the mock philosophy of Quentin's madness. The first passage, especially as it defines a line of subliminal action that suddenly erupts into Quentin's fight with Gerald Bland, as though the prose itself were waking from a dream, is the most brilliantly sustained part of Quentin's section. The second, however, takes the same germinal images in a direction unfortunately more representative of Quentin's character: a portrait of the artist as a young madman.

Quentin's section is altogether curious and perplexing. It contains beautiful, haunted writing that, as though to enact its own willed destruction, cannot resist drifting off into muddled self-examination; and we must be grateful for Faulkner's later admission that the preposterous conversation between Quentin and his father about incest with Caddy is imaginary,[19] though we have then to admit the provocative — indeed, the crucial — probability that most all of Quentin's recollections, surely including many of his conversations with Caddy, are imaginary. It is not incidental that Quentin grows in part from a merger of the characters of Bayard Sartoris and Horace Benbow in *Flags in the Dust* and prefigures the clairvoyantly insane Darl Bundren in *As I Lay Dying,* for Quentin at this point is one of Faulkner's self-consciously insane aesthetes and has only the suggestion of those traits that lead from neurotic aestheticism to the nightmare of patrimonial grief as he later matures as a character in the Sutpen saga and, later still, develops even more fully in the character of Ike McCaslin. The most intriguing thing about the novel is that each of Faulkner's major works for the next fifteen years, from *As I Lay Dying* to *Go Down, Moses,* seems a more complex and powerful reworking of material that would in retrospect appear hidden beneath the surface of Quentin's dilemma, largely unconscious and invisible, as it were, but nonetheless capable of arousing turbulent and creative emotions that Faulkner, at this point, cannot fully articulate. In this respect, the greater context of his career may be said virtually to create the significance of *The Sound and the Fury;* and far from failing to measure up to its high standard, his later novels, particularly *Absalom, Absalom!* and *Go Down, Moses,* probe and define the historical and psychological depths of the Compson tragedy in ways that are much more illuminating than either Faulkner's appendix or his romantic pronouncements of succeeding artistic failures could suggest.

Even so, the shadows of Faulkner's tragic world are here, and an extraordinary passion, physical and intellectual, lies hidden in this book and haunts this pair of failed sons and fathers. To speak of Mr. Compson and Quentin in this way is appropriate not least because their conversations, which approach and dwell in the *imaginary* whether or not we conceive of them as actually taking place, embody in their reduction to ridiculous romantic symbolism and whispers of gallantry the failure of a land, a people, a family — all of them known together as "the South" — to regenerate itself. Mr. Compson's cynical disinterest in Caddy's promiscuity and Quentin's narcissistic obsession with it represent, not opposing views, but views that are complementary to the point of schizophrenia: the father having renounced passion and patrimony altogether, the son attempting psychically to totalize it, to invest an entire family and its cultural role in an imaginary act of incest. The absence of Caddy as a character and the fantastic character of Quentin's passion are in this respect entangled, even indistinguishable, for the incestuous desire to father oneself or to be one's own family is here presented as correlative to, if not the cause of, the symbolic desire to absorb all creative energy into an invisible, ineffable presence — what is present only as desire, that perfect form into which all energy is channeled, all content sublimated, the vaselike erotic form Faulkner imagined his book itself to be.[20]

Quentin's suicide, therefore, should not be interpreted as a reaction against his incestuous desires or their failure to be actualized; rather, his suicide, like that of Melville's hero in *Pierre,* virtually *is* incest, the only act in which generation is thoroughly internalized (and prohibited) and the "father," as a consequence, killed. Here the rage that everywhere fractures the family and the book, the hatred of his past Quentin will deny in *Absalom, Absalom!* (or has already denied, if we merge the events of the two books), is folded into the act of love, in the bodily *image* of love: Quentin joins the water, the medium always associated with Caddy, as though he were lying down with it (one thinks of Millais's *Ophelia*), his bodily self falling to meet the enchanted corpse lying always beneath the shadowy surface of the prose. Death and love, murder and passion, are joined in incest, most of all in such an imaginary enactment and its sublimation in suicide. Quentin's death, of course, is offstage, just as invisible, in our experience of the novel, as Caddy herself; this is perfectly to the point, however, for as his reappearance in *Absalom, Absalom!* and the original stories of *Go Down, Moses* will suggest, Quentin's death, like his proscribed desires, is also *imaginary,* a symbolic distillation of the moral suicide diffused in later novels through the trauma of the Civil War, Reconstruction, broken promises, the failure of freedom and love — the encompassing drama that surrounds and defines for Faulkner the central act of grief.

The risks of such an aesthetic, one in part created retrospectively by the directions in which Faulkner was to take his initial impulses, are evident in *The Sound and the Fury,* a novel whose very essence is imaginary in that the "plot" or "story" is of almost no consequence but remains instead a way to project into actuality the inchoate states of grief and unfulfilled desire that are Faulkner's abiding subjects. Like Benjy's broken flower, his dirty slipper, and his fire, the story — by extension, the novel itself, as Faulkner would have it — is at once a memorial and a fetish; as it embodies loss without adequately containing or reproducing it, the story gets progressively more full and realistic in a traditional sense but cannot find an expression equivalent or superior to Benjy's opening inarticulate cry of Caddy's name. In the final image of Benjy circling the Confederate statue we recognize that, although the plot has unfolded and advanced, its essence still lies in section one, to which we nervously return. The returning to stillness, as to death, is the book's primary movement, and the style of Benjy's section, stillness on the point of death, enacts in narrative the hard, bright flame of symbolic intensity that Quentin imagines incest to be, and Faulkner wanted his book to be, the burning out in passionate stillness of the power to generate a family, a life, a story.

From a therapeutic point of view, if no other, it is quite plausible to maintain, as Maxwell Geismar does, that the novel speaks in accents "from the edge of the womb" that "recall and draw up from the abyss of the past our own forgotten memories"; [21] and the novel is surely, as David Minter suggests, a central point of departure among Faulkner's "strategies for approaching forbidden scenes, uttering forbidden words, committing dangerous acts." [22] The disjunction between these virtues and the novel's philosophical and rhetorical excess is a rather considerable one, however, and the greater one's attention to this disjunction, the more the novel resembles the Southern aesthetic predicament Faulkner spoke of in one version of his suppressed introduction: "In the South art, to become visible at all, must become a ceremony, a spectacle; something between a gypsy encampment and a church bazaar given by a handful of alien mummers who must waste themselves in protest and active self-defense until there is nothing left with which to speak." On a more positive note, Faulkner spoke in the other version of having learned to read, as though "in a series of delayed repercussions," his literary masters, "the Flauberts and Dostoievskys and Conrads." 23 This is exciting but somewhat spurious (it would, no doubt, have been indiscreet to add Eliot and Joyce, whom he had more obviously been learning to read); the important readings by repercussion would only come later, when Faulkner reread *The Sound and the Fury,* so to speak, and became his own literary master.

Faulkner's obsession with the unnameable, the inexpressible, is his own greatest hazard, and *The Sound and the Fury* is its most intricate expression. As it forecasts his preoccupation with form rather than plot, with modes of conflicting, antagonistic expression that depend on abrupt juxtaposition, sheer rhetorical energy, and exhaustive symbolic motifs, the novel embodies an incipiency of method that accords with its infantile accents and forbidden scenes. Still, it is difficult to tell why — or exactly at what point — its poignant memories get transfigured into neurosis or bizarre, overbearing symbolism. It quite often appears to have little to do with its own genetic myth, the image of Caddy in the pear tree that Faulkner claimed was "the only thing in literature which would ever move me very much," 24 even though it can easily be reduced to that image. Its interests remain largely unconscious, not just in the sense of intimating deep psychoanalytic drama, but also in the sense of deriving their power everywhere from such simple, abiding images, which as the novel tells us time and again are distorted and betrayed when they mature into stories. As Faulkner was fond of remarking, he wrote the "story" four times and gave up without getting it right. That, of course, is the novel's central myth; but it is worth considering, in the larger context of Faulkner's most important work — a context that has helped to create the myth — one reason why he could not get it right, why its interests may most be said to be unconscious, and why the obsession with Caddy was no mistake.

C LEARLY, the novel is about the doom of the South, but only *Absalom, Absalom!* provides the explosive historical setting in which this is fully evident. And as John Irwin has demonstrated, only an imposed strategy of assumptions about the nature of familial and temporal revenge can explicate Quentin's "ideas" at all. That pattern, Irwin argues, is put into perspective by the larger tragedy of Thomas Sutpen's family, which in retrospect — or rather, by an act of retrospection that is intimately involved with the desire for revenge — illuminates Quentin's suicide by proving to him, as it were, that it truly is a repetition of past doomed actions, just as his desire for Caddy is a repetition of past frustrated desires. Because he comes to realize that tragedy *is*

repetition and that its deepest level, in this case, lies in the "symbolic identification of incest and miscegenation," it may be said that Quentin's obsession with
Caddy's virginity is determined by forces that exist even further beneath the
nether reaches of consciousness that a good portion of *The Sound and the Fury*
dwells in, forces that only the historical depth of *Absalom, Absalom!* can reveal. As
Irwin points out, Quentin's attempt "to avenge his sister's lost virginity (proving
thereby that it had once existed) and maintain the family honor is an attempt to
maintain . . . the possibility of the existence of a virgin space within which one
can still be first, within which one can have authority through originality." But
the most tormenting denial of that virgin space, at the level of cultural history
the second novel adds to the first, lies in the fact that "the Civil War closed off
the virgin space and the time of origins, so that the antebellum South became in
the minds of postwar Southerners that debilitating 'golden age and lost world' in
comparison with which the present is inadequate."[25]

This dimension of the Compson tragedy is dramatically "repressed" in 1929,
however, and the larger importance of Irwin's reading of the novel's interior
myth must necessarily be pursued in the context of *Absalom, Absalom!,* in which
one might argue that the issue of miscegenation, which Irwin constantly alludes
to, is even more important than he claims; that it is more central to Quentin's
dilemma than the problematic of Oedipal revenge.[26] At this point, Faulkner
seems as much stymied by the theme of incest as Quentin is by his futile desire
to avenge Caddy's violation. If Quentin's obsession with Caddy's purity is to
move beyond the emotional lassitude and moral paralysis that William Taylor
has found to characterize the personality of the "Southern Hamlet," it will have
to engage something like the shock produced by the intrusion of modern morality into the closed cult of Southern sentimentality — the shock produced, for
example, when the dissipated college youth of the Prohibition era, as Cash suggests, confronted his own puritanical heritage:

> This bawdy outburst struck straight against Southern Puritanism and sentimen-
> tality — particularly the cult of Southern Womanhood — and so served to add to
> the sum total of fears on its own account. . . . For in the bottom of the minds of
> even the most flauntingly "emancipated" of these youths, the old sentimentality
> and Puritanism bred in their bones from youth still lurked, and often started up
> to torture the young woman with longing for the old role of vestal virgin, the
> young man with longing for the old gesturing worship of a more than mortal
> creature — to make them continually restless with the subconscious will to escape
> into being nearly whole again.[27]

It will be the burden of Faulkner's career to develop a rationale for the South's
paralysis and its resulting resurgence of sentimental longing. The nadir of the
shock of modernism, and its blasphemous inversion, Faulkner probes in *Sanctuary,* where the promiscuity of Caddy turns into the wild nymphomania of
Temple Drake and the purity of Southern Womanhood becomes a pornographic farce — and where, moreover, Faulkner disgorges himself in mockery of

his own initial psychoanalytic aestheticism. But the greatest shock he would save for *Light in August, Absalom, Absalom!*, and *Go Down, Moses*. There the shock comes in the abundantly evident bearing the threat of miscegenation has on Southern gynealotry and, we may surmise, on Quentin's incestuous desires.

In *The Sound and the Fury*, however, it is precisely this issue that is left inarticulate; and the most significant and tragic dimension of Southern narcissism Faulkner would later explore — the hallucinating, self-projected image of "the Negro" that the South created out of guilt and fear, the image so wonderfully and shockingly embodied in the monstrous, uncanny figures of the "white niggers," Joe Christmas and Charles Bon — lies speechless in Quentin's experience. In this instance as well as others one feels the force of Irving Howe's contention that there is nowhere in Faulkner's work "a copious and lively image of the old South. It remains forever a muted shadow, a point of reference rather than an object for presentation, perhaps because the effort to see it in fullness would be too great a strain on the imagination." [28] The shadow of the old South, and most obviously the shadow of "the Negro" it carries in forbidding proximity, are *in retrospect* (as Irwin argues) everywhere visible in the "shadow" self Quentin pursues and, finally, kills. By the time Faulkner's readers would be in a position to make such an assertion, though, the imaginative strain would have become so intense that Quentin's psychosis might well seem the best measure of Faulkner's painstakingly created design and his suicidal narcissism a mirror of the South's long-defeated dream.

Such a strategy is precarious and, to repeat, it only becomes visible over the course of Faulkner's career. Yet the shock produced by the intrusion of the modern into the domain of Southern puritanism and the Southern cult of memory is already evident in *Sartoris*, where the paralyzing disjunction between the new Sartorises and the old is sharply rendered by the novel's ability to hold the myth of memory at a point of perilous balance, neither endorsing it nor declaring it sheer fabrication. In doing so, it brings into view the most conspicuous feature of Faulkner's romantic mythologizing of the old South — that its power depends on his straining to the very limits of coherence those nostalgic legends of old Confederate times that were being offered up in all seriousness by his contemporaries. What one witnesses over the course of Faulkner's career is the increasing irrationality of the claims made on behalf of the old South as the new South approached the disillusioning realities of black civil rights activism and legislation, an irrationality for which his tortuous prose becomes a mirror but which also produces the bewildering effect that, the more Faulkner probes the myth, the more central it becomes, while the more he confronts its visceral elementary issue — the hallucinating figure of "the Negro" — the more he recoils into a form of outrage that is ambivalent in the extreme. By the time of his notorious public stands on desegregation in the 1950s, that ambivalence would come to seem painful indeed, and would seem as well to represent a retreat from the explosive moral stands his novels had already taken.

In *The Sound and the Fury*, then, incest is made to stand for something larger than itself, something having to do with the doom of "the South," but something we will not read of very explicitly until the early pages of *Absalom, Absalom!*, in which Mr. Compson remarks to Quentin, "Years ago we in the South made our women into ladies. Then the War came and made the ladies into ghosts."[29] The ghost-lady here is Rosa Coldfield, whose withering erotic fantasies seem to embody all that Judith and Ellen Sutpen are not allowed to say in the novel and, moreover, all that Quentin, perhaps, comes to think Caddy capable of saying if only she were allowed, by Faulkner, to say it. In between the two novels, Faulkner attributes versions of Caddy's suppressed confessions to Temple Drake and Joanna Burden, whose nymphomania — in each case prompted by her sexual violation by a "black man" — represents that underlying horror the revelation of which Quentin would prevent (and enact as surrogate) by enclosing his sister and himself in a state of damned, Pateresque purity: *"If it could just be a hell beyond that: the clean flame the two of us more than dead. Then you will have only me then only me then the two of us amid the pointing and the horror beyond the clean flame."*[30] Quentin's incestuous desires do, no doubt, define a libidinal Oedipal drama played out among the Compsons, father and son and preceding generations (we may later propose on the basis of the appendix), but this drama is argued and not acted by the novel; as of yet it has not completely engaged the central tragedy of the South and is more disconcerting than T. S. Eliot found Hamlet's problems to be. At best, it remains the aesthetic problem it had been for Horace Benbow, that unfathomable, transgressive state of artistic perfection with which Faulkner himself had been preoccupied from the beginning of his career[31] and that was now being passed through the furnace of Quentin's mind to reappear transfigured into more daring and dangerous forms in succeeding novels as the lost story of lost Caddy went on being told.

The Sound and the Fury is an apt title in more ways than one, for as Faulkner's remarks on the writing of *Sartoris* suggest, a creative convulsion of immense magnitude takes place between the two novels, as though Faulkner has entered the dream world, the limbo, that would make available his greatest materials. The new novel screens from view its most significant effects (for they have not yet been created); it also screens *Sartoris* by dissolving the linear structures of history, family, and the novel, and leaving a residue of first-person obsessions, fragments of identity that reach beyond the ghostly forms of consciousness that contain them but, touching nothing and no one, remain segregated and irreconcilable. Most significantly, in view of Faulkner's later development, they do little to touch the issues of race in which he would amplify those distortions and failures of sexual, generative power he had here found to constitute the crisis of Southern identity. The black characters in *The Sound and the Fury* do provide a context for the social and psychic decay of the Compsons, and that context is crucial; but as the marginal attention given to them in the appendix suggests, it would not be evident until *Light in August* why, as Quentin observes to himself, a "nigger" is not a person but "a form of behaviour; a sort of obverse reflection of the white people he lives among." At that point, Quentin's obsession with

Caddy's purity acquires a more subtle and provocative coherence, for the introduction of the theme of miscegenation reveals the absolute paradox in his obsession. Because the etymology and received meaning of *incest* suggest precisely the opposite, such purity is blasphemous by definition: incest is *impure*. To recognize this does not significantly change our perspective on Quentin's fantasy in Oedipal terms. It does, however, begin to alter Caddy's position as representative embodiment of Southern virtue and as ghostly echo of an honored ideal under severe contemporary pressures; and it begins to clarify why Quentin, as the appendix would put it, "thought he loved but really hated in her what he considered the frail doomed vessel of [his family's] pride and the foul instrument of its disgrace."[32]

Quentin's madness, as Faulkner came to depict it and as the retrospective vantage of the appendix could more justly assume, is primarily the South's, whose intense fascination with gynealotry increased in proportion to threats against it and created the peculiar situation in which the period of Southern history that came mythically to embody extreme virtue and honor, the antebellum years, was precisely the period whose virtue and honor, however they may have been manifested, were built on the most hideous corruptions of the human spirit imaginable. Like Quentin's conception of incest, such nostalgic conjuring makes "pure" what is thoroughly "impure" — though with this important complication: because incest defines a violation of purity or caste (*in* + *castus*), the integrity of the antebellum South, since it was projected in direct opposition *against* the violent threat of miscegenation that abolition and emancipation were said to entail, might well seem a clean, pure space of remembered innocence. Mr. Compson's contention that Caddy's purity is a "negative state" defined only by violation (a contention repeated in more complex form in *Absalom, Absalom!*) or that it is "like death: only a state in which the others are left"[33] (a contention *Absalom, Absalom!* seems designed to illustrate) is thus to the point: Caddy's purity and that of the South are defined by a transgression or violation of moral limits that virtually brings them into being, that define what is just as irrevocably lost, past, and "dead" as Caddy herself. Quentin's dilemma is to imagine that by committing the act himself he can preserve that purity by defining it in violation, much as the ideal poet (or the novelist obsessed with "unmarred" and "inviolate" sheets of paper) might preserve aesthetic purity in the consuming sacrificial flame of creation without properly generating anything except the perfect, sacred, unreadable utterance.

If it is to act thus in counterpoint to Quentin's obsessions, Caddy's moral fragility, like her near invisibility as a character, must be seen to portray the violent paradox upon which such conceptions of Southern innocence were built. This paradox would seem irrelevant to (or entirely at odds with) the issue of miscegenation if the contemporary fear of sexual mixing between blacks and whites did not entail a willful denial that Southern innocence, symbolized by its essential purity of white blood, had not already been irrevocably lost. As his work revealed, when Faulkner turned from *Light in August's* shocking exposure of the Jim Crow rape complex to the sins of the fathers that had set it in motion in *Absalom, Absalom!* and *Go Down, Moses,* this idealizing myth of innocence required the unconscious repression or deliberately conscious suppression of the miscegenation of white masters and black slaves, which not only counted for little or nothing in terms of human love but also made conceivable forms of incest that paradoxically could not be defined as such since the intimate family relationships incest assumes were, by further definition, declared utterly invalid. The transferal of threatened sexual violence to emancipated blacks revealed the idolatry of Southern Womanhood, in part, as a feverish sublimation of the lust of white masters for their slave women, a lust that could only be condoned by the insistence that it had no moral or emotional content but, because it inevitably did, therefore insured the ostentatiously proclaimed sanctity of white women and white marriage. In retrospect, that sublimation would be more severe than ever, for the logic of emancipation, in sexual terms as in others, created the specter of terrifying revenge, a specter far more monstrous than the actualization of such revenge would ever be.

By the time Faulkner began his literary career, the "lost" but feverishly maintained innocence of the South, so like Quentin's paradoxically puritanical concept of Caddy's purity, had become nothing less than the entire burden of white identity, and the threat against it was more and more obviously constituted, as Joel Williamson has noted, by the failure of "the myth of the mulatto demise." The historically prevalent Southern view that mulattoes were a dying breed, both biologically and culturally, and that the sins of the antebellum fathers were therefore passing from view, had begun to be exposed as a myth in its own right by the early twentieth century, with the result that miscegenation, whether instigated by whites or blacks, came to seem more heinous and the purity of white women more crucial than ever. "To merge white and black would have been the ultimate holocaust, the absolute damnation of Southern civilization," Williamson writes, and yet the mulatto made apparent "that white and black had interpenetrated in a graphic and appalling way," that "life in the Southern world was not [as] pure, clean, and clear as white people needed to believe." [34]

This interpenetration of the races need not, of course, require us to believe in the thorough interpenetration of either the twin themes of incest and miscegenation or the two novels those themes bring into troubled union. At this point they do not, in Faulkner's imagination, belong together as explicitly as *Absalom, Absalom!* will insist, and one need not believe that the threat of miscegenation is the repressed fear generating Quentin's incestuous desire in order to witness, as Faulkner's career unfolds, the absorption of a private, aesthetic neurosis by a potentially more volatile, comprehensive cultural disorder. That disorder, the threat to the fragile innocence of the white South, along with the historical dimension of tragic action it implies, is latent in *The Sound and the Fury* in the same way that the entirety of Quentin's tormented involvement in the conclusion of the Sutpen saga may be said to be latent, as if by imaginary projection, in the events of June 2, 1910. Miscegenation promised the slow but eventual extinction of the white race (few bothered to notice that the contrary might also be true); like incest, its exact opposite in the operation of prohibitions, it meant the suicidal failure of families and their caste to be perpetuated. It also meant the lasting extinction of a memory, a dream, in which half the South (and the nation) lived in an illusion, the other half in the long shadow it cast.

This complex situation, which Faulkner came to see as the heart of the South's damnation, in all its related mythical and contemporary extenuations, is left broodingly unconscious in *The Sound and the Fury*, which we only recognize at all in the larger context of later novels, where its shadow looms up in monstrous proportions. There is virtually no way to read it out of the novel itself, even though it adds a dimension of exceptional power to Quentin's theatrical agony; it is, so to speak, one of the novel's myths — paradoxically its most crucial and speechless. It is surely no mistake, however, that Faulkner some years later would burlesque Quentin's obsession with Caddy by describing his concept of honor as "the minute fragile membrane of her maidenhead," as precariously balanced as "a miniature replica of all the whole vast globy earth may be poised on the head of a trained seal," and then in the same vein of wretched prose describe Jefferson itself, and the anecdote it here produced, circa 1864, as "a bubble, a minute globule which has its own impunity" but which was also "too weightless to give resistance for destruction to function against . . . having no part in rationality and being contemptuous of fact." [35] The myth at the heart of *The Sound and the Fury* was as weightless and intangible (and as subject to grotesque caricature) as the lost dream it depended on. Nothing that Faulkner was to write would prove it otherwise, but he would certainly find better and more dramatically exacting ways to say it.

S ARTRE'S essay on *Sartoris*, though not as well known as his essay on *The Sound and the Fury*, is at once more penetrating and more capable of defining the peculiar relationship of the two novels as complementary points of origin in Faulkner's career. The "real drama" of Faulkner's work, says Sartre in passing from the particular case of *Sartoris* to a more general characterization of Faulkner's world, lies "*behind,* behind the lethargy, behind the gestures, behind the consciousness." His imposing tragic figures, Sartre points out, have only "exterior dimension" despite the obvious emphasis on their interior chaos; they have "secrets" that can neither be revealed nor "forced back into the unconscious," and Faulkner therefore "dreams of an absolute obscurity in the very depth of the 'conscious,' of a complete obscurity that we should ourselves create within ourselves." [36] These observations are entirely more instructive than Sartre's famous meditations on "time" in *The Sound and the Fury;* for the "conscious obscurity" of which Faulkner is master refers to both a method and a locale, and in the case of the transition from *Sartoris* to *The Sound and the Fury* perfectly describes the move away from a clear articulation of the Southern myth and toward its gothic complication in later works, where his expression of both the mind and the manner of the South is far from unconscious but engages instead the consciously created obscurity that is both the South's mind and our own American "self."

The shadow of "the Negro," because its capacity to figure as unconscious eruption, the sudden return of the repressed, is so powerful, magnificently marks this boundary for Faulkner; and his career up to *Light in August* might well be considered an extended repression of the figure of the Negro, who truly remains a *figure* for Faulkner since his great "black" characters are "white." But that novel, along with *Absalom, Absalom!* and *Go Down, Moses,* reveals a new depth of consciousness that is violent and haunting, that certainly has the characteristics of a gothic nightmare, but ought not, insofar as Faulkner's narratives are explicitly composed of formal modes of fictional consciousness, be considered "unconscious." That is to say, the depth of racial consciousness those novels engage is of explosive social, rather than strictly psychoanalytic, interest. On the other hand, as *Absalom, Absalom!* would prove in detail, *The Sound and the Fury* does force this central issue back into the unconscious, for there is almost nothing in the earlier novel — while there is everything in the later novel — to indicate that miscegenation or its shadowy threat is an important feature of Quentin's psychological disturbance. One might say that *The Sound and the Fury,* in this respect, *contains* the repressed that returns with increasing visibility over the course of Faulkner's career as he discovers the lost dimension of Southern experience *Sartoris* had failed to find. It is truly unconscious at this point, as though (we recognize in retrospect) Faulkner were passing toward the "depths of consciousness" through a melodrama of Southern family romance that cannot yet reveal its most peculiar and definitive secret.

More particularly, he was moving away from the autobiographical dilemma that *Sartoris* bogged down in; and while it is possible and quite profitable to detect recurring familial dramas throughout Faulkner's work that resemble his own in striking ways,[37] and while a number of his characters may be seen as authorial personae, the glimmers of autobiography left in *The Sound and the Fury,* in contrast to *Sartoris,* are tellingly marginal. Genealogical conflict has been compressed into a measured disintegration and restoration of temporality, and history has momentarily disappeared into the stalemate of psychoanalytic compulsion; but Faulkner seems also to have entered a cauldron of creativity and produced, in a white heat of experimental expression, the precipitous materials and their strained, immature forms that would allow him to write great novels. The most vital myth of *The Sound and the Fury* — one that we can neither rely upon nor confidently gainsay — is that it made possible everything else. His next creative efforts would produce a recasting of the materials of the Southern wasteland into the bitter and hateful denunciations of *Sanctuary,* and a perfectly tuned and controlled essay on forms of grief in *As I Lay Dying;* while each of his great novels that follow would refer back implicitly or explicitly to *The Sound and the Fury,* as intimately but tenuously connected to it as the novel is to its own germinal scene and its central, invisible character. The book is its own myth, as the design of Faulkner's career came to define it, a myth of tortured innocence explicated by earlier and later novels but at the same time self-contained and — intentionally, it seems — self-defeating.

It would, perhaps, be too much to speak of the novel as a kind of womb or genesis, for its avowed depictions of luminously failed beginnings, as well as the novel's accumulated myth of ecstatic purity, suggest that nothing could ever come of it or surpass it, that it is perfectly stillborn. This is certainly not true, and Faulkner's later comparison of the novel to a "child who is an idiot or born crippled" is more to the point.[38] Like Quentin's notion of incest, the myth of the novel's perfection is half bombast and hallucination, but its importance is literally inestimable, for the simple reason that "Faulkner" can be imagined apart from it no more easily than the novel can be imagined apart from Caddy, "the beautiful one, [his] heart's darling."[39] It contains brilliant, powerful writing that Faulkner would publically declare to be his best, writing that could, therefore, never be equalled. As though visibly enacting his own "compulsion to say everything in one sentence,"[40] and inevitably failing to do so, *The Sound and the Fury* defines his vision and its uttermost limits. It also contains the inchoate drama of the South that would mature into his best work over the course of the next decade. By the time Faulkner added the novel's appendix, that work would be several years behind him; and the design of Yoknapatawpha, obsessively recapitulating and shoring up earlier works, would more and more resemble the chaos from which it had sprung — with the paradoxical effect, of course, that only the furthering of the design could define its latent, magnificent failure and fix forever the myth of its original masterpiece.

chapter 2

Death, Grief, Analogous Form:
As I Lay Dying

> You know if I were reincarnated, I'd want to come back a buzzard. Nothing hates
> him or envies him or wants him or needs him. He is never bothered or in danger,
> and he can eat anything.
>
> — FAULKNER, *1956 interview*

FAULKNER'S desire to be reincarnated as a buzzard[1] may appear to
betray the kind of grotesque humor that *As I Lay Dying* (1930) has been
rightly accused of indulging. It is a noteworthy gloss not simply because the
novel's own buzzards pose a constant threat to the rotting corpse of Addie
Bundren as it is borne on its funeral journey to Jefferson, but also because
Faulkner's identification with the birds, when viewed in the context of the problems of narrative form posed by the novel, indicates immediately a grand, if
macabre, detachment from his materials. Such a detachment from materials
that are both dead and yet potently living — or to be more exact in terms of the
book, from materials that are in the process of dying — suggests an analogy that
is relevant to all of Faulkner's work (and, from the vantage of 1956, to his great
fictional design itself) but has particular interest for *As I Lay Dying* since the
novel itself seems curiously detached from his other major works. Although its
mood is that of savage burlesque, and thus represents a continuation of the intimate family brutalities Faulkner had already explored in *The Sound and the Fury*
and would make more violently shocking when he revised *Sanctuary, As I Lay
Dying* is rather a tender book. It can, more than any of his major novels, be read
independently, and it is his most perfect and finished piece of fiction. Perhaps
because of this, however, it is nearly a compendium of the problematic techniques that Faulkner had discovered in the sudden creative illumination of *The
Sound and the Fury* and would relentlessly pursue throughout the remainder of his
career. It is a virtual textbook of technique, one that displays all his talents and
their inevitable risks as they support and drive one another to the perilous limits
of narrative form Faulkner would require for his great novels on the prolonged
tragedy and grief of the South.

Complaints about Faulkner's rhetoric — its gratuitous contortions, its motiveless expanse, its tactless mix of pathos and ridicule — are common even among his admirers. Most often, such complaints proceed from one of two assumptions: that the author or narrator (the two are easily confused) has fallen victim to his own fantasies of technique; or that a character or speaker (these two are also easily confused) has been allowed a command of language utterly incommensurate with his place in the novel's realistic or representational scheme. In some notable instances the two difficulties are merged, as in the following passage from *As I Lay Dying*, in which the young boy Vardaman, "speaking" both as one of the book's fifteen main characters and as one of its equal number of narrators, describes an encounter with his brother's horse in the barn:

> It is dark. I can hear wood, silence: I know them. But not living sounds, not even him. It is as though the dark were resolving him out of his integrity, into an unrelated scattering of components — snuffings and stampings; smells of cooling flesh and ammoniac hair; an illusion of a co-ordinated whole of splotched hide and strong bones within which, detached and secret and familiar, an *is* different from my *is*. I see him dissolve — legs, a rolling eye, a gaudy splotching like cold flames — and float upon the dark in fading solution; all one yet neither; all either yet none. I can see hearing coil toward him, caressing, shaping his hard shape — fetlock, hip, shoulder and head; smell and sound. I am not afraid.[2]

Vardaman's narration presents an outrageous example of the kind of writing that has understandably led Martin Green to complain that Faulkner's rhetoric often appears to exist "*in vacuo*," that there is a "gap between it and the writer" so apparent as to leave him completely "alienated" from it.[3] What Green's complaint assumes, however, is in this case exactly what the form of *As I Lay Dying* so astutely challenges — a narrative consciousness formed by a supposed union between the author and his language, a union formalized and made conventional by the standard device of omniscient, or at least partly omniscient, narration, which the novel explicitly discards and disavows.

Vardaman's episode with the horse insists that we experience it as alienated language — alien in the sense of being disembodied, traumatically cut off from the conscious identity of character on the one hand and author on the other. The episode is remarkable but, in the context of the book's unique rhetorical problems, not extraordinary. And it has thematic significance insofar as the book is obsessively concerned with problems of disembodiment, with disjunctive relationships between character and narration or between bodily self and conscious identity. At extremity, Vardaman's trauma leads to the novel's shortest and most comically wrenching chapter — "My mother is a fish"[4] — and therefore suggests an intimate analogy between the absence of an omniscient narrator, a controlling point of view, and the central event of the book: the death of Addie Bundren, with respect to which each character defines his own identity. The relationship between absent omniscient narrator (or author) and dead mother does not, of course, consist of an exact parallel. Addie Bundren appears in the book, not only dying but speaking her own story in one chapter that appears more than a hundred pages after her literal death. It is important here to distinguish literal from figurative death, for the book's title — its adverb capable of being construed as *while, how,* or even *as if* — endorses the fact that Addie's death as it is experienced (one might speak of the phenomenology of her death) occurs over the course of the book and in relation to each character, thus rendering the distinction both necessary and hazardous. The title contains this possibility, moreover, by intimating an elegiac past tense where the collected acts of individual memory (the speaking "I" of each narrator) are disembodied and merged with the dying "I" of the mother, and by playing on the colloquial use of *lay* as an intransitive verb, so as to blur further the distinction between past and present events, a blurring sanctioned and exacerbated by the mixing of narrative tenses among the book's fifty-nine chapters. The action of the book occurs, that is, as Addie *lies* dying and as she *lay* dying, with each narrative "I" participating in the dissolution of her "I" by reflecting and partially embodying it.

It is in this respect that the dying maintains a figurative power far succeeding the literal event of Addie's death; and the chronological displacement of her single monologue alerts us to the possibility not only that we must understand the death itself to function as an act of temporal and spatial disembodiment, but that Addie's speech, as it were logically disengaged for the corporeal self that could have uttered it, is an extreme example of the way in which the novel's other acts of speech should be interpreted — as partially or wholly detached from the bodily selves that appear to utter them. One thinks for immediate comparison of Whitman's "Crossing Brooklyn Ferry," in which the speaker's violation of temporal and spatial boundaries generates the frightening sense of a truly disembodied, ever-present voice; but more so than Whitman's poem, the voices of *As I Lay Dying,* because they are detached even more obviously from a bounded authorial self, raise doubts about the propriety of referring to the novel's narrative acts as monologues. Such doubts are readily apparent in the example of Vardaman's encounter with Jewel's horse, where the utterance seems disembodied from the conscious identity of author and narrator alike. Yet it also works to enforce our understanding of Vardaman's traumatic reaction to his mother's death and by doing so provides an analogy for the narrative form of the entire novel. The horse that is resolved "out of his integrity, into an unrelated scattering of components . . . an illusion of a co-ordinated whole of splotched hide and strong bones within which, detached and secret and familiar, [there is] an *is* different from my *is,*" is emblematic, even symptomatic, of the body of Addie, in process of being resolved out of her integrity, the "*is*" of her self-contained identity; and it is emblematic of the "body" of the novel, itself disintegrated and yet carefully producing the "illusion of a coordinated whole."

Because the relationship between the bodily self and the conscious identity of Addie remains an issue throughout the book, because the self must continue both *to be* and *not to be* the corpse carried along on its self-imposed journey to Jefferson (a possibility disturbingly underscored by Anse's comic refrain "her mind is set on it"), one is tempted to speak of the body of the book as existing in an analogously fragile state and maintaining its narrative form despite the apparent absence of that substance one might compare to, or identify with, a central point of view embodied in an omniscient narrator. The horse's phenomenal dissolution and "float[ing] upon the dark" recalls other instances in the novel in which objects as experienced are detached from their fixed physical limits: for example, Addie's face in death, which "seems to float detached upon [darkness], lightly as the reflection of a dead leaf," or the flooded ford, where the road appears to have "been soaked free of earth and floated upward, to leave in its spectral tracing a monument to a still more profound desolation" — all of which contribute to our experience of the novel itself as an object whose uttered parts are radically detached from fixed limits and fully identifiable sources.[5] The novel, like the family whose story it tells, is held together in the most precarious fashion, its narrative components adhering and referring to an act that is simultaneously literal and figurative, just as the body of Addie is neither exactly corpse nor conscious self. The logic thus presents itself of speaking of the novel too as a corpse, as a narrative whose form is continually on the verge of decomposition and whose integrity is retained only by heroic imaginative effort.

Some early readers, misunderstanding the nature of Vardaman's reaction to his mother's death, took him to be another idiot, like Benjy Compson. Although one would not need Faulkner's certification to deny such a claim, the explanation he once provided is important. Vardaman reacts as he does, Faulkner pointed out, because he is a child faced with the intimate and perplexing loss of his mother, because "suddenly her position in the mosaic of the household [is] vacant."[6] This is true for all members of the novel's family, for whom Addie, at least in the portion of their history presented in the novel (the portion detached, as it were, from the fuller one we imagine by interpretive projection), is the center that no longer holds, that is defunct and yet lingers in stages of tenuous attachment. Vardaman's confusions between his mother and the fish, and between her seeming imprisonment in the coffin and his own recollection of being momentarily trapped in the corn crib —

> It was not her because it was laying right yonder in the dirt. And now it's all chopped up. I chopped it up. It's laying in the kitchen in the bleeding pan, waiting to be cooked and et. Then it wasn't and she was, and now it is and she wasn't.
>
> "Are you going to nail her up in it, Cash? Cash? Cash?" I got shut up in the new crib the new door it was too heavy for me it went shut I couldn't breathe because the rat was breathing up all the air. I said "Are you going to nail it shut, Cash? Nail it? *Nail* it?"[7]

— provide the most moving instances of the psychological disorientation that affects each of the Bundrens in his or her own way. And they bring into focus the two central problems of bodily integrity and conscious identity with which the novel is concerned: How can a body that still *is* be thought of as *was?* How can I, whose self has depended upon, and been defined in relation to, another self, now understand the integrity of my own identity? Vardaman, child though he is, consistently asks the most difficult and sophisticated questions about death in the book. He asks where Addie has gone; he in effect questions the farcical funeral journey, which is founded particularly on Addie's command to Anse that she be buried in Jefferson and sanctioned generally by the technically absurd and paradoxical notion on which funeral ceremonies are based — that the corpse both *is* and *is not* the self of the person; and he alone, innocently though mistakenly, assigns an agency to Addie's death by blaming Doctor Peabody, whose visit coincides with her death no less reasonably than the chopping up and eating of the fish.

P EABODY'S role in the novel is important quite aside from the comic relief provided when his obese body (again tangentially calling our attention to the importance of corporeal form in the novel) must be hauled up the steep hill to the Bundren house by means of a rope; important because, as Faulkner himself remarked, it gives "a nudge of credibility to a condition which was getting close to the realm of unbelief." Bringing in Peabody from what Faulkner called "comparatively the metropolitan outland" allows the reader to admit of the Bundrens that "maybe they do exist. Up to that time they were functioning in this bizarre fashion almost inside a vacuum, and pretty soon you wouldn't have believed it until some stranger came in as a witness." [8] Faulkner's explanation is a perfect indication of one of the novel's more instrumental effects: that in the absence of a controlling narrator the characters, who as narrators themselves participate in the dissolution of the book's integrity and yet by that very act define and maintain its fragile form, do indeed, as Darl says, "sound as though they [are] speaking out of the air about your head" [9] and appear to be acting in a virtual vacuum — the vacuum left both by the "author" who is not, as it were, present and by the integrated form that we as a consequence imagine would be there if he were. Without attaching too much importance to Faulkner's remarks we might nonetheless consider Peabody's appearance, apart from its other functions, in some measure a response to Faulkner's anxiety about the vacuum created by his own authorial absence, one that is bound up with the vacuum created by Addie's death. That is to say, the need to imagine a narrative rendered coherent by the controlling presence of an author — an authoritative *voice* — is not unlike the need to imagine, and the stricken reluctance to let go belief in, the integrated self of one who has died. Both needs may well be spoken of as conventional, as being formed by prior or habitual expectations, though it is precisely for that reason that both are so psychologically demanding.

Although Peabody need not necessarily be thought of as a figure for the author (a conventional way of meeting this demand), part of his role as witness consists of a most telling remark about the action of death in the novel: "I can remember how when I was young I believed death to be a phenomenon of the body; now I know it to be merely a function of the mind — and that of the minds of the ones who suffer the bereavement." [10] Of the two qualifications by which Peabody's remarks proceed, the second is the most striking and the most definitive with respect to the form of the novel; while the distinction raised by the first — that body and consciousness may present separable forms of identity — is one simultaneously entertained and held in abeyance by the book, the insistence that death demands the intimate participation of other minds virtually explicates the reactions of Addie's family to her demise and, correspondingly, the disintegrated yet tenuously coherent form of the novel. What dies in death, Peabody suggests, is not simply the body or even the mind attached to the body. Rather — and here again one might speak of the phenomenology of death — what dies are the connections between one mind and others. Thus it is that Addie dies not within a single, temporally bounded moment, but rather lies dying throughout the book, in that her death is not complete until the book ends. But even this is not a satisfactory way of putting it. For, although one could claim that her death is complete once she is buried, once her command is fulfilled, this would ignore the fact that many if not almost all the monologues, whether they are in the present or past tense, need to be understood as occurring, or continuing to occur, *after* the chronological end of the action. The process of detachment that grief involves must, that is, be understood as continuing beyond the physical limits of the story.

Peabody's definition suggests, moreover, that the mind that dies, the integral "I," depends on others for its dying (a metaphysical version of Addie's devoutly upheld command), and thus also undergoes a process of detachment. If this is so, then the self or the "I" existing prior to physical death is a self composed of others. Such a self is not isolated or solitary but communal; or, one should say, its integrity depends upon being integrated and its identity upon being constituted by identification, by a form of psychological or emotional analogy that works to extend the boundaries of identity. It is in death, as the novel tells us time and again, that this paradox is made manifest, that the need to imagine an integral self becomes most apparent even as the possibility of doing so passes away, a passing physically symbolized, as in Addie Bundren's case, by a decomposing corpse. And it is the action of grief, the refusal to let go those connections that once formed an integral self, that most painfully attests to the illusion of identity upon which our notions of self are founded. The "I" that lies dying, then, is the "I" of Addie and it is not; it is the "I" of each family member and it is not. As in the case of Anse, of whom Dewey Dell says, "he looks like right after the maul hits the steer and it [is] no longer alive and dont yet know that it is dead," [11] it is the "I" that each in his connection to her has formed and that now resists its own detachment and isolation even as it takes place. These paradoxes have their perfect analogous expression in the narrative form of the book, which both insists upon and yet prohibits our imagining that the fragmentary, disembodied episodes are — or to be more exact, *were once* — connected to the body or self of a story presented by a single controlling narrator. In taking this further risk, Faulkner perfects the formal strategy that the story of Caddy, lost in the grief-stricken maze of *The Sound and the Fury*, had suggested: like Addie, *As I Lay Dying* is both integrated and disintegrated; like each member of the family, each narrative episode participates in composing that integrated self at the same time it works out its own psychological detachment from it.

The theatrical collection of voices that the novel resembles not only reminds us that consciousness is largely memory, that the self is a fusion between a body with clear limits and a mind with unpredictable ones, and that the psychological chronology of our lives is easily more chaotic than that of the conventional novel; it does so by reminding us as well that although the novel, like any system of belief, offers an illusion of integrated form that may well be an improvement upon life, it is one that is precarious and requires our belief in things that do not exist. Or, as William Gass has remarked, "theories of character are not absurd in the way representational theories are; they are absurd in a grander way, for the belief in Hamlet (which audiences often seem to have) is like the belief in God — incomprehensible to reason — and one is inclined to seek a motive: some deep fear or emotional need." [12] *As I Lay Dying* is an exemplary case, because it is markedly a book in which characters exist on the basis of the briefest and most fragmentary physical descriptions and in which dialogue is constantly reported and often dislocated by narrative voices that, while they are careful to record identical dialects differently, nonetheless seem utterly severed from the peculiar bodily selves that ostensibly produce them. Vardaman's willingness to confuse the body of his mother with the body of a fish begins as a matter of temporal comparison (before the fish was "not-fish" Addie was still "is" [13]), but issues eventually in a spatial or corporeal integration of the two, dislocating one and the other from fixed limits in order to conceive a new form of identity. Vardaman's notion is absurd; yet it is only an extreme and traumatic form of the logic of analogy on which the book depends, a logic demanded by Faulkner's presenting his characters with powers of articulation that are literally inconceivable, by his splicing of reported action and dialogue with stream-of-consciousness narration, and, of course, by his dislocation of conventional prose limits through frequent violation of the rules of grammar and punctuation.

Among the three children most disturbingly affected by the death, Vardaman, perhaps because of the mechanism of transference, seems in some respects best able to maintain a hold on his own identity. He does so by a continual, prosaically simplified enumeration of his connections to, and understanding of, the actions around him. Darl seems technically his opposite and stands in much the same relation to him as Quentin does to Benjy in *The Sound and the Fury*. Although his sympathy with Vardaman becomes so pronounced that they ultimately listen together to the coffin, where Darl says Addie is "talking to God" and "calling on Him to help her lay down her life," Darl moves uncomfortably toward the tormented self-conscious posturings of Quentin Compson. Unable to contain his consciousness within the boundaries of sanity, Darl expresses his madness through hallucination and clairvoyance. As Tull puts it, "it's like he had got into the inside of you, someway. Like somehow you was looking at yourself and your doings outen his eyes." [14] In his clairvoyant knowledge of Dewey Dell's pregnancy and Jewel's illegitimacy; in narrating the events of Addie's actual death from a physical point that makes it impossible; and at last, on his way to a Jackson insane asylum, in speaking of himself in the third person, Darl tempts us to identify him with the omniscient author. But while Faulkner himself on one occasion associated Darl's visionary madness with artistic power, [15] it is important to note that this too is an instance of the novel's reluctance to meet the anxiety of omniscience. That is, by suggesting a link between omniscience and madness, Faulkner reveals what the novel backs away from as a form of disembodiment so extreme as to be terrifying and debilitating.

The tranquil side of Darl's madness, subtly and exactly expressed in his contention that "it would be nice if you could just ravel out into time," is countered by the more nightmarish character who, as Dewey Dell reports, "sits at the supper table with his eyes gone further than the food and the lamp, full of the land dug out of his skull and the holes filled with distance beyond the land." In psychological terms, the person of Darl offers the danger that the conventional boundaries between internal and external will become irremediably confused; while in terms of the novel, the character of Darl, who as Tull remarks "just thinks by himself too much," offers the danger that Addie's dying will be swallowed up by his consciousness, that her "I" and those of the other characters will become inseparable from his own. [16] Darl's omniscience is thus presented as a paradox that parallels, and takes its cue from, the paradox of death as it is explored in the novel: just as Addie's death calls into question the boundaries of the self by defining that self as a series of connections that appear even as they are disintegrated, Darl's intense consciousness, like that of an omniscient author-narrator, defines a self whose identity risks being lost in the act of becoming saturated with the ability to be connected to other minds. [17] The very form of the novel requires, of course, that the characters be understood as minds, as instances of narration or storytelling, but by constantly exposing as impractical our desire to fix the limits of each character's conscious identity, the novel also constantly refers us to the one identity, the one mind — that of the author — that has become so illusive as to be felt to be missing altogether.

I N SPEAKING of a corpse like Addie's that continues to seem both dead and alive, the difficulty of choosing between grammatical forms — *she* and *it, is* and *was* — keeps in view the central problem of bodily integrity, a problem explored insistently by the novel's blurring of boundaries between the animate and the inanimate, as in Anse's monologue on roads, Darl's on the river and the wagon, or Dewey Dell's on the dead earth. There are other examples we must turn to, but in all cases such blurrings increase our dependence on the rhetorical terms of the novel, preventing us from doubting the legitimacy of the absurd ritual journey as it unfolds and keeping us attached to the startling possibility of Addie's continued integral power. In this respect the most unnerving yet effective device is the sudden appearance more than halfway through the book, and chronologically (though it makes little sense to speak of it so) some four days after her death, of Addie's single monologue, one of the most emotionally charged pieces of writing in the novel and perhaps the one that comes closest to stating internally a theory of its narrative form.

The importance of Addie's diatribe against "words" — and particularly the word *love* — lies not simply in her belief that "words dont ever fit even what they are trying to say at," that we have "to use one another by words like spiders dangling by their mouths from a beam, swinging and twisting and never touching," [18] for these remarks add virtually nothing to the overwhelming effect already generated by the novel that this is the case. Nor does Addie's enumeration of her pregnancies and the manner in which each balances out or revenges another accomplish much more than providing a partial key to the various relationships of antagonism and devotion that exist among her children. While these relationships are important and finally have much to do with analogies one might draw between the family and the book as integrated forms, the instrumental significance of Addie's monologue arises rather in those sections of her utterance that may be said most to resemble the brooding, silenced voice of the narrator (or author) and are therefore most likely to be misread as moments of sheer invention for the sake of invention on Faulkner's part. The implied or explicit correlation between words and bodies that appears throughout Addie's monologue recalls similar dramatizations of Faulkner's authorial agony in *The Sound and the Fury*, dramatizations that in each case also prefigure the intimate analogy between creation and grief in Faulkner's most passionate explorations of wasted love and historical loss, *Absalom, Absalom!* and *Go Down, Moses*.

The technical wonder of *As I Lay Dying* and its relative thematic isolation among Faulkner's major novels may obscure its place in the development of his handling of loss and grief. The book elaborates those intimacies of loss that *The Sound and the Fury* had broached, but here the simultaneous rage and sentimental indulgence that unbalance the Compson's story are modified and merged; and the emotion spent in the sublimation of erotic passion in the earlier book, and later spent in the sublimation of the equally passionate tragedies of race, is brought to focus and distanced in the novel's extraordinary technique. This technique, fracturing that universal presence by and in which we constitute the essence of a story, defines grief as a characteristic of Faulkner's narrative form itself, a characteristic, that is to say, in which his forms find their fullest expressive power — that of articulating what is lost but lingering on the verge of memory, what will never be but *might have been*, what passionate word or act is harbored in that which remains, for fear or shame, unspoken or unactualized. While suggesting that the decaying corpse of Addie is emblematic of the burden of the Southern past, Faulkner at the same time comes closer to a full evocation of that feminine presence he everywhere associates with creative desire, its failure, and the resulting grief; identifying himself with that presence and yet barely screening his apparent hatred of it, he portrays in Addie the figure of *mothering* conspicuously absent in *Sartoris*, *The Sound and the Fury*, and *Sanctuary* — the figure his later novels will seek to actualize in a crossing of races and whose essence is the literal embodiment of the loss, the separation, and the grief Faulkner finds at the heart of cultural and familial history and acts out in the lives and form of fictional narrative.

Words like *motherhood*, *love*, *pride*, *sin*, and *fear*, Addie suggests, are just "shape[s] to fill a lack," shapes that, when the need for them arises, cannot adequately fill the void left by an accomplished act or a past event. Words "fumble" at deeds "like orphans to whom are pointed out in a crowd two faces and told, That is your father, your mother," and they resemble, in Addie's mind, the names of her husband and children, whose names and bodies imperfectly fill the lack in her bodily self they have caused:

> I would think: The shape of my body where I used to be a virgin is in the shape of a   and I couldn't think *Anse*, couldn't remember *Anse*. It was not that I could think of myself as no longer unvirgin, because I was three now. And when I would think *Cash* and *Darl* that way until their names would die and solidify into a shape and then fade away, I would say, All right. It doesn't matter. It doesn't matter what they call them.[19]

Although it might be too much to claim that the confused and sometimes contradictory remarks of Addie's monologue immediately explain anything, they do reveal that the novel, as John K. Simon has pointed out, is "the story of a body, Addie's, both in its existence as an unembalmed corpse and as it was — at least partly — conceived for passion."[20] That is, her remarks clarify what Addie implies and what Dewey Dell, in her own first pregnancy, has begun to discover — that the connection between sexual "lying" and lying dying is an intimate one, and that the violation is not simply sexual but generational, as Dewey Dell understands: "I feel my body, my bones and flesh beginning to part and open upon the alone, and the process of coming unalone is terrible."[21]

Pregnancy for Dewey Dell and for Addie involves a confusion of identity that inverts the one expressed in the process of death, in which the impossibility of conceiving of the self as a singular identity is made paradoxically conspicuous in the sudden need to preserve those connections that define the self even as they pass away. Standing at the other end of death, as it were, "the process of coming unalone" initiates in their most apparent physical form the connections without which one cannot fully imagine ever having been a lone, identical self existing apart from conscious and bodily ties to others. In extremity, the "coming unalone," the becoming more than one "I," leads to a threat of utter extinction through saturation, as in the case of Darl, whom we might think of as figuratively invaded by, and thus consciously "bearing" in distorted shape, all the novel's characters and events; or it leads to an extinction in which consciousness is completely severed from its own "I," as in Darl's meditation on sleep and in the nightmare that Dewey Dell's pregnancy, in conjunction with her mother's death, leads her to recall:

> When I used to sleep with Vardaman I had a nightmare once I thought I was awake but I couldn't see and I couldn't feel I couldn't feel the bed under me and I couldn't think what I was I couldn't think of my name I couldn't even think I am a girl I couldn't even think I nor even think I want to wake up nor remember what was opposite to awake so I could do that.

It is this predicament that Addie speaks of metaphorically when she cannot remember the shape of her body when virgin, cannot even articulate the word that might describe it. Words, that is, are inadequate not so much because they fail to "fit even what they are trying to say at," but because they fail to describe or fill the blank space that only the act of conceiving the need for a word can make manifest as irreparably lost or passed. Words are for something we are not or can no longer be: or as Peabody remarks, in a humorous variation on this potent analogy, when "it finally occurred to Anse himself that [Addie] needed [a doctor], it was already too late."[22]

As I Lay Dying speaks pointedly to the need for establishing and maintaining conscious attachments symbolically incorporated in bodily ties by constant reference, in both actual and formal terms, to the loss of the originating mother. Darl's claim that he has no mother and that the illegitimate Jewel has a horse for a mother; Dewey Dell's psychological merging of death and childbearing (both in her rhetorical association with Addie as mother and in her conceiving of the funeral journey as a means to get an abortion); Cash's obsession with Addie's coffin, as though its perfection and preservation will somehow save the bodily integrity of Addie; Jewel's heroic actions to save that coffin and its body from flood and fire; and Vardaman's transfiguration of mother into fish[23] — all of these reactions identify grieving as foremost a process of detachment, of disembodiment, in which the act of *expression* is central. Supported by the chaotic chronology of the novel, which prevents us from knowing "where" the characters are speaking from, the community of voices itself participates in the paradoxical action that grieving is, an action that expresses connections in order both to make them and let them go. Like the voices of the women singing at the wake described by Tull, the voices of the novel that tell Addie's story (including her own) seem to "come out of the air, flowing together and on in sad, comforting tunes. When they cease it's like they hadn't gone away. It's like they had just disappeared into the air and when we moved we would loose them again out of the air around us, sad and comforting."[24]

This is true whether we conceive of the characters as talking, as thinking, or — in some instances — even as writing their stories; and the confusion as to which is the more appropriate conception makes it clear that grief seldom has an appropriate form or a distinct chronology. What Faulkner once spoke of as characteristic of his entire work is particularly relevant to *As I Lay Dying:* "The fact that I have moved my characters around in time successfully, at least in my own estimation, proves to me my own theory that time is a fluid condition which has no existence except in the momentary avatars of individual people. There is no such thing as *was* — only *is*. If *was* existed, there would be no grief or sorrow." [25] The form of the novel keeps *is* from becoming *was* as Addie's corpse is kept dying beyond the physical death and — because the stories have no fixed temporal origins but rather are desperately detached from them — even beyond the supposed chronological end of the action, Addie's burial and Anse's remarriage. Grief itself seems disembodied from its object precisely because the boundaries of that object have ceased to have specific meaning and now receive abnormally deliberate, if displaced, attention. The dislocation of conscious attention that grief can produce makes Vardaman's psychological transferences from mother to fish, for example, or Cash's from body to coffin plausible and even necessary, and helps explain what André Bleikasten has referred to as Faulkner's possession by the "demon of analogy" in the novel. [26] The action of grief responds to and reflects the demand for analogy, for the possibility of relocating the lost integrity of one object in another as a way of expressing the maintenance of emotional connections that are threatening to disappear.

Because the novel refuses to settle on a point of view, a narrative focus that gives immediate coherence to the story, but on the contrary forces us to develop that coherent identity by an act of imaginative identification, piecing it together from disparate parts, it too might well be regarded as a family without a mother, as it were, without a single source from which we can clearly say the parts have sprung. And yet of course we do say just that: we say Faulkner is the author, these all are parts of him, products of his creation. To say this, however, is both necessary and speculative, for the parts — disembodied from the act that apparently produced them — are in their own way as much orphaned as Addie's own children or the words that she speaks of as filling a lack left by a deed that has passed. The self that produced them, or the integral point of view that we imagine as controlling them, has "come unalone" in that act, which is now a lack filled by shapes. We know and need it only in retrospect; because this is the case, the process of grieving that the Bundrens undergo — a process in which their breaking of connections with Addie at once defines her self as composed of them yet requires each of them to lie dying along with her — is analogous to the narrative unfolding of "Faulkner's story," a process in which the shape of the book is built up by accumulation and connection but paradoxically participates in the disintegration of that imagined single form, leaving each episode in isolation, tenuously attached to the others and at the same time orphaned — referring to, yet failing properly to "fill" and complete, the lack that they make manifest. Because they exist in the novel's form as disembodied both from the bodies that utter them *and* from the one body that we must understand as having once produced them, the narrative episodes do indeed seem a collection of voices in the air.

As I Lay Dying is best understood, then, as a book in which death is the story and the story is a death, a book in which the authorial "I" also lies dying; that is, he is dead as Addie is dead, dead as a single identity but still alive in the episodes that continue to refer themselves to that identity and continue to constitute it even more emphatically in our desire to locate Faulkner's own "language," his own "story," in the voices of his characters. To speak of the book as a corpse is to recognize that such an expression is at once appropriate and inadequate, for just as Addie's corpse is not what dies (except on one occasion) in the book, the words that fill the book, like the family that continues to fill and be filled by Addie Bundren, are alive, however disembodied, fragmented, and comically bereaved. The expressions of grief that work out their own disembodiment from a lost, decomposing object by the insistent desire for analogous experience find analogy in the novel's form, which, like the action of grief, relocates the limits and power of that object in the stories of which it is now composed. Those expressions continue to have and to acquire meaning, and continue to make connections, despite the absurdity of doing so and appearing to act, as Faulkner recognized, in a virtual vacuum.

I T IS A measure of the novel's magnificent power that it leads us to recognize Faulkner's mastery in the very situation in which we are tempted to say he has surrendered control of the book, has himself become disembodied as "author." Wright Morris has spoken quite rightly of such examples of stylistic power in Faulkner's work as moments in which "the technique is so flawless that the effect is incandescent. Craft and raw material are in such lucid balance that it seems the craftsman himself is missing." [27] A more appropriate way of characterizing As I Lay Dying is difficult to imagine, for Faulkner is indeed missing — missing as Addie is missing, nonetheless commanding our attention and our attempts to account for his seemingly invisible control. His own notorious remarks (in the preface to Sanctuary) about the ease and speed with which he wrote the novel are no doubt slightly overstated; but Faulkner's admission on another occasion that the novel is an example of that creative situation in which "technique charges in and takes command of the dream before the writer himself can get his hands on it" [28] corresponds to our sense that the book's craft and material, its form and substance, like the form and substance of Addie, are working in brilliant accord, at once engagingly distinct and emotionally inseparable.

It is such power, charged by the activity of grieving that expresses itself analogically, that compels us to seek analogues for the author in the work, connections between Faulkner and Peabody, Faulkner and Darl, Faulkner and Addie, for example — or perhaps just as appropriately, as the lucidity of Faulkner's technique may suggest, between the author and Cash, the patient, meticulous builder of Addie's coffin. Faulkner's many references in letters and interviews to himself as a craftsman, as a user of "tools" and materials and a virtual builder of tales, makes the analogy unavoidable; though this analogy is not as immediately central as the formal analogy between Faulkner and Addie, it amplifies that one by bringing into focus the relationships between body and coffin, and perhaps more notably between coffin and book, as objects of extraordinary fragility and devotion. Against flood, fire, and scavenging buzzards, the coffin, though hiding it from view, preserves its rotting cargo long enough to get it buried in Jefferson — preserves the integrity of the object it both literally contains and figuratively renders absurd *as* an object in the same way that the form of the book, elaborately pieced together, both literally contains its central event, Addie's death, and figuratively renders absurd the physical limits of that event. Darl's early characterizations of his dead mother's body as "spent yet alert," "volitional," or "lightly alive, waiting to come awake," [29] as well as the novel's continual unpredicated reference to the coffin and its body as "it" (or to both as "her"), all work to blur the distinction between body and container, the animate and the inanimate, in a fashion that is completely analogous to the novel's formal blurring of distinctions between its own structure of expression and the ongoing event that is expressed. The coffin "contains" the object of the family's quixotic devotion as absolutely and precariously as the book "contains" the dying of Addie Bundren. Like the book, the coffin is both the shape filled by the fragile self of Addie and a "shape to fill a lack," the lack that death makes manifest and *is*, but in which those of whose minds it is a function refuse fully to believe.

The coffin and the book, each in its way, maintain the integrity of Addie's bodily self. But if we keep in mind the example of gentle Cash, who admits that there is "a fellow in every man that's done a-past the sanity or the insanity, that watches the sane and the insane doings of that man with the same horror and the same astonishment," the coffin and the book must also be seen as maintaining, in moral terms, the integrity of the funeral journey — and against rather overwhelming odds. For quite aside from the preposterous physical threats to the journey, the family's own intentions are continually betrayed as shallow and self-serving. Anse wants new teeth and a new wife; Dewey Dell wants an abortion; Cash wants a gramophone; and Vardaman wants to eat bananas and see a toy train. Only Jewel and Darl seem immune from mixed motives for reaching Jefferson, the one determined to complete the burial, the other determined to prevent it. Although the effort may succeed precisely because of these base intentions, it is also the case — as in Vardaman's wish to see the train, which he says "made my heart hurt" — that the intentions themselves may have become bound up with the forms of analogous experience and expression that grief both makes possible and necessitates. There seems no other explanation for Faulkner's most masterful stroke in the novel, the complete deletion of the actual burial of Addie, the act that her command set in motion and to which the entire action of the book is devoted. Yet as Vardaman unwittingly suggests early on when he asks Dewey Dell, "Did [Addie] go far as town?" [30] it is not the burial that matters but the journey, the heroic effort to sustain the fragile community of the family in the face of physical and psychological trauma. Each of the Bundrens participates in the journey as he or she participates in the dying of

Addie; each journeys and each dies, and in doing so testifies to the continued integrity of the dead mother, memorializing the passing of the body by expressing the emotional ties that continue to compose the self.

The novel's treatment of the corpse of Addie must thus be understood in the same light as Vardaman's boring of holes through the coffin into her face — as an act of love whose grotesque expression is at once perversely comic and at the same time utterly sincere. What the book poignantly exposes is the precarious nature of ritual expression, particularly that of funeral rituals, in which an absurd possibility — that the corpse of the person nonetheless *is* the person — is maintained not because anyone believes it but because no one can immediately, emotionally deny it. The trauma of grief, in which death most clearly *is* a function of other minds, makes the irrational conventional; and the elegy that the expression of grief may become must itself, as the novel certainly does, harbor the eventuality of seeming comic or grotesque. It is "only when the ritual is disengaged from its symbolic function," Olga Vickery has remarked of the novel, "that the comic aspect becomes apparent." Vickery goes on to note that the distinction between empty and significant ritual is not unlike the distinction Addie's monologue draws between words and deeds,[31] an analogy that is completely appropriate if — and only if — we understand words to be capable of more than Addie admits; that is, only if we understand words, the shapes that fill a lack, as the possible expression of an identity that is most intensely and passionately present even as it passes away. The ritual of the book threatens at every point to become disengaged from its symbolic function and thus to appear simply absurd or grotesque; yet this is perfectly in keeping with the various characters' precarious and traumatic attachment to the central object of the ritual, and moreover in perfect keeping with the novel's formal disengagement of its narrative expression from a controlling consciousness, a consciousness that would more clearly and conventionally stabilize the meaning of the death and its ritual enactment. The absurdity of the characters' reactions, as well as the absurdity of the journey itself, register in unmediated form the paradox of death that the book struggles so hard to contain.

At one point Darl describes Anse's face as having been "carved by a savage caricaturist [in] a monstrous burlesque of all bereavement."[32] If one is tempted to say that this applies equally well to each of the characters, and that Faulkner's modern parable produces only a travesty of its characters' efforts and a virtual parody of itself, it must be kept in mind that, because parody works by a form of analogy that is more successful the more fragile are the boundaries between the mockery and the object, the tale of the Bundrens is one that preserves that fragile equilibrium and expresses it formally in the extenuated distinctions between voice and character, between corpse and self, and in this case most of all between the conventions of ritual and their burlesque. "There's not too fine a distinction between humor and tragedy," Faulkner once remarked, for "even tragedy is in a way walking a tightrope between . . . the bizarre and the terrible."[33] It is difficult, of course, to read *As I Lay Dying* as tragedy, but its bizarre and terrible humor keeps before us the fact that comedy itself is often a means of releasing pressure and relieving anguish. The contortions of language that break down boundaries between the outrageous and the awful, that is to say, are not unlike the emotional trauma associated with death, for the instability of the expression of grief makes it particularly susceptible to the potential comedy of analogy.

Such contortions tend easily toward the tall tale; but then Faulkner, in an age dominated by "The Waste Land" and by Hemingway's cold-blooded and often futile heroism, might well have felt the necessity of exaggeration in order to render a parable of heroic effort in the modern world. Of course much of Faulkner's fiction tends toward the tall tale, but what is extraordinary about *As I Lay Dying*, particularly when we recall that it follows *The Sound and the Fury* and falls between the composition and revision of *Sanctuary*, Faulkner's most unrelentingly brutal parable of the modern world, is that the comedy itself could come to seem the finest, most passionate expression of grief and — with precarious extremity — of love. In this respect, the novel projects a world of tragic compassion Faulkner would not find again until *Absalom, Absalom!* and *Go Down, Moses*, in which the intimate entanglement of grief and love, and the scattered family passions they reflect, are so anguished as to appear almost beyond redemption. For the moment, however — perhaps the only certain moment in his career — Faulkner's own compassion became brilliant, powerful, and unabashedly moving.

chapter 3

Sanctuary:
An American Gothic

W HICH of Faulkner's major novels is not an American gothic? The phrase would apply as well to virtually any of them — most particularly, perhaps, to *Light in August* or *Absalom, Absalom!,* in which Faulkner intimately engages those problems of slavery and race relations that constitute America's central gothic experience, enacting patterns of convulsive passion, repressed guilt, and violently released hatred, the darkest side of the soul of American history from its moments of origin. Like *The Sound and the Fury, Sanctuary* (1931) takes up Faulkner's major theme in a peripheral fashion, but it stands nonetheless alone among his better novels in forsaking at nearly every point the complex psychological dramatizations and convoluted narrative forms that characterize the others. *Sanctuary* is indeed psychologically disturbing, and its form presents a special kind of problem, yet both theme and form, thoroughly entangled as they are, seem intentionally to resist elaboration and explanation; rather, they jut into our consciousness with all the blunt pain of fated horror. As Clifton Fadiman put it in an early review, "the coiled and deadly prose" of *Sanctuary* reveals "an artistic temperament so icy as to induce in the reader nervous terror rather than aesthetic submission." [1]

There is no relief from the terror and — what is more frightening, to the point of burlesque — no purposeful explanation of it. There is no sanctuary. Faulkner's revisions of the novel, far from toning down the violence, only, and quite deliberately, increased it; and the major addition to the revised version — the section devoted to a psychobiography of Popeye as a child — only, and quite wonderfully, renders the novel's mysterious horror more stunning. The story of Popeye's childhood is, in effect, something of a joke on the reader, for its exposes in perverse extremity the limits of "naturalism" as a literary form and a philosophical position. To get a sense of Faulkner's strategy in *Sanctuary,* we need only to note, for instance, that he may well have drawn his title and, to some extent, his plot from a short story by Dreiser, whose "Sanctuary" was written in the early 1920s and encountered the usual objections from magazine publishers before being collected in *Chains* (1927). Dreiser's story concerns a young woman who initially grows as a "flower" amid the "dung-heap" of her tenement childhood. Succumbing to the ill fortunes of urban life, Madeleine Kinsella is eventually driven to prostitution after being deserted by her beau. When she is arrested, Madeleine is put under the care of the Sisterhood of the Good Shepherd; once she returns to the cruel outside world, she is taken up by a "hawk of the underworld," one of those "Fagins of sex . . . who change their women as they would their coats." He forces her into prostitution once more, but in the end Madeleine does indeed find "sanctuary" — by returning to the Sisterhood, where, inspired by "an image of the Virgin," she decides to stay.[2]

Dreiser's story has little of the power of his novels, for his characteristic creative virtues depend on a monumentality of prose that reflects the uncontrollable forces of urban, capitalistic life in America; and his great novels — *Sister Carrie* and *An American Tragedy* — portray characters who succeed or fail, not because they are crushed by the machinery of social forces they oppose, but because they desire exactly what the machinery of their society offers: sex, power, and money, the three things Dreiser finds everywhere synonymous in modern American life. "Sanctuary," casting back in detail after detail to Crane's *Maggie*, nevertheless offers a happy ending that neither Crane nor Dreiser often found feasible or useful, and it has neither the accumulated force of Dreiser's longer works nor the precise virtues of Crane's shorter ones, in which, from their different but complementary perspectives, the ruthless and irresponsible violence of urban America is subtly embodied in the work's style. Certainly, the peculiar poetry of Crane's fiction differs radically from the prehistoric, blocklike prose of Dreiser, but each style has the effect of flattening or submerging characters within a landscape of economic and biological action they cannot control. Characters in Crane and Dreiser are manipulated by the world they live in and the prose that creates them.

It is not at all fortuitous that naturalism, as style and as doctrine, moves in its greater moments toward an aestheticism of expression, a symbolic consolidation or concentration of immutable forces, for the naturalistic novel relies heavily on a gothic intensification of detail, which, like the symbolist poetry some of Faulkner's early fiction aspired to, expands time, stops it, or threatens its very existence in order to recapitulate the history of the species (or the hero's society) in the life of the individual. One finds this in Norris and Dreiser, and more frequently in Crane and London, when social criticism gives way to intense impressionism. Such moments understandably lead in turn to a style that strives for stark, simplified points of view, complete moral detachment, and violent, hard-edged forms of expression. They lead, that is, to Hemingway, Cain, Farrell, West, and, perhaps most of all, to Hammett. And in one strange but logical case, they lead to Faulkner. *Sanctuary* is less dependent on Faulkner's native Southern traditions than his other major novels, and it engages more directly than any of them the violent realities of contemporary life, in this case the realities of a country poised at a point of passing from the Roaring Twenties to the Depression Thirties. It belongs emphatically to the genre of "hard-boiled" fiction of that period; the most distinctive feature of its technique is a cold, intense observation that does not mimetically reproduce reality but, as Camus remarks of this school, cultivates instead "the most arbitrary form of stylization." The hard-boiled style takes the aesthetics of observation to their limit and intentionally obliterates the inner life of its characters; and to the extent that the psychological and the emotional are subordinated to the purely physical, the novels Camus describes tend toward a philosophy of pathology. Because "the life of the body, reduced to its essentials, paradoxically produces an abstract and gratuitous universe," Camus remarks, such "novels of violence are also love stories." [3]

But then all of Faulkner's central works, as well as most of his others, conform to such a loose definition. Although they greatly diverge from the novels Camus has in mind, his major novels on the problems of race are all explicitly violent love stories. They are "romances" of Southern history and Southern passions — romances in the sense defined by Hawthorne and Twain, depicting the lost world of the possible, the marginal real, the "might-have-been" that still is, but also romances in the more singular sense of their derivation from historical and contemporary assumptions about the threatened violation of white blood by black blood. The hysteria over miscegenation, which provides the basis for the South's own peculiar gothic tradition, is evident in *Sanctuary* only in eccentric ways; but the naturalistic theories that underlay and promoted that hysteria by converting providential design into evolutionary proscription are prominent indeed. Without tracing in detail here naturalism's paths as it moves toward a variety of modernisms, let us note simply that, since Popeye descends directly from Norris's Vandover or McTeague, for example, and more distantly from Hawthorne's villains, Norris's well-known definition of naturalism as a form of romance aptly characterizes *Sanctuary* as it anticipates Faulkner's romances of race. Far from being a variation of popular sentimentalism, Norris contends, the romance is an "instrument, keen, finely tempered, flawless," which pierces "through the clothes and tissues and wrappings of flesh down deep into the red, living heart of things," and uncovers "the unplumbed depths of the human heart, and the mystery of sex . . . and the black, unsearched penetralia of the soul of man." [4]

Norris's "black soul" is biological, as Hawthorne's was theological; in Faulkner the two come together in the "black soul" of Southern man, the complex shadow of "the Negro" that occupies a position at the very sex and heart of Southern life. *The Sound and the Fury* revolves around that discovery in widening circles that would only come into focus in *Absalom, Absalom!* But one may suggest that *Light in August* and, less obviously, *Sanctuary* were the means of Faulkner's discovery, the one prefiguring Charles Bon in his contemporary manifestation as Joe Christmas, the other reworking the narcissistic, incestuously disturbed Quentin Compson in the character of Horace Benbow by bringing him into confrontation with impenetrable evil in a way that forecasts Quentin's confrontation of the

Sutpen tragedy. Like the rereading of Quentin's life that the doubled figure of Henry Sutpen makes available, such a reading of *Sanctuary* is possible only in the larger, retrospective context of Faulkner's career. The novel deflects this interpretation as skillfully as it does others, and it is first of all an exemplary document of American modernism, which presents a brutal, resistant surface. While it is no less shocking — rather, it is more immediately shocking — than Faulkner's best novels, its shock derives not from the deep social and psychological nightmare of Southern history but from the crude intangibility of contemporary violence, which seems to have no particular explanation and no identifiable origin. Like Popeye's violent life and death, it simply happens.

ALTHOUGH it certainly remains the "cheap idea" and the "most horrific" tale Faulkner claimed in his notorious preface that the original *Sanctuary* was,[5] the revised version is startlingly better and demonstrates, now that the original text is available, his keen judgment in making the changes that he did.[6] Aside from increasing the episodes of violence and their intensity, the most critical change Faulkner made was to reduce drastically the organizing presence of Horace Benbow. The original text is largely subservient to the character of Horace, more particularly to elaborations of his psychological and aesthetic problems, many of which had wisely been removed from *Flags in the Dust* when it became *Sartoris* but now reappeared, indicating that Faulkner had not exorcized them in the character of Quentin Compson and was reluctant to discard them altogether. What remains of Horace's pathology in the revised version — his incestuous attachment to his stepdaughter, Little Belle, and his still troubled relationship with his sister, Narcissa — is just enough to make plausible, without overwhelming, his futile entanglement and interest in the grotesque criminal worlds of Frenchman's Bend and Memphis. In the original version, it is far too clear that Faulkner himself is reconstructing for Horace "an edifice upon which he would not dare to look, like an archaeologist who, from a meagre sifting of vertebrae, reconstructs a shape out of the nightmares of his own childhood."[7]

Such speculations and such writing are what Faulkner fortunately excised from the novel in rearranging episodes and reducing Horace's role. In doing so, he partially freed himself from one of his most unsatisfactory characters, redirected the overbearing aestheticism of his earlier work, and gave to the stories of Temple and Popeye the violent prominence that made the novel sensational and, indeed, good. For the power of *Sanctuary*, like that of other hardboiled fiction, derives from a presentation of problems or strategies that one must characterize as "psychological" but that cannot by any clear means be described in therapeutic terms. Such descriptions may well arise in critical readings of the novel, but it is important that they not be thematized by the author in a particular character. The story must remain, in essence, a mystery; while it may be that *Sanctuary*, as Malraux remarks, is "a novel with a detective-story atmosphere but without detectives,"[8] it need also be a pathological story without a pathologist — or, as Malcolm Cowley puts it, "an example of the Freudian method turned backward, being full of sexual nightmares that are in reality social symbols." [9]

Cowley also contends, in a way that summarizes one faction of opinion about the novel, that Popeye represents "the mechanical civilization that has invaded and conquered the South" and seems "a compendium of all the hateful qualities that Faulkner assigns to finance capitalism." [10] This seems rather a long jump to make, and it may only be possible if we assume Popeye to be an extension of Jason Compson and a harbinger of Flem Snopes. However, *Sanctuary* appeared at a time when the nation was beset and fascinated by organized crime, and more exactly at the point that finance capitalism, in the stock market crash of 1929, had just suffered a catastrophic setback. The novel culminates a decade of public attention to crime and criminals — the era of Prohibition — in which the nation itself, in Stephen Marcus's words, had "committed itself to a vast collective fiction," a "collaborative illegality"; [11] and it prefigures a decade of great economic turmoil that to some observers made the blurring of the legal and the illegal at the heart of American capitalism more apparent. The glamor of the one era and the bleakness of the other, both productive of criminal heroes, are fused in *Sanctuary* in a way that is more distinctively American than Southern, and the featuring of Popeye and Temple that Faulkner accomplished by reducing the role of Horace is crucial to that effect. The literature of crime that dominates this period of American social history is most characterized by a thorough lack — or at least an existential denigration — of psychology, the two assumptions being that the pseudo-Freudian and Darwinian deliberations of Dreiser, for example, could only lead to a position of philosophical despair; and that, because this was true and because American society was apparently collapsing into lawlessness (or, from the Marxist point of view, was innately lawless), the self was as much a fabrication as the society it inhabited.

As the product of a society that was lawless by nature (that is, in which laws themselves came to seem natural forces designed to benefit the fittest), the representative Dreiserian hero, who survives only by manipulating the social and economic "laws" of survival, might well give way to the criminal hero — the gangster, the Hemingway tough, or the Hammett detective, who operates on both sides of the law and of necessity constructs his own moral universe. In extremity, it might give way to what is simply perverse — to Popeye, an impotent, violent, pathetic creature. The psychobiography of Popeye that Faulkner appended in his revisions of *Sanctuary* extends the horror of the novel, but it neither explains nor justifies his life as a criminal. This addition is precarious, for it poses, with all the portentous shock of a case study, as the "cause" of evil. Son of a syphilitic strikebreaker who deserts his family; grandson of a pyromaniac; given to cutting up small animals with scissors; and venomously allergic to alcohol, Popeye is rather a compendium of naturalistic doom. One might argue, as Cowley does and as the novels of Norris and Dreiser often do in more dramatic ways, that so spectacular a doom is inherent in the deep laws of naturalism that gird the structure of American capitalism; but Faulkner's positioning of the chapter, an extraordinary stroke, requires us to understand that such an "explanation" is an afterthought, that the moral universe has extreme need of such explanations but that they have practical limits and ultimately cannot describe the true source of evil or even reveal whether the evil of the modern world has a particular source.

In the context of the other revisions of the novel, the addition of Popeye's psychobiography suggests, moreover, that Faulkner saw the near dead end of Horace as a character and as a dramatic measure of the book's social terrors. Horace precedes Quentin Compson (who seems in *The Sound and the Fury* to have grown from a merging of the characters of Horace and young Bayard Sartoris) but, as the revisions of Quentin's life in *Absalom, Absalom!* would reveal, the troubled aesthete needed firmer grounding than any clinical specification of his "complexes" could offer. The historical depth of his psychological disturbance that the Sutpen tragedy affords makes Quentin the magnificent modern figure that he is; on the other hand, Horace remains — particularly in *Flags in the Dust* and the original *Sanctuary* — a highly literary creation who is stifled by his own, and his author's, self-conscious display of currently fashionable Freudian ideas. The revisions of the novel leave Horace's psychological disturbances as mysterious as the general evil of the novel by embedding them in much larger failures of "law, justice, [and] civilization," which at best can only be ascribed to "that irony which lurks in events" and at worst require Horace to admit that there may be "a logical pattern to evil." [12] The absurd miscarriages of justice and civilization that propel the novel's plot, as Faulkner came to see, have no clear dramatic relation to Horace's psychological problems. Faulkner increased the one by inserting the violent lynching of Lee Goodwin and reduced the other, bringing both together in the case study of Popeye, who ironically gets what (according to the laws of man and nature) he deserves and absorbs the profound shock of the book into a dark moral pit.

The transferring of the burden of psychological case study to Popeye extends the horror of the book not merely by adding sensationalistic details but also, more importantly, by exposing the moral void of psychoanalysis and social science, the conspicuous fields of inquiry that bring naturalism into the twentieth century and conspire to make justice a subject of pathological study. It is no accident that the primary technique of such inquiry, the technique of scientific observation, derives from the methods of the naturalist and, in literature, conforms to the careful techniques of recorded observation advocated, for example, by Zola in his influential essay "The Experimental Novel." Such techniques make a necessary virtue of apparent moral neutrality, of unflinching attention to the degradation that exists in the social world, and in doing so they unavoidably — in fact, intentionally — blur distinctions between the moral and the pathological. In a larger sense, they blur distinctions between the legal and the illegal by assuming that laws, after all, are social constructions, that deviant behavior, criminal or not, is utterly relative, and that the moral world is a series of fabricated ideals that cover up or repress the gothic turbulence of instinctual life.

Sanctuary borrows on the assumptions and techniques of naturalism in its evolving contemporary forms, most notably its great American expression in the form of the hard-boiled detective novel, where the technique of observation, the moral skill *par excellence,* is concomitantly a method of survival and a means of administering justice. As they grow out of the nineteenth-century novel's own incorporation of administrative techniques of surveillance,[13] both the detective's and his novel's plotting of action depend on a manipulation of evidence in order to create a logical pattern in which problems or crimes can be solved and justice carried out. In the representative case of Hammett, such action depends on going outside the law — the "law" as both ordained structure of justice and preconceived fictional plot — in order to create a "plot" that could conceivably be resolved in any of a number of ways but in the end seems to have only the resolution, the "solution," offered by the detective, who has in effect virtually created it. The assumption in the world of Hammett's novels, as Marcus writes, is that the "reality" given to the detective is "a fabrication, a fiction, a faked and alternate reality," which it is his job to deconstruct and reconstruct into a "true fiction" — not, as in the classical detective story, by discovering what "really happened," but by substituting his own version of the real, by creating a fiction, like that of the novelist, that is more plausible and persuasive.[14] To the extent that his methods are themselves "illegal," the detective's posture circumscribes a moral universe of extreme relativism, an extenuation of the survival of the fittest in which the hero, instead of falling victim to crushing, uncontrollable economic and political powers, masters and exploits those powers to his own ends, defining the morality of power by embodying it himself.

As Malraux observed, however, *Sanctuary* has no detectives. Or rather, it has a detective, Horace Benbow, who is powerless to prevent grotesque misapplications of justice and incapable of revealing why such evil as the novel continually dwells on should occur. One might say that *Sanctuary* is the underside of Hammett's novels; its interests are much the same, and its obsession with impotence reflects the masculine domination of the hard-boiled novel at the same time (in Faulkner's revisions) that it marks the passing into futility of psychological concerns that is the hallmark of Hammett's neo-Hobbesian world. Hammett's detectives frequently recall from their own lives, or encounter in the lives of their clients or criminals, an incident suggestive of buried psychological problems, but such problems almost without exception either become part of a series of "clues" that are dismissed as formally irrelevant to the plot as it unfolds or are made thematically subject to ridiculing scrutiny. At one point in *The Dain Curse* (1929), for instance, the Op encounters the novelist who will ultimately be revealed as the "criminal" and finds him writing an article, for the *Psychopathological Review,* "condemning the hypothesis of an unconscious or subconscious mind as a snare and a delusion, a pitfall for the unwary and a set of false whiskers for the charlatan," which makes it impossible "for the sound scholar to smoke out such faddists as . . . the psychoanalyst and the behaviorist." [15] The novelist, of course, turns out to be insane, but his project is not at all dissimilar to that of the Op (just as the Op's methods are, strictly speaking, neither legal nor illegal: they simply get the job done), whose techniques everywhere render morally meaningless the mitigations of behaviorism and the claims of unconscious or disturbed motivation.

In the case of *Sanctuary*, such claims are not declared altogether irrelevant but are shown to be nonetheless impotent. As Horace reconstructs the role of Temple Drake and merges her sexual violation with his own troubled desires for Little Belle, his defense of Lee Goodwin becomes more and more futile almost in precise measure of his own increasing psychological involvement in the case. After Temple's account of the night of crime, Horace broods over a photograph of Little Belle, which appears "to swoon in a voluptuous languor, blurring still more, fading, leaving upon his eye a soft and fading aftermath of invitation and voluptuous promise and secret affirmation," thus initiating for Horace a rape fantasy that so verges on criminal participation as to unsettle completely the illusion of his legal objectivity. The assumed objectivity of the aesthetic of observation is, however, exactly what is at stake in the novel; for Horace's narcissism, as this scene suggests, is patently a figure for that of the reader, who is invited to witness and indulge in fantasies that may well have personal, psychological motivation (as in the case of Quentin's fantasies of incest with Caddy) but have no public, moral explanation. Not only is there no justice, no law, and virtually no civilization in *Sanctuary*, there is also no justification for evil. It simply exists, infecting everyone; and as Horace remarks to Aunt Jenny, "there's a corruption about even looking upon evil, even by accident." [16]

L OOKING upon evil is precisely what the novel asks us to do. Its endlessly creative elaboration of scenes and metaphors of observation and voyeurism induces a kind of paralysis that is at once repelling and enticing. The central figure of that pattern, as his name suggests, appears in the peculiar sexuality of Popeye, who can arouse himself (though he cannot physically do so at all) only by watching Temple and Red fornicate, "hanging over the foot of the bed without even his hat off making a kind of whinnying sound." Popeye does indeed turn Reba's whorehouse into a "peep-show," as she puts it, but what else does the entire novel do? From the moment she is introduced, we are watching Temple along with everyone else — watching particularly "her long legs blonde with running, in speeding silhouette," as she cavorts with her university beaux, dashes frantically about the Old Frenchman place, seeking one sanctuary after another, and struggles invitingly to escape the pending, inevitable horror, all the while taunting her men and her readers with "a grimace of taut, toothed coquetry." [17] To remark that Temple too gets what she deserves may be true but is somewhat beside the point; certainly Faulkner's critique of Southern Womanhood is raised a fierce notch from *The Sound and the Fury*, but it is here subordinated to the novel's own techniques of observation, which have as their aim the creation of a moral shock whose ramifications exceed the collapse of Southern gynealotry even as they circle around it.

Temple takes her place among Faulkner's many heroines, from Caddy Compson to Eula Varner, whose distinctive characteristic is the aura of tragically — often comically — violated sexuality at the heart of Faulkner's gothicism. In the cases of Joanna Burden and Rosa Coldfield he would make painfully explicit the convulsive passions of racial fantasy that lie behind the peculiar premium placed on the purity of Southern Womanhood, and in this respect as well *Sanctuary*'s revisions draw the novel back from the vision of degenerating aristocratic ideals that Faulkner had already portrayed in *Sartoris* and *The Sound and the Fury*. This revision seems equally deliberate, for it entails the discarding of two signal passages in which Horace sees the Old Frenchman place as a house vaguely haunted by collapsed Southern dreams.[18] These deletions, like the reduction of Horace's psychological turmoil, have the effect of further divorcing the corrupt modern world of the South from the spent glory of its origins and making the contemporary horror all the more inexplicable. In the larger context of Faulkner's fiction, we recognize the tormenting relationship between the two worlds — recognize, as Delmore Schwartz points out, that the conflict between old and new South "brought Faulkner to the extreme where he can only seize his values, which are those of the idea of the Old South, by imagining them being violated by the most heinous crimes"[19] — but in the novel itself, as in *The Sound and the Fury*, we are given few indications that the faded Confederate dream could have any bearing, except a completely negative one, upon present reality.

This may, of course, be the most obvious form of critique; but the "spent ghosts of voluptuous gestures and dead lusts" that linger in Temple's whorehouse bedroom lack the fuller historical resonance of those in Joanna Burden's bedroom (where much the same words characterize the climactic phase of her affair with Joe Christmas),[20] and the sexual violation of Caddy Compson, or Rosa Coldfield's long-remembered, long-denied fantasy of violation, are in this case drained of Faulkner's more embracing vision and reduced to a nearly clinical voyeurism. *Sanctuary* is decidedly a study in the pathology of history, but here again one must note (to extend the analogy) that it is a historical novel without a historian, that its vision is one that works on all levels to resist the longer, deeper vision that may well surround it and leaves the collapsed dream of the old South part of the novel's hidden evil mystery. Unlike Rosa, who "heir[s] too from all the unsistered Eves since the Snake" and lives an entire life in the fantasized moment of an "unravished nuptial,"[21] Temple is made to experience the most horrible of rapes — an experience that releases in her the nymphomania that, Faulkner forces us to assume, the pretentious conventions of Southern Womanhood have created.

Temple's virginity, like that of Caddy, is a moot point; it must be violated to have existed at all, much as the grandiloquent dream of the old South — as the next ten years of Faulkner's career would corroborate — must have been destroyed to have existed at all. Temple herself suggests this in one of the novel's more intriguing figures of voyeurism. As she lies in her whorehouse bed watching the "mirror-like" glass face of a broken clock, "holding in its tranquil depths a quiet gesture of moribund time . . . the ordered chaos of the intricate and shadowy world upon whose scarred flanks the old wounds whirl onward at dizzying speed into darkness lurking with new disasters," Temple recalls the hour of dressing for a dance. More particularly, she recalls the girl who prefaced her account of a sexual experience (which terrifies and sickens her audience) by pointing out that boys like girls best when they are dressed, that "the Snake had been seeing Eve for several days and never noticed her until Adam made her put on a fig leaf." [22] Faulkner's complication and inversion of the Edenic myth is perfectly to the point, for the covering of innocence, which *follows* violation, is here made to *precede* it, virtually bringing innocence into being as that which will and must be violated, which must be subject to violent temptation and destruction to have existed at all. In novels to come Faulkner would probe the greater passions of the lost Eden of the South, as well as its requisite creation of gothic incest fantasies. But in *Sanctuary* the more resonant historical logic of the myth is once again initially subordinated to the aesthetic logic of voyeurism, the distinctively modern version of sin that allowed D. H. Lawrence to argue, in his discussion of *The Scarlet Letter*, that the original sin of Adam and Eve was one of "self-watching, self-consciousness" — a narcissistic voyeurism in which "they peeped, pried, and imagined." [23]

This is the strategy of *Sanctuary* throughout a variety of configurations, perhaps the most notable of them the very style of the novel, which presents a hard, glassy surface of sensational temptation but refuses to reveal the least erotic excitement or, for related reasons, to offer satisfactory explanations of its horrible brutality. As Joseph Reed remarks, the novel "will not become pornography and its generic structure refuses to conform to that of the dirty joke." [24] Reed's observation comes in response to Leslie Fiedler's contention that *Sanctuary*, besides being "a brutal protest to the quality of American life written in the pit of the Great Depression," is also "the dirtiest of all the dirty jokes exchanged among men only at the expense of the abdicating Anglo-Saxon Virgin." [25] It is doubtful that Reed's objection holds up, for *Sanctuary* is a dirty joke in almost every way imaginable (including a more than slight suggestion of the racial hysteria that provides the context for the "dirtiest" of the American jokes Faulkner himself had in mind). But Reed may well be right to insist that the novel is not pornography — neither legally nor, as it were, aesthetically — for it quite cunningly backs away from depicted sexuality, leaving only its horrible vestiges, its frenetically twisted states of desire, it sublimation in violence. Still, *Sanctuary* may simply reveal the immense difficulty of defining pornography, and, because the novel's very purpose is to expose a world of no redeeming virtues or values and to present only the most degraded of erotic stimulations, there is equal reason to believe that it is excessively pornographic. (The case of *Ulysses* was recent enough to suggest that Faulkner, as his notorious preface intimates, was exploring the limits of taste on native ground.)

Like the corncob rape itself, the book borders on a comedy of disgust and thus points forward to the shocking sexuality of *Light in August* and the pastoral perversions of *The Hamlet*. Its grotesquery extends the dark humor of death in *As I Lay Dying* but unavoidably assumes social and moral responsibilities that the tall tale of the Bundren family could leave aside. In doing so, it continues to raise a host of aesthetic problems at the heart of Faulkner's major novels, all of them tied here to the central metaphors of voyeurism and impotence, tied most of all to their implied correlation. Such problems, and such a correlation, may again be understood to present questions of "realism" — or, more exactly, of "naturalism" — for the aesthetic of observation, reduced to primitive essentials, leads by immediate logic to the shocking, spare impressionism of Hemingway or Hammett, the fictional world of total control in which everything is on the precarious verge of psychic and moral collapse. The extreme masculinity of that stance depends on reducing or denying the emotional and on *mastering* every detail that is brought into view — including women, who are, therefore, exceptionally on view.

Sanctuary moves toward this extreme by leaving behind the world of Dreiserian naturalism, in which Popeye would be the crazed, immoral capitalist some readers have thought him to be, and Temple would be the fallen woman who succumbs to the enchanting lure of wild life or consumer madness and prostitutes her body, as one desirable item among others, in order to survive and thrive amid predatory forces. This does not happen; rather, Temple remains a victim in the more traditional gothic sense of the imperiled maiden, the virgin who is not quite willing to be seduced but who gets what the novel says she really wants and needs. She is violated and mastered by a fiend wielding an inanimate object in the place of his person; but this is only the requisite extension of the book's intense superficiality, its fascination with flat, blurred, or metonymic characterization — in fact, its denial that it deals with characters at all, but rather deals throughout in things, in allegories of modernism, in the style of the cartoon. It is no mistake that Corey Ford could parody *Sanctuary* in a sketch called "Popeye the Pooh," or that Faulkner himself could suggest that the part of Popeye ought to be played in film by Mickey Mouse, for the novel invites such comparisons.[26] That is not to say *Sanctuary* is simply a bad joke but, on the contrary, that it reveals a special hazard of the new realism, whose decided misogyny may be what later led Faulkner to remark that the best job he had ever been offered was that of "landlord in a brothel," which he claimed is "the perfect milieu for the artist to work in."[27] The new realism depicts a world of art outside the world of law and nearly outside the world of feeling, a two-dimensional world in which faith in transcendent ideas or beliefs is grotesquely distended and the depth of human passions is reduced to clinical dissection at best and crude allegorical caricature at worst.

The hard, angular surface of *Sanctuary* works continually to deny more than the briefest intimation of the fading theology that defines Hawthorne's world or even the redefined evolutionary theology that characterizes the romance of naturalism for Norris and Dreiser. Its obsessive focus on eyes that seem to be rubber knobs, clots of phlegm, clay marbles, inkwells, holes burned with a cigar, electric bulbs, tiny wheels, holes in a mask, empty globes, and so on is emblematic of this strategy, inscribing in the characters themselves the voyeuristic shock that belongs to the reader and suggesting that the depths of the human soul and heart are, when exposed, completely empty. *Sanctuary* is a parody of depth in formal terms that parallel its displayed rejection of historical meaning and convincing psychological motivation. As it arouses expectations only to shatter them in crudeness or obscurity, the narrative is instilled with a form of suspense that, rather than being resolved by the clarification of details or the denouement of plot, veers off into impotent shock and numerous miscarriages of justice. In this respect, the gothicism of *Sanctuary* is most conspicuously modern and, perhaps, American in its illumination of those primitive, atavistic strains of violence and sexual obsession that may be the most essential underlying feature of American culture but cannot — not yet, for Faulkner — be articulated in convincing historical terms. The novel's breathless flurry of action constantly reveals — nothing, leaving only the seizures of thwarted desire, corrupted ideals, and reverberating pain, only "a voice of fury like in a dream, roaring silently out of a peaceful void." [28]

It is quite understandable, given the novel's elaboration of sexual nightmares in which masculine and feminine roles are reversed and its expressed interest in a violent eroticism whose most definitive characteristic (for Popeye and Horace alike) is voyeuristic impotence, that readers should have recourse to psychoanalytic interpretations that dwell on the conversion of castration fears into cruel fantasies of rape, [29] or that go one step further and suggest, as Fiedler does, that Popeye's perverse voyeurism projects "a brutal travesty of the American artist, helpless and fascinated before the fact of genital love." One need not agree with this arcane speculation in order to endorse Fiedler's further contention that the rape of Temple (which he calls a "love scene") portrays "the hysterical masculine protest of [Faulkner's] time in the image of the maimed male." [30] In this regard, Faulkner's novel is another, particularly awful instance of the modern sexual catastrophes to be found, for example, in Eliot, Hemingway, Fitzgerald, and West. Nevertheless, it is Horace, not Popeye, who bears the burden of Faulkner's authorial projections, such as they are, and defines the greater themes of impotence — the impotence of justice, of art, of human sympathy, the impotence of feeling and memory themselves.

The reduction of Horace's childhood memories and the addition of Popeye's psychobiography in Faulkner's revisions have the effect of bringing the two characters into the narcissistic mirroring posture that the first chapter defines. That chapter provided the opening scene only in revision; there is thus reason to think that Faulkner did indeed come to see Horace and Popeye as opposing forces, allegorically positioned for a fight over the representative embodiment — indeed, the very body — of white Southern Womanhood, and that such a melodrama entailed a disjunction in formal terms as severe as the implied disjunction between traditions of honor in the old South and their sterile perversion and collapse in the modern world. By diluting the historical context that Faulkner's larger career provides and by largely transferring Horace's defense of tradition into the arena of neurotic obsession, the novel resists a deliberate spelling out of these issues. To the extent that the form of the novel divides itself between the stories of Horace and Temple before bringing them together in violent merger and conflict, *Sanctuary* recalls and prefigures the structure of antagonistic forms that is characteristic of almost all of Faulkner's novels. In particular, it casts forward to *Absalom, Absalom!*, in which the gothic sexual fantasies of Miss Rosa Coldfield are the medium of Quentin's immersion into the Sutpen tragedy. The later novel gives Quentin the historical depth that *The Sound and the Fury*, like *Sanctuary*, cannot provide and further reveals that Faulkner's best mystery novels are not, to be exact, detective novels at all, that the closer he comes to the actual detective story — in *Knight's Gambit, Intruder in the Dust,* and particularly the extension of Temple's story in *Requiem for a Nun* — the more unsure are his methods and his vision. That vision derives in his best moments from an exploration of crimes that are problems neither of legal guilt nor personal neurosis alone, but rather represent a moral catastrophe at the heart of Southern and American social history.

Like Quentin, Horace is stalled in a narcissistic nightmare that the events of the book can only exacerbate, and his posture of impotence (which is also Quentin's, who would preserve Southern purity from violation by indulging his own incestuous desires) may thus be said to resemble Faulkner's artistic predicament in one significant way. The clash between Horace and Popeye may be seen as the clash between the ideals of civilization and their complete betrayal, or between the richness of memory and the blank stare of pointless, sourceless evil; but it is also the clash between modernism and the older form of romance that the rest of Faulkner's major novels draw on and incorporate, between the hard-edged naturalism of Hemingway and Hammett, and the different psychological gothicisms of Thomas Dixon and Hawthorne. In this respect, Horace may resemble no one more than Miles Coverdale, impotent voyeur, for *Sanctuary's* setting and action, as well as its stunted confessional mode, suggest a modernist Blithedale, a deranged and degenerate utopia in which the hypocritical ideals of Southern and American civilization find their crystallized expression, an expression that has no redeeming features and therefore cannot become legitimately tragic.

S UCH a comparison would perhaps be out of order if Faulkner's career had ended with *Sanctuary* or had taken a different direction after it. It seems, however, to have taken a necessary direction, for his next novel, *Light in August,* would make formally and thematically central that clash between the modern South and its dark original sins, the clash that hangs suspended throughout Faulkner's work up to *Light in August* and then leads him resolutely back toward the nineteenth century, notably toward the Civil War, much as Hawthorne had been led to his Puritan origins in search of the buried secrets of contemporary life. In both instances what is revealed is evil — or rather, a particular set of attitudes about evil — and in both instances the discovery issues in an extraordinary ambivalence about that evil, at once its scathing condemnation and its celebratory remembrance. As Faulkner works through *Light in August, Absalom, Absalom!*, and *Go Down, Moses*, the American and Southern myths of lost innocence will eventually become superimposed upon each other, and he, as Hawthorne did, will more and more project himself through his work as the contemporary "representative" of the failed, magnificent, cruel generations that produced him. Although similar arguments could be made for both, as the earlier example of *Sartoris* demonstrates, such projection need be considered no more strictly autobiographical in Faulkner's case than in Hawthorne's. Instead, it need only engage the most vital configurations of a past that is simultaneously familial and historical as they pass into impotent, enslaving contemporary forms.

Just as the shocking sexuality of Temple prefigures that of Joanna Burden, the introduction of Popeye's psychobiography brings into partial view the tortured childhood of Joe Christmas. Although Faulkner once remarked that Joe Christmas was legitimately "tragic," while Popeye was simply a "monster,"[31] it is no mere coincidence that each of them — the one for obvious reasons, the other for reasons at first glance inexplicable — is characterized as a "black man," for Faulkner was moving toward his great, magnificently ironic novel of "passing" in which the domains of theology and naturalism would be collapsed into the embodied evil of Christmas, the "monster" who represents the South's shocking contemporary threat by representng as well its gravest moral sins and their consequent guilt. Temple's description of Popeye as a "black man" does not, of course, initially suggest more than momentary confusion; and Horace's first confrontation of Popeye — in which his eyes appear to be "soft black rubber" and his skin has "a dead, dark pallor," in which he wears his usual "tight black suit" and even "smells black . . . like that black stuff that ran out of Bovary's mouth and down her bridal veil when they raised her head"[32] — reveals no significant evidence that Popeye is part Negro. Two minor passages early on in the original text, in which Horace recalls "Popeye's black presense lying upon the house," filling the darkness "in black and nameless threat,"[33] suggest what the novel rather assumes — that Popeye is an incarnation of evil with no source, no explanation, no mythology to back him up. And far from providing such a mythological structure, Temple's later recollection of the Edenic analogy only insures its inability to offer any useful moral frame of reference. Like virtually everything else in the novel, Popeye's evil and its originating significance are left ambiguous, cut off after momentary insinuation. But it is not at all misleading to emphasize that, because Popeye is a white man who is, as it were, black, just as

Joe Christmas is a black man, as it were, who is white, Faulkner has begun exploring the central mystery of the Southern gothic experience, the mystery of "blood."

An even less obvious, but potentially more revealing, ambiguity along these lines appears in Temple's report to Horace of the fantasy she employs to resist her impending violation at the Old Frenchman place. Her fantasy is complicated, perhaps pointlessly so, but it involves imagining that she can ward off the phallus that threatens her, the "little black thing like a nigger boy," by becoming a man herself, so that "the little black man got littler and littler." Even here the "black man" is more clearly the nameless evil of sexual violation in any form whatsoever; yet in the context of Faulkner's fallen South, and especially in the context of Temple's risqué portrayal of Southern charm and temptation, the fantasized resistance of violation by a "nigger boy" — and, more obviously, the metonymic identification of "the Negro" as a sexual organ — acquires disturbing meaning. The potent ramifications of that violation and its resistance will become Faulkner's explicit subject for the next ten years as he probes first the frantic hysteria over, and tragic actualities of, miscegenation in the contemporary South, and next their turbulent origins in the violent acts of master against slave. As miscegenation emerges as the South's own peculiar version of original sin — and as Temple's frantic invocations of "Daddy. Daddy . . . Give it to me, daddy," are transfigured into Joanna Burden's erotic exclamation of "Negro! Negro! Negro!" — the dimensions of Southern gynealotry become more viscerally complex than either Horace's or Temple's fantasies can reveal.[34]

The lost innocence of the Confederate South projects a world that never existed or, if it did, was quite certainly a mockery of innocence. The projected remembrance of that innocence requires, with all the vengeance of extreme repression, the substitution of one myth for another, requires that black violence against white pose as the horrible consequence of emancipation and that white violence against black — brutal in every respect, but most visibly an outrage in sexual acts that were, more often than not, simply expressions of white lust — be subsumed under the tearful memory of persecuted ideals and lost grandeur. While *Sanctuary* does not clearly depend on the convulsive passions that engender the Southern myth of lost innocence in order to create any one of the many brutalities it revels in, the depiction of Popeye as a "black man" forecasts the most important theme in Faulkner's career. As Claude-Edmonde Magny has remarked, the various sanctuaries of Faulkner's world "assume their sacred character only through the profanation which despoils them forever."[35] The Confederacy is one such sanctuary; and to the extent that white Southern Womanhood is its characteristic embodiment, the profanation of Temple Drake by the grotesque representative of the modern world, the ceaseless hemorrhage that follows her rape, and the wild nymphomania the act releases are a fitting expression of the rape complex of the postbellum South, that most strikingly disordered version of the lost American Eden.

Sanctuary, one might say, should have appeared as a chapter of the agrarian manifesto *I'll Take My Stand* (1930), for Faulkner would spend the next decade of his career, as Allen Tate there suggests a Southerner must do, taking hold of his tradition "by violence."[36] With the important exception of Robert Penn Warren's contribution, "The Briar Patch," this collection of last stands, written from the heart of the South's experience of the Depression, has disturbingly little to say about slavery and blacks — so little, in fact, that it often seems as eccentric as *Sanctuary*, which is also a profoundly conservative document. But the conservative stance of Faulkner's novel — exaggerating the more abstruse or better concealed tendencies of most of his fiction — is the stance of intimate, loving hatred, which in any event is more promising and more illuminating than the stance of reactionary vendetta. *Sanctuary* may take the form of an attack on modern forces that continue to destroy the dream of the old South, but it assumes an extraordinary degree of complicity in that destruction, even sees it, as Faulkner's work would increasingly suggest, as a providential judgment or, at the least, a self-inflicted punishment. In the language of the detective novels it resembles, *Sanctuary* is an inside job.

While it often seems intentionally incapable of bearing the burden of interpretation it calls for, and while it may never be construed as a great novel, *Sanctuary* remains thoroughly fascinating: because it is shocking and thrilling; because it invites a number of thematic approaches, none of them completely satisfactory; and most of all because it displays an authorial frenzy, a revelling in the modern that prepares Faulkner for his great works of historical retrospection, his true "romances." Malraux's famous declaration that *Sanctuary* depicts "the intrusion of Greek tragedy into the detective story" seems largely irrelevant unless we read the novel in the broader context of Faulkner's fiction, where the reciprocal cycles of vengeance, the fulfillment of curses, and the familial doom that characterize Greek tragedy are more openly utilized. But the remarks that precede this comment are absolutely relevant to *Sanctuary* as it gathers together tangential forces and anticipates the work to come. The novel, Malraux points out, poses the

> question of a psychological state on which almost all tragic art depends and which has not ever been studied because esthetics do not reveal it: fascination. . . . The tragic poet expresses what obsesses him, not to exorcize the obsession (the obsessive object will reappear in his next work), but to change its nature: for, by expressing it with other elements, he makes the obsession enter the relative universe of things he has conceived and dominated. He does not defend himself against anguish by expressing it, but by expressing something else with it, by bringing it back into the universe. The deepest form of fascination, that of the artist, derives its strength from being [an expression of] both horror and the possibility of conceiving horror.[37]

Sanctuary marks a point of passing toward the peculiar gothic traditions of the South, which are revealed as Faulkner's career develops to be exceedingly

American as well, and it portrays him in poised confrontation with the modern, immobilized before it, much as Horace is impotently fascinated, trapped, and entangled by the melodramatic brutalities of Popeye and Temple. *Sanctuary* seems resolutely the novel in which Faulkner "conceived and dominated" the horror and anguish of his native country's life and times. In his next major novel that horror and that anguish would seem instead to have conceived and dominated him.

part 2

chapter 4

The Strange Career
of Joe Christmas

I am invisible, understand, simply because people refuse to see me. Like the bodiless heads you see sometimes in circus sideshows, it is as though I have been surrounded by mirrors of hard, distorting glass. When they approach me they see only my surroundings, themselves, or figments of their imagination — indeed, everything and anything except me.

— RALPH ELLISON, *Invisible Man*

E LLISON'S protagonist, speaking to us from behind the veils of his creation and from just beyond the stark visibility sanctioned in law, if not in fact, by *Brown* v. *Board of Education* in 1954, betrays an anguish in which acquiescence and attack are merged. The subtlety of that anguish and the long accumulation of power on which it depends are prefigured in one of the epigraphs Ellison chooses for *Invisible Man* (1952), one that also looms in monstrous proportion behind *Light in August* (1932). In citing Captain Delano's perplexed question, "What has cast such a shadow upon you?" while deleting Benito Cereno's stunned reply, "The Negro," Ellison winds the explosive power of silence in Melville's tale one notch tighter and renders the ambiguous protest of his own narrative all the more invisible and threatening. The century that falls between the publication of *Benito Cereno* (1855) and the Supreme Court decision casts a shadow the American nation quite certainly has not yet escaped, a shadow, just as certainly, that some can never know except, perhaps, by radical acts of imaginative sympathy. "You wonder whether you aren't simply a phantom in other people's minds," says Ellison's protagonist. "Say, a figure in a nightmare which the sleeper tries with all his strength to destroy." [1] The extremities of psychological enslavement articulated in these passages from Ellison's prologue are penetrating and remarkable not only because they present a form of lived alienation few whites could ever understand but also because they embody — from the other side of the mirror, as it were — the frightening responsibility for that alienation by coming as close as possible to enclosing in one revealed image the burdens of black and white alike.

The single image enclosing (but never quite merging) those burdens constitutes the tragic center of Faulkner's major work, a center he may be said to have worked toward but only properly discovered in the early stages of a noval first entitled "Dark House" and ultimately *Light in August.* The discovery came with the introduction, into a story first devoted to a demented minister, of Joe Christmas, the character whose tragedy, Faulkner later said, was that "he didn't know what he was . . . which to me is the most tragic condition a man could find himself in — not to know what he is and to know that he will never know." [2] To debate the relative tragedies of Joe Christmas and Ellison's protagonist is probably futile; suffice it to say here that Faulkner may be right and that in Joe Christmas he discovered a character whose tragedy was the most powerful and ambiguous he could conceive. Both the power and the ambiguity of Christmas, as well as the imaginative courage that compels *Light in August,* only appears in proper perspective, however, when we recall that Faulkner, in 1955, would distinguish Ellison from Richard Wright, who "wrote one good book . . . [then] stopped being a writer and became a Negro. Another one named Ellison," Faulkner told his audience in Japan, "has talent and so far he has managed to stay away from being first a Negro, he is still first a writer." [3] It is hard to say, here, how much of either *Native Son* or *Invisible Man* Faulkner had absorbed; he may have felt their power deeply, as deeply as he felt the Supreme Court decision of 1954, which he rather reluctantly endorsed but also put into critical perspective by noting that it "came ninety years too late. In 1863 it was a victory. In 1954 it was a tragedy." [4]

This is indeed a peculiar remark, and it is only tolerable (not to say understandable) if we keep in mind that Faulkner was born in 1897 and virtually grew up with the resurgence of Jim Crow. The "tragedy" Faulkner refers to is the only tragedy he could thoroughly imagine — the tragedy of the South that includes but, from the perspective of white Southerners, can never literally embody the tragedy of the Negro: certainly not literally, but perhaps by a figurative embodiment that so engulfs and subsumes the literal as to bring them into perilous union. The further tragedy that Faulkner's best work from *Light in August* through *Intruder in the Dust* sought to express lies precisely in what must be, what can only be imagined or felt but never fully lived; and it is in the simultaneous rhythms of repulsion and union, of hatred and embrace, so vividly carried to their extremities of contact and failed resolution in Faulkner's style, that his most visceral understanding of that tragedy is realized. Those rhythms, which readers have quite rightly (but often for the wrong or less relevant reasons) assumed to be distinctly "Southern," create and sustain an act of imaginative vision that has no parallel in modern American writing. They do so because they re-create a moral and psychological sympathy that is at once courageous and, as Faulkner often claimed, inadequate, a sympathy that pervades his major works of the 1930s and 40s, but whose paradoxical contours can best be felt, once again, by placing side by side his later assertions that the fulfillment of *Brown* v. *Board of*

Education could come "maybe in three hundred years," because "in the long view, the Negro race will vanish in three hundred years by intermarriage."[5]

These contours are familiar to readers of Faulkner's fiction, and particularly familiar to those acquainted with his much publicized comments on desegregation in the 1950s. They are worth bearing in mind here simply because it is easy to take them either too lightly (and thus divorce his fiction from the realities it constantly struggled to incorporate) or too seriously (and thus convict Faulkner of a lapse in moral vision) when, on the contrary, they must be understood to continue to express both a defiance and a tragic sympathy that is completed and extended by their powerful ability to bring into further focus those conflicts arising between a novelist's "private" imaginings and his "public" postures. In some cases, as the history of literary criticism and biography demonstrates, the fiction itself may give way to ideas that have arisen against an author's will or without his consent; in others, like that of Faulkner, an author's adamant claim that he is not "merely telling a story to show a symptom of a sociological background"[6] must be acknowledged but also balanced against the probability that his material itself, if not his public declarations, will define conflicts that are simply beyond his control. Faulkner's notorious "go slow" attitudes toward desegregation diverged little from those of the country at large and were not far out of keeping with the language of the *Brown* decree of implementation in 1955 ("a prompt and reasonable start," "good faith compliance at the earliest practicable date," "with all deliberate speed"), whose ambiguity momentarily revived the shattered dreams of Southern segregationists. By the time Oxford, Mississippi, became the scene of an insurrection that C. Vann Woodward has called "the most serious challenge to the Union since the Civil War," Faulkner had been dead nearly three months. The bloody rioting that accompanied the enrollment of James Meredith at the University of Mississippi in the autumn of 1962 confirmed once again — this time despite a nationally televised plea from President Kennedy and with the equally public complicity of Mississippi's states-rights governor, Ross Barnett — that Faulkner's native state, historically a leader in legal and illegal segregation, was now more than ever no state at all but virtually a country within a country.[7]

According to Joseph Blotner, Faulkner a few days before his death had attributed the violent opposition likely to arise against Meredith's impending enrollment to a minority of white supremacists whose children did not attend the university;[8] this is largely true, and we must certainly assume that Faulkner would have been appalled by the "Battle of Oxford" (in Woodward's phrase) that took place on 1 October 1962. It had not been so clearly the case in 1956 when Faulkner, contemplating the rioting that accompanied Autherine Lucy's enrollment at the University of Alabama, wrote in his famous *Life* magazine "Letter to the North" that "the first implication, and — to the Southerner — even promise, of force and violence was [not such rioting but] the Supreme Court decision itself."[9] Yet it is exactly that wrenching division of loyalties — dramatized in

Oxford a century after the Civil War, as though to magnify more than half a century's struggle to reenslave and reliberate Jim Crow — that had become and would remain Faulkner's life in the form we know it best: his fiction. Mississippi, at the time of Faulkner's death, as it had been throughout his life, was to some observers a country within a country within a country; that is, a closed society still fierce in its isolation within the often closed society of the South itself, which for over four years in reality and well over a hundred years in its own imagination remained a nation socially and psychologically outside the nation that enclosed it legally and physically. The ratio between Mississippi and the United States, like the ratio between Faulkner's public statements and his fiction, describes a state of precarious union, one by which the form of Faulkner's career must be measured and in which we may find the rudiments of an analogy pertinent to his fictional encounter with the continuing problem of American slavery. For the state of being, the state of mind that Ellison's protagonist expresses — containing as it does nearly hallucinating layers of psychological involvement and complicity between slave and master — is an exemplary representation of the further and fiercer enslavement of black within white, and of *white within black within white,* that Faulkner discovered in *Light in August* and confronted until his death on Colonel Falkner's birthday in 1962.

The shadow of "the Negro" that descends upon Melville's Benito Cereno had long been and would long remain the central metaphor of America's most visible and continuing outrage, one that describes a union of responsibility and fantasy in which shadow and object, like black and white, are so inseparably fused as to be meaningless without each other. It is a metaphor Faulkner employs relentlessly in *Light in August* and one whose psychological power Ellison, a few years before *Invisible Man,* had sensed when he wrote that a "ritualized ethic of discrimination" enforced on whites as well as blacks led Faulkner, among other Southern artists, to discover in the Negro "a symbol of his personal rebellion, his guilt and his repression of it." [10] More recently, Daniel Aaron has focused attention on the most striking of the glaring deficiencies and failures of direct confrontation in a century's worth of literature on the Civil War — the marginal role of the people whom that war, as it progressed, came to be about. For most writers, Aaron points out, the black man was at best "an uncomfortable reminder of abandoned obligations, or a pestiferous shadow, emblematic of guilt and retribution," and even for Melville, Twain, Cable, and Faulkner, haunted though they were by racial nightmares, he "served primarily a symbolic function and seldom appeared from behind his various masks." [11] Such "black invisibility," as Aaron rightly puts it, is not very surprising in a genre dominated for obvious reasons by white authors; but it is not for that reason any less revealing of a conspicuous feature of Faulkner's fiction — that he seldom chose to meet the political and military realities of the war face-to-face but rather enveloped himself in the perhaps more profound realities of veiling myths, the twisting corridors of the *might have been,* the long agony of history lived and relived in retrospective fantasy. Most like Twain in this regard, he chose to

measure the past dream by the present nightmare, measuring both as they con-
flicted and merged like black and white, shadow and self, in the tangled rhythms
of fact and fiction.

TO SAY that Faulkner first discovered the full burden of his central
tragedy in the midst of writing *Light in August* is of course misleading; he
had detected (without extending) it much earlier, certainly as early as *The Sound
and the Fury*, in which Quentin Compson realizes "that a nigger is not a person so
much as a form of behaviour; a sort of obverse reflection of the white people he
lives among." [12] The startling effect of this realization, which in retrospect
appears to lead directly to Faulkner's major works of the next twenty years,
comes into dramatic perspective in *Absalom, Absalom!*, in which Faulkner
reimagines and redirects Quentin's dilemma and suicide with an obsessive historical fury, enclosing it within the more haunting, more feverish and far-
reaching story of Sutpen's Hundred. It is not misleading, however, to imagine
that Faulkner's own rereading of his first great novel in the context of his greatest would not have been possible without the extraordinary deepening of style
and theme that *Light in August* afforded. Like the story that revolves around Joe
Christmas, the story that revolves around Charles Bon was first entitled "Dark
House," as though Faulkner had been moving toward the stunted, explosive
encounter between Quentin and Henry Sutpen ever since Quentin's suicide,
and had found his way through the mediating figure of Christmas, a figure
neither black nor white who (as Faulkner would later say in a remark that also
bears upon the case of Quentin Compson) "deliberately evicted himself from the
human race because he didn't know which he was." [13]

Quentin's realization that "nigger" is a form of behavior, an obverse reflection
of the white people surrounding him, resembles the brooding comments of
Ellison's invisible man in that it too articulates two separate and parallel, but
mutually dependent, phenomena: first, that the impenetrable mask of "Negro,"
however it divides the theories of historians and novelists, springs from a political reality that inevitably overleaps its varied social, physiological, and custom-
ary justifications; and second, that this masking is hallucinatory to the extent
that, from a white perspective, it manifests the interiorization of racial trauma
that led Faulkner, among others, to recognize that "nigger" — like all such
epithets and possibly in some instances no more or less than "Negro" or "black" —
describes not a person but a projected image. We might well speak, then, of two
masks, one covering the other, which in turn appears to cover the invisible. The
second is a kind of masking Ellison rightly situates in a more universal context of
diversionary social and political behavior that for him includes the examples of
Benjamin Franklin, Ulysses, and Faulkner (who, for instance, posed as the
"farmer") and finds to be motivated, in the case of the "dumb act" of the Negro,
by "a profound rejection of the image created to usurp his identity," a rejection
that makes possible "the secret of saying the 'yes' which accomplishes the expres-

sive 'no.'" [14] The first is a masking that grows out of a responsibility for, and confrontation with, the second; and it develops by the paradox that, the more strenuous and intricate the probing of oppressed by oppressor becomes, the more the black mask may become fixed until it seems a reflection of the white, distortion upon distortion in an endless recession of mirrored images.

Such a masking of masking, in fiction and in fact, may blur into near incoherence the very best of intentions, as in the case of a notorious remark in preface to a pioneering revisionist study of American slavery: "I have assumed that the slaves were merely ordinary human beings, that innately Negroes *are*, after all, only white men with black skins, nothing more, nothing less." [15] To be a white man with a black skin — one of the potential absurdities that *Invisible Man* explores, and one that Faulkner himself appeared to encourage when he remarked in 1958 that the Negro's "burden" is that "it will not suffice for him to think and act like just any white man: he must think and act like the best among white men" [16] — is in some respects precisely the threat that has motivated most racist hysteria since the Civil War. But its most compelling and, as Faulkner saw in the 1930s, tragic dimension was revealed in the obverse absurdity: to be a black man with a white skin, to be a virtual caricature, not only of an inhuman social and political system, but also of what in some minds was the most menacing result of that system's abolition. That such a menace inevitably contained more fantasy than actuality is neither surprising nor mitigating; far from it, for it is precisely the hallucinating "possibility" of miscegenation, which in the white mind has often maniacally exceeded its grasp of the facts, that forms and propels the strange career of Joe Christmas. From one point of view it hardly matters that the evidence of Christmas's "black blood" boils down to the second-hand testimony of a circus owner who had employed his reputed father, and that we receive that testimony from Christmas's fanatical grandfather, who has murdered the father; what matters is the other point of view, the climate of fantasy in which the evidence, whichever way it may point, counts for little beside the suspicion that overwhelms and submerges it, repressing and distorting it at the same time.

Light in August is an extended meditation on this fantasy, extended by Faulkner's desire to work out every conceivable variation, on every level he could imagine, within the limits of one sustained narrative. But Faulkner's desperate infusion of form with theme in *Light in August* only releases the full power it holds, and only — like Christmas at his death — rises forever into our imaginations, when we recall that the novel appeared approximately at the crest of a forty-year wave of Jim Crow laws that grew in part out of a threatened economy, in part out of increasingly vocal demands for black equality during and after World War I, and in greater part out of reawakened racist fears that had, at least in contrast, simmered restlessly for a generation between Reconstruction and the twentieth century. To be more exact, they grew out of the Supreme Court's decision in favor of the doctrine of "separate but equal" in *Plessy* v. *Ferguson* (1896) — a decision that rested the burden of its argument on a case involving a "Negro" who was "seven-eighths white" and could pass as white. [17] Those years, which more or less encompass the lives of Joe Christmas, Quentin Compson, and Ike McCaslin, belong to Faulkner, who became a major novelist over the same period of time but did so by reminding us how old the new fears were, how little they had changed, and how long they were likely to last.

In probing those fears as they generate the turbulence of *Light in August,* let us risk citing one more remark by the Faulkner of the 1950s. Drawing an analogy for a University of Virginia audience between unassimilated blacks as "second-class citizens" and unassimilated dogs among a population of cats (or vice versa), Faulkner qualified his belief that, for "peaceful coexistence," it must be one way or the other (either first-class or second-class, "either all cats or all dogs") by adding that "perhaps the Negro is not yet capable of more than second-class citizenship. His tragedy may be that so far he is competent for equality only in the ratio of his white blood." Faulkner went on to qualify this qualification, just as on other occasions he made it clear that he thought the issue of "blood" was irrelevant; [18] and it should be unnecessary by now to add that nothing is to be gained by accusing Faulkner of blatant racism. His analogy here rescues itself from embarrassment by mixing dogs with cats (rather than dogs with people), but in doing so it brings to mind the examples of the seemingly marginal, yet finally indispensable, animal analogies Twain invokes in *Pudd'nhead Wilson* (1894), a world of cats who can "prove title" and "miserable dogs" and curs who cannot. "I wish I owned half of that dog," David Wilson declares to an astonished group of blockheads when an "invisible dog" makes a howling racket, "because I would kill my half." [19] This remark, of course, is fatal to Wilson's legal career, gets him branded a "pudd'nhead," and is only proved wise, not to say prophetic, when it is ultimately brought to bear upon the tragedy of the black-and-white, white-and-black "twins," Tom and Chambers.

There are numerous and abundantly evident points of contact between *Pudd'nhead Wilson* and *Light in August;* the one worth bearing in mind here is the resemblance between the lawyer Pudd'nhead Wilson and the lawyer Gavin Stevens, both of whom endorse a theory of "blood" behavior to account for the tragedy of each novel's central character. Twain's complete title has usually been recognized to be *The Tragedy of Pudd'nhead Wilson,* and one must assume that Twain, adding irony to irony in the novel that "changed itself from a farce to a tragedy" as it developed (not unlike *Plessy* v. *Ferguson,* first heard in Louisiana in 1892 and then pending before the Supreme Court), fully intended us to confront a legal and moral abyss when Wilson unmasks the white Negro Tom, convicts him of murdering his stepfather-owner, and ultimately gets him sold down river to offset the indebted estate of his original owner. From a position hopelessly outside the community of Dawson's Landing, Wilson heroically moves to its center and becomes public spokesman for, and executioner of, its deepest fears and hatreds, endorsing by further and more brutal implication the theory — held even by Tom's mother — that his various disgraces and misdeeds are the result of his blood: "It's de nigger in you, dat's what it is. Thirty-one parts

o' you is white, en on'y one part nigger, en dat po' little one part is yo' *soul.*"
Because Roxy goes on to trace Tom's confusing but prestigious genealogy
through his father, Colonel Cecil Burleigh Essex, to Captain John Smith, to
Pocahontas, and to "a nigger king outen Africa," it has to be noted that Twain's
irony, which continually slips back and forth between convention and creation,
between social conditioning and blood, is more complicated than this condensed
summary can indicate.[20] Quite certainly it is more complicated than the theory
of Joe Christmas's behavior on the day of his execution offered by attorney
Gavin Stevens:

> But his blood would not be quiet, let him save it. It would not be either one or the
> other and let his body save himself. Because the black blood drove him first to the
> negro cabin. And then the white blood drove him out of there, as it was the black
> blood which snatched up the pistol and the white blood which would not let him
> fire it. And it was the white blood which sent him to the minister. . . . And then
> the black blood failed him again, as it must have in crises all his life. He did not
> kill the minister. He merely struck him with the pistol and ran on and crouched
> behind that table and defied the black blood for the last time, as he had been defy-
> ing it for thirty years. He crouched behind that overturned table and let them
> shoot him to death.[21]

Whether Faulkner had Twain's lawyer in mind when he created Gavin Stevens
(whose role in *Intruder in the Dust* rather seems to support this possibility), we can
only guess. But Stevens speaks, as Pudd'nhead Wilson does, in service of an
unbearable anxiety that, because it constantly threatens to dissolve into anarchy
both a social and a psychic structure, can only be contained by the simplest of
theories — one that is necessarily rendered farcical by renouncing the dangerous
complexities generated in the surrounding actions of the novel.

Like the "fiction of law and custom"[22] that turns white Roxy and her even
whiter son into "Negroes," the fiction of Joe Christmas's black blood — "I think I
got some nigger blood in me," Christmas tells his first lover, Bobbie, "I don't
know. I believe I have" — subsumes within it a burgeoning historical reality that
cancels out what is undeniably *visible*. In his case the ascendancy of that fiction is
doubled because, though the evidence is utterly doubtful, even to the point of
the darkest of comedy — "If I'm not," Christmas tells his last lover, Joanna
Burden, "damned if I haven't wasted a lot of time" — it overwhelms not only the
community that destroys him but Christmas himself as well. The climate of fantasy that cancels out what is visible, what is "white," makes the sacrifice of Joe
Christmas all the more necessary and haunting — necessary because the blasphemous visibility of violent social disorder must be met with greater violence in
order to totalize its repression; haunting because the narrative that contains the
tragedy of Christmas at a constant, precarious edge does so by merging its own
fictions with his, as in the metaphor chosen to describe Christmas's full passage
into "blackness" after his apparent murder of his stepfather, McEachern:
"vanishing as he ran, vanishing upward from the head down as if he were run-

ning headfirst and laughing into something that was obliterating him like a picture in chalk being erased from a blackboard." This erasure, plunging Christmas into some fifteen years of life as a "Negro," must nevertheless be posed against its opposite, the more brilliant and potent metaphor Faulkner chooses to describe Christmas when, on the night before his murder of Joanna Burden, he bursts forth naked into the headlights of an approaching car: "He watched his body grow white out of the darkness like a kodak print emerging from the liquid. . . . 'White bastards!' he shouted. 'That's not the first of your bitches that ever saw . . .'"[23]

The figure of the photographic negative is so apt that we may hardly notice it at first. What it offers is a figure of simultaneous concealment and revelation, a figure that marks with explosive precision, at a point of passing from one to the other, the ambiguity of Joe Christmas, who — like Jim Crow, yet with the doubled ironic pressure of already appearing to be what he must but cannot become — virtually is a *figure* rather than a person. He is at once a reminder (of the amalgamation of white fathers and black mothers during slavery) and a threat (of the amalgamation of black fathers and white mothers ever since); as a "white" man fathered by one apparently only slightly more "black" than he himself is, Joe Christmas passes not simply between two races but also between two conflicting, complementary forms of anxiety. As a monstrous figure embodying at once an image and its opposite, a full measure of equality and its absolute denial, Christmas at a psychological level is a literal embodiment of the uncanny; while at a sociological level he is an emblem of his country's heightening trauma, containing "within" himself the fantasized projection of a further, invisible country within. It is necessary, in suggesting that *Light in August* is the greatest American treatment of the problem of "passing," to bear in mind what is obvious — that it is written by a white man often slow to sort out his own doubts and confusions about Jim Crow; for the enslaving myth of racial hysteria in the twentieth century necessarily surrounds and contains "within" itself the literal horrors of slavery it refers to but suppresses at the same time. The paradox, in this respect, seems almost a simple one: not how can a black man be a white man, but how can a white man be a black man?

THE LITERATURE of passing had become relatively common by the publication of *Light in August*, most prominently in gothic romances such as Cable's *The Grandissimes* (1880) and Chestnutt's *The House behind the Cedars* (1900), but one of its most penetrating expressions had appeared in James Weldon Johnson's *The Autobiography of an Ex-Coloured Man* (1912). Johnson's protagonist, embodying the struggle with invisibility that Faulkner and Ellison would only be able to approach from their contrary positions of visibility, succinctly depicts his first thoughts on discovering that he is no longer white but black: "I did indeed pass into another world. From that time I looked out through other eyes, my thoughts were coloured, my words dictated, my actions limited by one dominating, all pervading idea which constantly increased in force and weight until I finally realized in it a great, tangible fact." [24] Although the novel is hardly Johnson's own autobiography, it acquires more force by posing as such and by offering testimony whose singular authority makes the frenzy of Faulkner's version all the more pointed and inevitable. The relevance of the *Autobiography*, whose hero more prosaically but certainly more convincingly passes back and forth between black and white, gains further power from the fact that Johnson once projected in his notebooks a novel to be entitled "The Sins of the Fathers," which was to involve unknowing incest between the white daughter and the bastard Negro son of a Southern planter, culminating in the accidental death of the son and the suicide of the guilty father. Thomas Dixon had already used the title and a very similar theme, and Faulkner, familiar with Dixon if not with Johnson, would later write nearly the same novel — namely, *Absalom, Absalom!* To reach the novel he never wrote, Johnson, like Faulkner, was moving from the twentieth century to the nineteenth, from Jim Crow to the slumbering nightmare out of which he had sprung. He was moving, then, toward a more historical understanding of the entangling myths of race that only the passing of several generations could make wholly visible; and he was doing so, as Joseph Skerrett points out, by dramatizing in the *Autobiography* the tragic strategy of true irony, which Kenneth Burke rightly insists is based on "a sense of fundamental kinship with the enemy, as one needs him, is indebted to him, is not merely outside him as an observer but contains him *within*, being consubstantial with him." [25]

It is worth focusing all the attention we can on the irony Burke describes, for like Faulkner's metaphor of the photograph and its negative it elucidates a "kinship" — in the actuality of blood, in the legalities and illegalities of "separate but equal," in the embraces and denials of racial hysteria — whose generative power permeates Faulkner's major works. In *Absalom, Absalom!* and *Go Down, Moses* Faulkner would expose, in flashes of released cultural anxiety, the draining intimacy of that kinship; but in *Light in August,* where the stark sensuality of the sexual encounters between Joe Christmas and Joanna Burden is more shocking than intimate, kinship is continually denied. Although the entire novel strives prodigiously, in detail after detail, to connect its characters by merging their responsibilities and actions, and by embedding their lives within one another in almost ridiculous ways, the effect of such exertions is quite simply to render the endless analogous details superfluous and the embedded lives fruitless. No sooner are the stories of two or more characters brought together than they are torn away from one another, creating in the novel, as in the problem of race it maintains at an agonizing pitch, an energy of fusion and division in which opposites appear to be created neither by emotional merger nor by extreme alienation but rather by holding both in generative, ironic proximity. What Irving Howe says of the book's social, religious, and sexual levels — that they can be distinguished for the purpose of analysis but actually "work into one another as the materials of estrangement, the pressures that twist men apart" [26] — expresses this paradoxial tension well and defines, moreover, the true torment of Christmas's invisibility: the explosive pressure of containing the invisible in the visible and, more to the point, the visible in the *in*visible.

The circle of bondage that Joe Christmas at first seems to have broken in murdering Joanna Burden only leads him fatefully back to his place of birth. In returning to Mottstown in the borrowed shoes of a Negro — "the black tide creeping up his legs, moving from his feet upward as death moves" — he has "made a circle and he is still inside of it." Having been carried by fate to what seems his last destination, Christmas is finally called by his true, schizophrenic name — the "white nigger" — and, as an anonymous narrator appropriately assuming the collective title of "they" tells us, he acts accordingly: "He never acted like either a nigger or a white man. That was it. That was what made folks so mad. For him to be a murderer and all dressed up and walking the town like he dared them to touch him, when he ought to have been skulking and hiding in the woods, muddy and dirty and running. It was like he never even knew he was a murderer, let alone a nigger too." [27] Finally Christmas does "act like a nigger" and allows himself to be beaten and jailed, as though in brief anticipation of allowing himself to be shot and castrated, an act in which Gavin Stevens, we recall, would have us believe he "defied the black blood for the last time." The posture of Christmas in his seemingly insane passivity, fusing the contradictory tranquillities of Stowe's Uncle Tom and Nat Turner but in essence resembling neither, can be construed as a kind of psychological exhaustion motivated as much by the spent fury and defeat of his character in the novel's formal terms as in terms of any fully conscious (from his own point of view) or fully conceived (from Faulkner's point of view) ideological decision. This is not to say that his death — or its manner, or particularly its mode of presentation — is insignificant but, rather, that it must be viewed as representing a continuation of the formal crisis that Faulkner pursues frenetically throughout the book: the crisis of containing the dominant story of Joe Christmas *within* a book he threatens to tear into dispersed fragments and, consequently, of containing the novel's excessive physical and emotional violence *within* a meaningful and legitimately tragic structure. [28]

The extreme ambiguity of Christmas's behavior on the streets of Mottstown and in Hightower's kitchen (whether or not he acts like a "nigger," and why, is a point we must return to) can only be approached in abstract terms for the very good reason that the intense pressure of the novel, which resembles classical tragedy insofar as it leads Faulkner to a precarious invocation of Fate, appears to have grown out of the unexpected eruption, into "another" story, of the character Joe Christmas. To describe this eruption as a return of the repressed, the sudden casting over a story of the South of its long, peculiar shadow, is appropriate but, in formal terms, inadequate; aside from the special case of Joanna Burden and Joe Christmas there does not exist in the novel the kind of psychological union (and its inevitable inversion) between master and slave that compels *Pudd'nhead Wilson* and *Benito Cereno*. In terms of composition Twain's novel, because it began as a farce about Siamese twins and ended as a brilliantly botched meditation on slavery and miscegenation, offers the best comparison, but it is bound in contrast to appear, as it were, more psychologically integrated. When Faulkner wrote to his editor, Ben Wasson, that *Light in August* "seems topheavy" because "this one is a novel: not an anecdote," [29] he not only brought into perspective the work of his career up to that point but also indicated an important formal development. Growing out of the violent superficiality of *Sanctuary*, which had itself been reworked in terms of the struggle in *As I Lay Dying* with loving, antagonistic analogous form, the new novel represented a hybrid of the two in which Faulkner mastered the realism of form by seeming to surrender to something beyond his control. The many complaints voiced by readers that *Light in August* struggles desperately but fails to bring the story of Christmas even into contact with the story of Joanna Burden (and more notably the stories of Hightower and Hines, and most notably those of Byron Bunch and Lena Grove) are perfectly justified: perfectly, for how else can Christmas's strange career, as man and as symbol, be characterized? The plunging, ravaging appropriation of larger and larger blocks of historical material, the summoning of one after another approach toward and withdrawal from the stranglehold of the past, leave Christmas no less mysterious than when he is discovered on the steps of the orphanage and christened with his blasphemous name.

It is not clear whether Faulkner thought the material devoted to Christmas or that not devoted to him was responsible for making the novel "topheavy," but it hardly matters. It is precisely these two bodies of material, like the body of Christmas himself, that express in tangled and repulsive contradiction the novel's precipitous achievement of the only union possible between form and theme, between black and white, between the community and its sacrificial object. The best critical comment on *Light in August* appears almost incidentally in a 1945 letter to Faulkner from Malcolm Cowley, who was then preparing *The Portable Faulkner*. Although he declared *Light in August* "the best of your novels as novels," Cowley was frustrated because, while it seemed to him at first that the novel "dissolved too much into the three separate stories" of Lena, Hightower, and Christmas, he ultimately found that they were "too closely interwoven" to be pulled apart. "It would be easy for you to *write* Joe Christmas into a separate novel," Cowley remarked, "but the anthologist can't pick him out without leaving bits of his flesh hanging to Hightower and Lena." [30] The suggestive brutality of Cowley's metaphor is no doubt equally incidental (surely more so than his decision, with Faulkner's approval, to anthologize the story of Percy Grimm), but it is nonetheless telling; for it describes, first, the wrenching physical union between Christmas and his community that is violently longed for and realized, and with more than equal violence rejected, in the novel; and second, it describes the formal union that drives into fusion with others the story of Christmas and yet leaves his story, like his self, isolated, naked, living nowhere and murdered everywhere.

The formal violence that is needed to include Christmas within the novel's plot (which is less a plot than a puzzle put together under the strain of forced analogy) is most evident in the single link between Christmas and Lena Grove, the character with whom the novel begins (as did Faulkner's composition) and ends, and whose story provides the frame and the filtered domestic warmth that makes Christmas's story all the more terribly ironic. The alienating contrast between Joe and Lena, who never meet except throught the novel's relentless probing of mediated psychological union, has led Cleanth Brooks, with oxymoronic precision, to characterize *Light in August* as "a bloody and violent pastoral."[31] More immediately, it led Faulkner to what is at once the most improbable, haunting, and necessary scene in the book. When she mistakes Lena's baby for her grandson, "Joey . . . my Milly's little boy," Mrs. Hines brings the anguish of Joe [Hines]-McEachern-Christmas into a heightened relief that is only surpassed by Lena's consequent confusing of Christmas himself with the child's father, Lucas Brown-Burch: "She [Mrs. Hines] keeps on talking about him like his pa was that . . . the one in jail, that Mr Christmas. She keeps on, and then I get mixed up and it's like sometimes I can't — like I'm mixed up too and I think that his pa is that Mr — Mr Christmas too — ".[32]

The union of Christmas and Lena exists only in — one might rather say, between — these two confusions about him as father and as son, a significant coupling because throughout the novel it is exactly the ambiguity of the filial relationship that determines the burden of his life. Moreover, and more importantly, it is also the relationship that is made to represent the trauma of the South in its acute sexual crisis — the threat that an invisible menace will become all too visible. Because the novel constantly raises the specter of miscegenation, that menace appears before us on every page, in nearly every line of Christmas's story with paradoxical clarity; but precisely for that reason — and even in spite of the vivid, lurid trysts of Joe and Joanna — we may forget, may want to forget what looms in the background of Christmas's life and his novel. Like the early illustrator of *Pudd'nhead Wilson* who either failed to read the book or was stricken by moral vertigo when he depicted the decidedly beautiful *white* Roxy as an Aunt Jemima figure, we may (certainly in the 1930s if not in the 1980s) simply not believe our eyes. The one doubtful and unverified fact of Christmas's existence that is responsible for Mrs. Hines's mad confusion (that he is the *son* of a "nigger") also sets in motion the menace unwittingly articulated in Lena's confusion (that the "nigger" will *father* a white woman's child) and compels Faulkner, on the verge of failing to bring his novel into any coherent focus, to risk a connection that is perfect to the very extent that it is the product of desperate fantasy. The power, as well as the necessity, of such a fantasy is the single feature that holds the fragmented, momentary crossings of plot in place and saves the novel from wasting every one of its passionate efforts at characterization. As he exists in this more extreme form of "passing" between worlds — from son of a "nigger" to "nigger" as white father — Christmas seems nearly a perverse caricature of white racial hysteria. Not so perverse, however, as the amendment to a typical "racial purity" bill introduced into the Virginia legislature in 1925 that would have required all citizens to register, with the state Bureau of Vital Statistics, all racial strains, however remote, that had ever entered their families; and not so hysterical as the climate of anxiety that led to the measure's rejection — because it was clear that many fine Virginians, living and dead, would be classed as Negroes.[33]

THAT hysteria in part determines the elegantly distorted shape of the novel, a shape determined (it might also be said) by the complementary pressure of containing Christmas, as character and as fantasy, who seems passively to bend the lives around him into a form capable of expressing his own, which in itself, if it is not nothing, is certainly left veiled and intangible. Irving Howe has noted that the "mulatto" excites in Faulkner "a pity so extreme as often to break past the limits of speech" and thus produces some of his "most intense, involuted and hysterical writing."[34] Simply at the level of syntax this observation applies more exactly to *Absalom, Absalom!* and parts of *Go Down, Moses;* but it is with respect to the form of *Light in August,* which may in the end pose more interesting formal problems, and which in any event appears to have made the later novels possible, that the importance of Howe's claim must be judged. In the novel that turned Faulkner's career toward its greatest materials and their most significant expression, the crisis of blood works jointly with the crisis of form, both turning Faulkner back toward the 1860s in search of a solution, however partial and fragile, to the continuing crisis of history in the South.

By way of passing to a more explicit consideration of the problem of the novel's form, let us note again that the intersection of the three crises — of form, of blood, of history — lies in the embracing crisis of sexuality, which compels the confusions that bring Christmas and Lena into their first, fantastic moment of contact and which generates a second, more oblique but more conclusive one, the contact made in the mediating presence of Hightower when Christmas is lynched. Although Brooks has rightly insisted that Christmas's death is a "murder" rather than a lynching,[35] I want to use the word with full deliberation in order to stress the climate of fantasy the book assumes and depends on for its power. In his 1929 study of lynching, dedicated to James Weldon Johnson, Walter White reported that the issue of sex "in the race problem and specifically in lynching is distorted by [a] conspiracy of semi-silence into an importance infinitely greater than the actual facts concerning it would justify." That conspiracy both results from and produces something of a willful blindness to what clearly exists (the historical fact of the rape of black women by white men during and after slavery) and a hallucinatory frenzy about what exists more in fantasy than in fact (the inexorable craving for and rape of white women by black men), thus making it nearly impossible, White noted, to elicit from many Southerners any kind of response on the subject but one of "berserk rage."[36]

There is no more need to point out that White's formulation is not intended to be definitive of an entire people than there is to add that it is true enough as an abstract representation, not of the South alone but of the entire nation that brought Jim Crow into visible existence, to warrant our attention. Before the character Christmas can bring these tensions and fears to their climactic expression in the outraged cry of his priestlike executioner, Percy Grimm — "Has every preacher and old maid in Jefferson taken their pants down to the yellowbellied son of a bitch?" [37] — he must himself be made to represent, to embody from both sides of the mask, the distortions of feeling and fate that the crisis of sexuality can release. He does so in the long, long plunge into his past that Faulkner requires seven chapters (almost exactly the middle third of the book) to negotiate. The flashback of Joe's earlier life centers him "within" a novel pervaded by frames, by memories of memories, by stories embedded within stories embedded within stories; that is, it brings him, as the novel does each of its major characters, out of the resonant darkness of the past and into the slight but explosive moments of contact before communion breaks in denial by rendering formally visible his unknown or unrecognized being already *within* them.

As Christmas exists as a fantasy of black within white, he comes in the novel's action to inhabit and create the critical moments of the lives of others — fortuitously in the case of Joanna Burden, fatefully in the case of Doc Hines, tragically in the case of Hightower, by the gamble of tenuous analogy in the case of Lena Grove, and with apparently preordained justice in the case of Percy Grimm. Faulkner's surging narrative dislocations of time have received more attention than any other aspect of the novel, [38] and rightly so, for they are all that can make dramatically plausible the lives of characters that are otherwise stunted by gorgeous but deadening obsessions. What is noticed less often is that the lives of those characters who most embody the life of Christmas as a racial fantasy (Joanna Burden, Hightower, Hines, Percy Grimm) are also the ones that Faulkner seems able to treat only by analogously disjointed plunges into the past. Once this is seen, however, we recognize as well that the shape of the novel is more distorted than ever. Aside from her functional act of childbearing, which reveals the potential contamination of Christmas as it appears and passes away in its most unnerving, because radically peripheral, form, Lena Grove serves simply and beautifully to frame and contain the violence of the novel; [39] and Byron Bunch, the displaced narrator on whom much of the burden of Faulkner's story falls, appears hardly more than the medium of Lena's containment of that violence, which centers in Christmas and reaches back toward chapter one and forth toward chapter twenty-one through the subsidiary frame of Hightower's life. The book's symmetry, of course, is not perfect, and there is no particular reason to wish it were; for though we may object to the narrative's chaotic detours and its forcing into probability coincidence upon coincidence, particularly in the aftermath of Joanna Burden's murder, the possibility ought also be entertained that it is only those diversions from a single line of action — into the extended recapitulative histories of Hines, Hightower, and Grimm — that can make visible the complete alienation of Christmas in formal terms. In order to eventuate in its appropriate sacrificial function, the story of Christmas must set in motion the stories that surround his not so much by merging, but rather by colliding, with them. Joe Christmas must be both central and marginal, sacred and profane, galvanizing and menacing: he must momentarily release into the public horror of revealed story those distorted passions of a community that are otherwise hidden and suppressed.

In recognizing that *Light in August*, like *As I Lay Dying* before it and *Go Down, Moses* after it, contains four or five incipient novels, we need to note that Faulkner's psychological chronology works toward an approximation of life rather than the seamless web of "fiction." As Byron Bunch realizes of his own increasingly perilous involvement with Lena, "*it was like me, and her, and all the other folks that I had to get mixed up in it, were just a lot of words that never stood for anything, were not even us, while all the time what was us was going on and going on without even missing the lack of words.*" This remark applies just as clearly and appropriately to Joe Christmas, who, like Addie in *As I Lay Dying*, almost willessly determines the shape of the stories that surround and impinge upon his own. The novel's expressed antagonisms between public and private, along with the attendant misunderstandings and hypocrisies they make possible, are realized in a narrative form whose rhetorical melodrama creates stories as they are needed, virtually at the moment they come into the action of being. Joanna Burden's story thus becomes "public" (as her life becomes meaningful) in the novel's terms by being expressively contained in Christmas's and released by her murder; the stories of Hines and Grimm, and the more significant depth of Hightower's, are similarly released by and into the public crisis precipitated by that murder and their own fated involvement in it. In an early scene that clarifies the degree to which *Light in August* represents an extension of the formal experiments of *As I Lay Dying*, the novel itself forecasts the form these expressions will take when Lena waits for a wagon that will take her to Jefferson. As the wagon approaches, "like already measured thread being rewound onto a spool . . . as though it were a ghost travelling a half a mile ahead of its own shape," Lena thinks to herself, "*it will be as if I were riding for a half mile before I even got into the wagon, before the wagon even got to where I was waiting, and . . . when the wagon is empty of me again it will go on for a half mile with me still in it.*" [40] There is no need to elaborate the way in which the novel, in story after story, in a recollective form that insists on the sudden and precarious violation of one life by others, gathers and rewinds the potentially random but critically connected threads of its lives. Any one of the characters might be compared to the wagon as a ghost traveling ahead of, and therefore determining, its own shape; they each "contain" already within themselves the lives that will be made manifest in strained momentary contact, and this containment, as well as the strain it expresses, is reflected in the visible, literal containment enacted by the novel's form.

In stressing that the issues of race and miscegenation are fully involved in the novel's form, there is no reason to suggest that this involvement is an explicitly causal one; *Light in August* might well have had a similar form without the ambiguity of Christmas's blood, without his being "Negro" at all. Obviously, though, it would not be the same novel, nor would it be capable of expressing with such haunting social and psychological complexity, with such power to contaminate and bring to crisis, the radical internalization of black within white. In this respect, the issue of blood, the epitome of the many spurious connections and analogies that fuse the novel's divergent lives, appears to be the only feature that rescues much of the narrative from a collapse into cascading, uncontrolled rhetoric. It does so by keeping that rhetoric at the tenuous edge of collapse and thereby measuring the fragility of the South's social and psychological order. Faulkner himself intimated the formal crisis the novel expresses when, in response to a question about the "style" of *Light in August,* he characteristically replied that he didn't "know much about style" but went on to speak vaguely of something "pushing inside him to get out."[41] Since Joe Christmas says almost exactly the same thing of his contaminated blood, there is nothing to prevent us from saying that this something, bluntly, is the "nigger in him" — "nigger" not as blood, as enslaving memory, as the simultaneously feared and needed *other,* but as all of these, as the formal and psychological embodiment of a crisis that became even more acute in the life of Jim Crow than it had been in the second generation of slaves and masters Cash speaks of: "Negro entered into white man as profoundly as white man entered into Negro — subtly influencing every gesture, every word, every emotion and idea, every attitude."[42]

T HE FORM of Joe Christmas's early life, released in a flashback constituting a third of the novel and framed by his murder of Joanna Burden, is itself pervaded by stories within stories that enact in further significant detail the interiorization of lives with which the remainder of the novel struggles. The most important of those stories, the story of Joanna Burden's heritage as it is placed within the context of her sexual ravishing, bears almost the entire moral weight of the issue of miscegenation. It ties together the different religious zealotries of Christmas's two surrogate fathers, McEachern and Hines, and it is forced into more explicit genealogical parallel with that of his last figurative father, Hightower, both in its antebellum depth and in the aroused suspicion of "nigger-loving." Like the corncob rape of Temple Drake in *Sanctuary,* what we remember most — are perhaps most meant to remember — about *Light in August* is the violent sexuality of Joe and Joanna, whose analogous expression is the ecstasy of religious fanaticism. This analogous relationship is amplified as soon as we notice in turn that the story of Hines, representing the obverse merger of the two, has a function similar to the psychobiography of Popeye that Faulkner appended in his revisions of *Sanctuary.* Although it is not the ironic joke that the story of Popeye's childhood seems to be, the story of Christmas's fated origin, placed within that of the maniacal Hines, represents an excursion into religious naturalism that expands, but cannot possibly explain, the horror that has already been revealed.

Extending the naturalistic tragedy of *Pudd'nhead Wilson* by enveloping it in an aura of Calvinistic damnation, Faulkner creates for Joe Christmas the prominent place in the classic American tradition many readers have sensed he has. He does so, however, in a way that has seldom been taken into full account, for Hines's obsession with the "bitchery" of original sin, raised to an extreme pitch by the specter of miscegenation, brings into view a very peculiar strain of Southern racist thought. Among the many bizarre and scandalous efforts to justify white supremacy by evicting the Negro altogether from the human species (and surely something of a highpoint in centuries of "scholarly" and "scientific" research into the subject), the most notorious at the turn of the century were those of Charles Carroll, who argued in *The Negro a Beast* (1900) and *The Tempter of Eve* (1902) that Eve was seduced by an apelike Negro, not a serpent, and that the whole history of man's long fall from grace therefore derived from this original sin of bestial miscegenation.[43] Such a distant tainting of white blood obviously raised questions answered only by a fanatical devotion that is more preposterous than its own germinal theory. It was a devotion the South was familiar with in less extravagant forms; and as we have seen in the case of *The Sound and the Fury* — and more particularly in the case of *Sanctuary*, where Popeye at several points is described with deliberate ambiguity as a "black man" — Faulkner had already begun developing a psychology of American original sin that would include its most troublesome, because undeniably "real," form — the mixing of white masters and black slaves. Faulkner invokes the hysteria of miscegenation as original sin only tangentially in *Light in August* (without further clarifying its broader historical import, as he would in *Absalom, Absalom!* and *Go Down, Moses*), but it is important to note that it, too, determines the form of Christmas's life by determining the form that the dependent crises of blood and sexuality take.

In the long act of narrative memory devoted to Christmas's life as he consciously knows it, both the resonant sexual terror of Joe and Joanna, which the whole novel strives to encompass and contain, and the "womansinning and bitchery" of Hines into which Faulkner's fascination with this terror eventually dissolves, are prefigured by an act of formal interiorization enveloping what may be the book's most preposterous and penetrating scene. In chapter eight, approximately in the middle of Christmas's story, his affair with Bobbie moves toward its violent climax — the apparent killing of McEachern — by moving first into the recent past. The chapter begins with Joe "passing swift as a shadow" down the rope he uses to escape his bedroom, and the next chapter begins with McEachern, the full power of his "bigotry and clairvoyance" turned on, recognizing Joe's shadow and following him to the dance. In between, we are carried back into a recollected account of Joe's affair with Bobbie, and in the middle of that account we are carried back to a peculiar moment earlier in Joe's life that is also framed on the one hand by his first surreptitious meeting with Bobbie and on the other by his physical attack on her when she reveals on that occasion that she is having her period and cannot make love. The brief flashback that interrupts the larger flashback, which interrupts yet larger flashbacks, is nothing less than a primitive act of sacrifice. Horrified by one of his adolescent friend's description of menstruation — "the temporary and abject helplessness of that which tantalised and frustrated desire; the smooth and superior shape in which volition dwelled doomed to be at stated and inescapable intervals victims of periodical filth" — Joe slaughters a sheep and kneels to it, "his hands in the yet warm blood of the dying beast, trembling, drymouthed, backglaring. Then he got over it, recovered." He does not forget what he has been told, but simply finds that he can "live with it, side by side with it." This strange act of purification, which is presented with little irony but which seems nonetheless flagrantly absurd, thematically recapitulates Joe's earliest memory (the parodic primal scene between the doctor and the dietician); it refers more immediately back to his refusal of a sexual encounter with a black girl ("enclosed by the womanshe-negro," he is overcome by "something in him trying to get out, like when he had used to think of toothpaste"); and it points forward to his future sexual exploits — in which he will insist to lovers and whores alike that he is a Negro, through which the twisted passion of Joanna Burden will be released, and for which he will in the end be killed and castrated.[44]

The scene of the sheep slaughter is not particularly well conceived, and it is typical of Faulkner's lapses into obfuscation at critical moments in his plotting of symbolic action. It has little of the sacrificial significance of the hunt in *Go Down, Moses* and cannot carry the burden Faulkner apparently wants it to unless we recognize the figurative function of the blood sacrifice. We should emphasize, in this regard, that the novel's focus on sexuality at its climactic moments represents both a furthering and a containing of the form of violence it continually refers to more obliquely — the violence of slavery and racial hysteria, which either immediately or more remotely is dependent upon sexuality; that is, on "blood." The importance of this sacrificial scene thus lies in part in the fact, as René Girard has pointed out in a different context, that menstrual blood may easily be taken "as a physical representation of sexual violence," a representation whose "very fluidity gives form to the contagious nature of violence."[45] It is precisely such contagion that is rendered doubly powerful in the specter of miscegenation, the specter yoking violence with sexuality under whose aegis Joe Christmas is sacrificed in a violent denial of sexuality. The nature of that sacrifice requires further examination; but to see it clearly we must first see clearly the one union between two characters in *Light in August* that determines the warped shape of all the others: the relationship of Joe Christmas and Joanna Burden.

Their union is, of course, the book's center. It is a union of two masks, of mirror images (even in their names), that also parodies the possibility of real, loving union by reducing it to violent sex between a spinster living in "an old colonial mansion house" and a small-time hood living in its deserted "negro cabin." The enervating compulsion of their relationship arises as Faulkner, apparently striving to counter one myth, creates another that necessarily includes, extends, and makes more terrifying the first. For in countering the violent sexual desires of Christmas with the ever more frantic desire for violation he arouses in Joanna, Faulkner produces a psychological amalgamation that responds to the menace of physical amalgamation by internalizing it as a brutal struggle between conscious repression and unconscious eruption. As they exist in a bizarre replica of slave and master, enacting and passing between the South's own version of original sin and the contemporary threat it makes credible, Christmas and Joanna represent at a psychological level the tangle between *repression* and its failure that corresponds to the tangle between *oppression* and its failure at a social and political level. The fact that Joanna is a "nigger-loving" descendant of New Englanders is important to the extent that it reflects Southern accusations both before and after the war that the North endorsed miscegenation, and manifests in the mind of the South exactly that emancipation, in fact and in fantasy, which makes Christmas a monstrous figure; but this in turn is only fully dramatized when, once Joanna has been murdered, the community's antiabolitionist sentiments are forgotten and completely engulfed by racial hysteria. As the narrative puts it, she is killed "not by a negro but by Negro"; and when the community, hoping "that she had been ravished too," begins to "canvass about for someone to crucify,"[46] Joanna becomes more than anything else a "white woman," archetypically embodying Southern gynealotry and its concomitant "rape complex."

That complex, the result of an intense confusion between guilt and self-justification, has been analyzed by a number of social historians,[47] but prior to Faulkner it achieved its most popularly significant (though far less interesting and complicated) expression in the racist novels of Thomas Dixon, which had a prominent place among the racist sociological literature that quickened the rebirth of Jim Crow. The climactic scene of *The Clansman: An Historical Romance of the Ku Klux Klan* (1905), for example, involves the rape of a white heroine by a black "animal": "A single tiger-spring, and the black claws of the beast sank into the soft white throat and she was still." In the wake of such moral horror and degradation, the girl and her mother commit suicide rather than face the public humiliation it entails.[48] When Dixon's novel became *The Birth of a Nation* in 1915, the image of "the Negro as beast," long a stock figure in the South and elsewhere, was visibly fixed as the icon to which almost any justification of Jim Crow could ultimately be referred. Although the climate of hysteria that existed probably did not require it, the iconography received ample support, not just from obvious lunatics like Charles Carroll, but also from more respected commentators like William Hannibal Thomas, who dedicated *The American Negro: What He Was, What He Is, What He May Become* (1901) to "all American men and women of Negroid ancestry who have grown to the full stature of manhood and womanhood" but maintained, among other things, that "negro nature" is so "thoroughly imbruted with lascivious instincts" and "so craven and sensuous in every fibre of its being that a negro manhood with respect for chaste womanhood does not exist."[49] After endorsing Thomas's views, the novelist Thomas

Nelson Page added that, although the actions of lynch mobs are indeed shocking, there is a deeper shock "at the bottom of their ferocious rage — the shock which comes from the ravishing and butchering of their women and children." The problem arises, Page observed in a characteristic mixture of frenzy and delicacy, because the teaching of equality means but one thing "to the ignorant and brutal young Negro" — "the opportunity to enjoy, equally with white men, the privilege of cohabiting with white women."[50]

Although there was considerable disagreement as to whether the "pure black" or the "mulatto" was most degenerate, and therefore most likely to violate white women, miscegenation was, at the height of Jim Crow, hardly seen as a serious solution. The point was nearly moot, however, since in the wake of *Plessy* v. *Ferguson* the "one-drop" rule prevailed in fact if not in every courtroom: as Thomas remarked, "a mass of white negroes would . . . merely add to an already dangerous social element," because "the variegated freedman would still be a negro in mind, soul, and body."[51] This, of course, is Joe Christmas's problem. And in *Can the White Race Survive?* — like White's *Rope and Faggot,* also published in 1929, the year in which *Light in August* appears to be set — James D. Sayers picked up the old and still predominant argument that civilization would eventually be destroyed unless the "frightful cancer" of miscegenation was eradicated with a surgeon's knife wielded "vigorously and with a steady hand . . . before it gets so spread into [our] vitals that it cannot be rooted out."[52] This, of course, is Percy Grimm's theory — not an uncommon one, either, even though the statistics on lynching, such as they were, showed that between 1900 and 1930 fewer than one sixth of the blacks lynched could actually be accused of rape.[53] But "those who believe in the visibility of ghosts," wrote Frederick Douglass, "can easily see them," for race prejudice "creates the conditions necessary to its own existence" and "paints a hateful picture according to its own diseased imagination."[54]

This is nearly the language of Hawthorne, and as such it clarifies one aspect of the "romance" of race in the South and in the nation, clarifies it even more brutally when we recall that Dixon's white supremacy novels were subtitled *Romances.* No more appropriate term can be imagined, however, for *Romance* in this case brings together in the "diseased imagination" Douglass invoked a virulent nostalgia, the menace of sexual violation, and a twisted utopian vision, which, to say the least, make the Southern penchant for Walter Scott pale in comparison. Such a characterization perfectly describes Dixon's *The Leopard's Spots: A Romance of the White Man's Burden, 1865–1900* (1902), the language of whose preface is calculated to arouse fantasy — "It will be a century yet before people outside the South can be made to believe a literal statement of the history of these times. I have tried to write this book with the utmost restraint" — and whose abiding message is the threat of the "mongrel breed" articulated most vividly by the Reverend John Durham: "*In a Democracy you cannot build a nation inside a nation of two antagonistic races; and therefore the future American must be either an Anglo-Saxon or a Mulatto.*" The test of a man's belief in equality, Durham later asserts, is "giving his daughter to a Negro in marriage. . . . When she sinks with her mulatto children into the black abyss of Negroid life, then ask him!" That Dixon's "test" seems nearly a parody of the stock question hardly discredits its power; on the contrary, it reenforces the obvious continuity of Southern thought on its most elemental, visceral issue. The war transformed the Negro into a "Beast to be feared and guarded," wrote Dixon, and now, as then, "around this dusky figure every white man's soul was keeping its grim vigil."[55]

That this "dusky figure," this shadow, is indeed a *figure* rather than a person is what generates the ambiguous power of Faulkner's own "romances" of race. It is in *Absalom, Absalom!* and *Go Down, Moses,* which like Dixon's romances spread across the entire history of the South, that the contagion of the racist imagination must be measured; but it is in *Light in August* that Faulkner found the key to the mysterious country of Yoknapatawpha by finding in Joe Christmas and Joanna Burden the climactic realization of a hysteria that had necessarily been building since Reconstruction. He found in Christmas the utter, alienating paradox of that contagion, and he found in Joanna Burden its gestating, enclosing receptacle. To put it in such sexual terms — thus literalizing the anxiety implicit in Cash's figurative assertion that "negro entered into white," as white had into Negro — is not at all unwarranted; for the complementary converse of Joe's repeated aversion to both black and white women ("the lightless hot wet primogenetive Female" that seems to enclose him "on all sides, even within him") is Joanna's nymphomania, which reaches its rhetorical climax in her frenzied erotic exclamation: "Negro! Negro! Negro!"[56] By making Joanna a "nigger-lover" before making her a "nigger's lover," Faulkner deflected attention away from a more unsettling possibility he had already explored in the brilliant story "Dry September" (1931), in which the "rape" of a white Southern spinster by a black man is clearly suggested to be a product of her own diseased imagination.[57] It may be that Faulkner found this possibility too dangerous to elaborate in *Light in August* and thus countered Joanna's explicit desire for violation with her New England abolitionism. As we have noted, however, it hardly matters; once she is murdered, she becomes as white and respectable and Southern as the communal hysteria requires.

In Joanna Burden's frenzied embodiment of a state of seizure that, with all the characteristics of released repression, expresses a direct counterpoint of the South's greatest fear, we also find an ironic emblem of the more far-reaching observation of James Weldon Johnson: "The South today stands panting and almost breathless from its exertions."[58] Just as Joe has spent much of his life in a state of "physical outrage and spiritual denial," "trying to breathe into himself the dark odor, the dark and inscrutable thinking and being of negroes, with each suspiration trying to expel from himself the white blood and the white thinking and being,"[59] Joanna's correlative breathless exertions engulf and internalize him as the alien *other* — the invisible seed of black blood that should be, that *must be* mixed with her own. Their physical union enacts a "pantomime of violation," as Howe remarks,[60] but it represents as well the vivid climax of the historical fantasy that created it. Entering the "gutter filth," the "sewer," the "bottomless morass," the "swamp," the "pit [of] the hot wild darkness" of Joanna's desire, Christmas enters the actualization of a fantasy that creates his life and leads to his death: "It seemed to him that he could see himself being hunted by white men at last into the black abyss which had been waiting, trying, for thirty years to drown him and into which now and at last he had actually entered." The surge of "pent black blood" that accompanies his execution, rushing "from out the slashed garments about his hips and loins . . . like a released breath," expresses the origin and end of racial violence as it is transformed from twisted fantasy into grim reality, as it is raised from invisible menace into visible sacrifice. The medium of that transformation, the shocking sexuality of Joe and Joanna, bears all the fateful weight of inherited tragedy as their affair nears its conclusion, the two of them "peopled, as though from their loins, by a myriad ghosts of dead sins and delights, looking at one another's still and fading face, weary, spent, and indomitable." And her false pregnancy with his "bastard negro child," apparently the result of menopause, is the ironic culmination of the novel's romance of blood.[61]

Maxwell Geismar is thus absolutely right, for the wrong reasons, to complain that the tragic union of "the Negro and the Female, the twin furies of Faulkner's deep southern Waste Land," leads to no redemption or proper catharsis in *Light in August,* but rather can express only "the world of human perversions whose precise nature is that they are also infantile emotions . . . the reflections of our early animal instincts which have been blocked and forced out of their normal channels of maturing."[62] The failure of emotional catharsis in the mating of Joe and Joanna, because it holds in tension the adolescent rite of purification Joe performs and the greater communal effort at purification performed by Percy Grimm, makes further evident the infantilizing relationship between white and black, which in some respects the abolition of slavery could not eliminate but could only intensify. It is therefore essential that the brutal gothicism of *Light in August* — which grows out of a union among Calvinism, racism, and naturalism — be seen to derive from "infantile emotions," for it is these very emotions that require a (white) system of social and political convention to be justified on the basis of (black) primitive, animal, "natural" instincts. This has been the argument of every racist commentator from antebellum years through the twentieth century; it even lies behind the most disturbing aspects of Thomas Jefferson's thoughts on black slavery in *Notes on the State of Virginia* (1787). Troubled that emancipation might not be possible without the freed slave "staining the blood of his master," Jefferson was driven to an analogy whose apparent absurdity nevertheless had the sanction of centuries of thought on the origins of blacks. Situating his understanding of the natural difference between black and white in the neoclassical language of beauty, Jefferson noted that the superiority of elegant, symmetrical white physiognomy was proved even by the Negroes' own "judgment in favour of whites, declared by their preference of them, as uniformly as is the preference of the Oranootan for the black woman over those of his own species." [63]

Jefferson did not bother, or could not bring himself, to unpack the details of this explosive analogy. Perhaps for him, rumored to be the father of mulatto children — and so portrayed in one of the first novels by a black American, William Wells Brown's *Clotel, or, The President's Daughter* (1853) — the emotions were too complex and personal to admit of extended analysis. His assertion in any event, as Winthrop Jordan remarks, recapitulates with a "geyser of libidinal energy" some of the "major tenets of the American racial complex" and at the same time may transfer to others his own repressed "desires, unacceptable and inadmissible to his society and to his higher self," thereby draining them "of their intolerable immediacy." [64] Such a dramatic transfer of repressed desire to its complementary paranoid fantasy describes rather exactly the progression of racist thought from slavery through the equally tenuous justifications of Jim Crow. The myth of excessive virility and lust in the Negro as "beast" derived historically from his presumed direct descent from the ape, most commonly the orangutan; and Jefferson's minor displacement of that theory of descent into more liberal distinctions — the black man preferring the white woman, as orangutans prefer black women over their own species — did little to hide its bluntness. Confronted with "that immoveable veil of black which covers all the emotions of the other race," [65] Jefferson retreated to the safety — behind the further veil — of primitive, infantile fantasy.

There may be no reason now to take Jefferson too much to task — and there would have been less reason, say, in 1940, the year Richard Wright's *Native Son* exploded into the American imagination, releasing the Jim Crow nightmare in splendid horror. Described by the press in the novel as an "ape," a "missing link in the human species," a "jungle beast . . . in the grip of a brain-numbing sex passion," Bigger Thomas is the paradoxical cry of oppression and its violent protest, of fantastic fear and its requited realization. His "rape" and murder of Mary Dalton is terrible precisely because of the double pressure of fate and coincidence that brings it about; but in the press it is ascribed to the "minor portion of white blood in his veins, a mixture which generally makes for a criminal and intractable nature." Exposing the brutal rebellion a misconceived liberalism can produce, *Native Son* nonetheless transcends the actual violence it depicts in the hallucination of protest that, like a mirroring image, like the mask of a mask, pervades and creates the character of Bigger: "He wished that he could be an ideal in their minds; that his black face and the image of his smothering Mary and cutting off her head and burning her could hover before their eyes as a terrible picture of reality which they could see and feel and yet not destroy." The prosecution's assertion that Bigger burns Mary's body in order "to destroy evidence of offenses *worse* than rape," to obliterate the "marks of his teeth . . . on the innocent white flesh of her breasts," reminiscent as it is of *The Clansman*, is unnervingly countered by the greater, more legitimate violence in Bigger's own mind: "He committed rape every time he looked into a white face. He was a long, taut piece of rubber which a thousand white hands had stretched to the snapping point, and when he snapped it was rape. But it was [also] rape when he cried out in hate deep in his heart as he felt the strain of living day by day." [66]

Had it been Jefferson, Mississippi, rather than Chicago, Bigger would perhaps not, as the prosecutor goes on to remark, "have been accorded the high honor of sitting here in this court of law!" and of being executed by the machinery of deliberate justice. The difference between Joe Christmas and Bigger Thomas as deliberate, even stylized symbols of requisite sacrifice should not be ignored; but the enslaving fate that surrounds each of them, expressing a thorough interpenetration of fantasy and reality, is as similar as the details of their crimes—similar to the point that Bigger, in what seems a deliberate echo of Faulkner's refrain concerning the fate of Christmas, says early on, "Sometimes I feel like something awful's going to happen to me." [67] Of course everything that happens to Bigger and to Joe Christmas is awful. But whereas Wright's risk lay in the lure of a Marxist ideology that threatens to flatten out Bigger's tragedy, the risk in the case of Faulkner's novel is that the awful, forced to extremity in the grandiose rhythms of the prose and in the relentless probing of depravity, will become comic. Indeed, *Light in August* often verges on the burlesque horror of *Sanctuary,* but only at two points—in its delineation of Joanna Burden's murder and in Percy Grimm's bicycle chase of Christmas— does it slip over the edge, at both points in recoil from the greatest acts of violence the novel contains. The second, because it leads to the slaughter of Christmas, has the greater significance as an ironic, anticipatory release of pressure; the first, however, increases in splendor for having come straight out of Faulkner's Southern precursor, Poe.

The passerby who discovers the fire and then the nearly decapitated body of Joanna Burden is afraid "to pick her up and carry her out because her head might come clean off." [68] Her throat slashed ear to ear, Joanna seems an intentional mirror image of Madame L'Espanaye, who in "The Murders in the Rue Morgue" (1841) is decapitated by an orangutan wielding his master's razor. When her corpse is picked up, the head falls off. Insofar as Poe's story should be read in part as an oblique, libidinous racial fantasy, the details of the murder, the fear of whipping that initiates it, and the focus on the beast's mimic shaving with his murder weapon all have their relevant analogues in *Light in August*. [69] Faulkner does not bring the razor into such powerful symbolic focus as Melville had in *Benito Cereno,* and nowhere in *Light in August* does he directly compare Joe Christmas to an orangutan: he did not have to, so much was the "Negro as beast" a part of Southern—and American—racial iconography. And though we should note as well that he was probably drawing on a similar murder of a white woman by decapitation with a razor (followed by the lynching and castration of the black murderer) that occurred near Oxford in 1908, [70] it is the heritage of racial violence, surrounding this actual murder as well as its fictional counterpart and enveloping both in the convulsive fantasies of blood violation, that must be seen to contain *within* it the power of *Light in August*. As Christmas himself both contains, and is contained within, a myth, so the novel embodies within itself the many threads of a racial myth — unwinding and rewinding in both Faulkner's career and his nation's history — that in a larger way embodies it.

The murder of Joanna Burden, which appears as a kind of shadow play of weapons, revolver and razor,[71] and which follows from her final attempt to get Christmas to kneel with her in prayer, is the last, antagonistic expression of the violence their combative sexual affair has mimicked all along. As such it casts back to the ritual sacrifice Joe performs to cleanse himself of the horror of menstrual blood ("It's something that happens to them once a month," his companion had said) and forecasts the ambiguous absolution he finds kneeling behind a table when he is murdered in Hightower's house. Enveloping the two murders and the affair that produces them, and enveloping the novel and the heritage that produces it, is the potent symbol of "the black shadow in the shape of a cross" that Joanna invokes at the climax of her family's story. Although the shadowed cross is black, the crucified are white; the "shadow in which" all live, black and white, is the perfectly ambiguous expression of the burden of white *within* black *within* white — of what her father calls "a race doomed and cursed to be forever and ever a part of the white race's doom and curse for its sins."[72] There is no need to go through the contortions some readers have to see Christmas as a Christ figure; his career simply includes that potential significance (as, in a different fashion, Lincoln's career did) but surpasses any actual relevance it could have — except (here again like Lincoln) as the ironically tortured emblem that releases into the surging rhythms of racial fantasy the degeneration of Southern gynealotry (Joanna Burden), the tautological frenzy of zealous racism (Doc Hines), the last gasp of the Lost Cause (Hightower), and the dream come true of the Invisible Empire (Percy Grimm). What it does more conclusively is continue to depict the psychological confusion in (and quite nearly the inversion of) the relationship between master and slave, in which a literal and visible ascendancy is engulfed by one that is figurative and invisible. Joe Christmas lives between these two possibilities, passes between them, and it is there that he dies.

F AULKNER began *Light in August* in August of 1931, the centennial anniversary of Nat Turner's bloody rebellion in Southampton, Virginia. The Turner insurrection, in which some fifty whites were murdered, erupted out of nowhere — or so it seemed to many Southerners. A religious fanatic who early in his life had apocalyptic visions of "white spirits and black spirits engaged in battle," of lighted figures in the sky stretched "from east to west, even as they were extended on the cross on Calvary for the redemption of sinners," Turner claimed in the purported confessions recorded by Thomas Gray that he was divinely inspired to take up Christ's yoke and "fight against the Serpent, for the time was fast approaching when the first should be last and the last should be first."[73] The threat of Turner's rebellion was thus mitigated in some minds by his madness; only insanity could lead otherwise contented slaves to such brutal atrocities. Aside from the crazed rebel slave in Harriet Beecher Stowe's *Dred* (1856), Turner received little significant literary attention until the appearance in 1967 of William Styron's *The Confessions of Nat Turner,* a novel designed to reassure no one, black or white.

The aspect of Styron's searing fictional account of Turner's life that has aroused most controversy is his explicit portrayal of Turner's imagined sexual attraction to several white women, most particularly to the white girl who appears to be the only person Turner himself actually killed. If this part of the novel is to be deprecated, however, it must also be measured, for example, against the portrayal of "rape" in *Native Son.* Turner's desire (as Styron depicts it) to fill his future victim with "warm milky spurts of desecration" or, in another instance, to repay the "pity" and "compassion" of a weak white woman with "outrageous spurts of defilement" and produce in her "the swift and violent immediacy of a pain of which I was complete overseer,"[74] is nothing less than the actualization of a fantasy that may have existed during slavery (although Turner's insurrection, among others, was remarkably free from such sexual retribution) but arose more clearly in the twentieth century *between* black and white, making deceptively confused the masks that faced and reflected each other, and enclosing both in the violence the threat of amalgamation could release. Without minimizing the important differences between the situations and the historical renderings of Bigger Thomas and Styron's Nat Turner, we should note as well that from the standpoint of their creators they are two sides of a coin, two masks of violence turning against itself in redoubled, nearly tautological frenzy. The power driving this frenzy, as James Baldwin has observed in the case of Bigger, is simply that of a "complementary faith among the damned," which may lead them at last to a forcing "into the arena of the actual those fantastic crimes of which they have been accused, achieving their vengeance and their own destruction through making the nightmare real."[75]

Faulkner was dead by the time Styron's novel appeared; he thought well of *Native Son;* and there is no evidence, aside from the coincidence of the date he began *Light in August,* that he knew or cared much about Nat Turner. But the psychology of amalgamation, and the violence it responds to and extends, are rendered visible on nearly every page of Faulkner's novel. It is a psychology that thoroughly depends on the paradox of retributive violence — a paradox Faulkner often described in response to questions about violence in his fiction as something "man must combat" even when "he has been strangled by degradation and violence, when he has hated the violence he participated in, when he has resisted the violence, when he believed in something like honor and pride and compassion, even in degradation."[76] Sex, he added, has much the same function; indeed, it is difficult to conceive of their separation in his novels, so completely do they penetrate each other, like white and black. Because violence and sexuality determine the contours of the South's romance of blood, it is worth pointing

out again that the relationship between *Sanctuary* and *Light in August,* Faulkner's
two most violent and sexual novels, is an important one. As we noted earlier,
the ambiguous delineation of Popeye as a "black man" casts back in the
American tradition toward Hawthorne's probing of the secret thrills of Puritan
repression, and at the same time prefigures Faulkner's confrontation in *Light in
August, Absalom, Absalom!,* and *Go Down, Moses* of the more haunting, more
historically immediate complexity of that repression. By making literal in Joe
Christmas the figurative coloring of Popeye and extending by a single degree
the nymphomania of Temple Drake into the comic depravity of Joanna Burden,
Faulkner himself passed the color line that would define his major work and
extend the boundaries of classic American fiction to include a tormenting problem that underlay each successive challenge to the failing vision of democratic
freedom.

Faulkner's struggle with the problem of narrative form up to and including
Light in August must therefore be seen to contain as well his evolving effort to
include a tradition that is both larger than his own and yet in the twentieth century completely dependent on it. *Light in August,* heaving and bulging with the
effort to integrate those traditions, barely survives the pressure it produces, but
it turns Faulkner, as it would Styron, back toward the century in which the
amalgamation of America and the South seemed least likely and became most
crucial. The accounts of those readers of *Light in August* who have tried to
emphasize that Christmas is characteristic of the "isolated, doomed heroes" of
classic American fiction; that he takes his place in the "descending spiral of isolation, rebellion, and denial" that is "the heritage of American negation"; or that
he personifies "the most extreme phase conceivable of American loneliness," [77]
are thus correct but require a different emphasis. The critics I quote from here
hardly deny the importance of race, but they focus on a problem of literary characterization that in the case of *Light in August* both contains, and must be subordinated to, a more particular social one. "The problem of the twentieth century,"
W.E.B. Du Bois remarked in *The Souls of Black Folk* (1903), "is the problem of
the color-line." [78] By embodying that problem in a character whose very physical
and emotional self embodies the sexual violence of racial conflict, Faulkner
made the problem painfully visible and immediate.

He did so most evidently by enacting in the novel's form the crisis that moti-
vates its action. We have already noted that Christmas both dominates the novel
and threatens to tear it apart, and that the peculiar form of the novel derives in
large part from the way in which the characters of Joanna Burden, Hines,
Hightower, and Grimm come into being in the long plunges into the past that
contact with Christmas brings about. The actualization of their lives, in bold,
alienating movements away from a line of integrated narrative action, expresses
in the novel's form a crisis responding to the violent crisis of blood that the contagion of Christmas represents. Donald Kartiganer is thus right to say that,
because the novel's isolated characters and scenes all "revolve around, and blur
into, [the] impenetrable center" of Christmas's story, even as that story itself

"dissolves into expanding configurations of meaning," *Light in August* is a novel whose form "feeds on its own dissolution." [79] What is most striking about the novel is that despite the later novel's extraordinary increase in narrative and syntactical complexity *Light in August* is much harder to keep in focus than *Absalom, Absalom!* The radical involution of fiction within fiction in the story of Charles Bon has no equal moment in *Light in August*, in which the crisis of blood, the "containing" of black within white, white within black, derives its power from collision, penetration, and withdrawal rather than from the dramatic marriages of opposing forces that Faulkner would strive for in Quentin's and Shreve's imaginative reconstructions. Both the action and the form of *Light in August* answer violence with violence, tearing away from each other lives and stories as they threaten to become joined. At a psychological level they do indeed blur into each other; but at a narrative level that responds to the deepest need of that psychology, they remain vivid and powerless in their segregation.

It is for good reason, then, that in accounting for Christmas's flight to Hightower's house Faulkner first raises the possibility of "like to like" and then replaces it with Gavin Stevens's equally inadequate theory of a battle in Christmas between white blood and black blood. The long, most isolating plunge into the past of Hightower that follows Christmas's death offers little that is relevant to Christmas's life, or even to Hightower's act of providing him with a futile, last-minute alibi — little, that is, but one of the many tortured myths that lie behind the enslavement in which Joe Christmas, like Jim Crow, is still trapped. Christmas's act of striking down Hightower, like a "vengeful and furious god pronouncing doom," issues only in the overcharged, overcompensating rhetoric of Hightower's final visions of the haloed wheel and the tumultuous rush of cavalry. As though spending in wild abandon the accumulated fury he could not bring into the focus of dramatic involvement, Faulkner tears away from each other the two characters who might most conceivably have been linked. They remain connected only by the slender threads of Faulkner's recurring plot of skipped generations, tied and untied with merciless haste, and by the fanatical exclamations of abomination and bitchery that mercilessly isolate Christmas's grandfather. Both the sexual frenzy of Hines and the visions of Hightower that are its ironic, sublimated correlary are surpassed in significance by the act of sacrifice that the one leads toward and the other falls away from. The "single instant of darkness" in which each of them continues to live can neither approach nor further elaborate the visionary scene of Christmas's death that grows out of Percy Grimm's violent act and his swift, brutal proclamation:

> "Now you'll let white women alone, even in hell," he said. But the man on the floor had not moved. He just lay there, with his eyes open and empty of everything save consciousness, and with something, a shadow, about his mouth. For a long moment he looked up at them with peaceful and unfathomable and unbearable eyes. Then his face, body, all, seemed to collapse, to fall in upon itself, and from out the slashed garmets about his hips and loins the pent black blood seemed to rush like a released breath. It seemed to rush out of his pale body like the rush

of sparks from a rising rocket; upon that black blast the man seemed to rise soaring into their memories forever and ever.[80]

Christmas's passive, suicidal participation in this act is one of several features that have led readers to envision him as a Christ figure. When he was once asked about this, Faulkner simply replied that because there are, after all, very few plots in the world of literature and because "that Christ story is one of the best" that has been "invented," it is likely that "it will recur."[81] When Christmas rises "forever and ever" into the memories of his executioners, the Christ story recurs in a fragmented form that depends on it ironically at best. It certainly depends upon it less, for example, than does *Uncle Tom's Cabin* (1852), whose author quite rightly claimed to have depicted nothing "that equals the frightful reality of scenes daily and hourly acting on our shores, beneath the shadow of American law, and the shadow of the cross of Christ," but seemed also to believe that only the "sons of white fathers" among slaves, only those with the "haughty feelings" of Anglo-Saxon blood "burning in their veins," could rise in revolt "and raise with them their mother's race."[82] Stowe, of course, meant to increase her rhetorical power by these remarks rather than undermine it. But as Baldwin has trenchantly observed of the novel whose hero acquires his superhuman powers of humiliating endurance from a vision of the suffering Christ, *Uncle Tom's Cabin* wears the secret "mask of cruelty." Although it poses as a catalogue of actual crimes and heart-rending violence, its emphatic racist sentimentalism betrays a "theological terror, the terror of damnation," which in the end is "not different from that terror which activates a lynch mob." As Baldwin's challenging remarks suggest, the terror behind Stowe's mask may be the distinguishing characteristic of a drama of repression, which when it is inverted leads directly to Bigger Thomas, who is so much Uncle Tom's contemporary descendant, "flesh of his flesh," that if the books are placed together it seems Stowe and Wright (not at all unlike Joanna Burden and Joe Christmas, we might add) "are locked together in a deadly, timeless battle; the one uttering merciless exhortations, the other shouting curses."[83]

To see this inversion clearly and to measure the changing climate of racial fantasy that makes it possible, we need only to place *Light in August* between the two books and their authors. Welding together the suffering passivity of Uncle Tom and the violent rage of Bigger Thomas, Joe Christmas, his own blood violently released in retribution for the blood he has spilt and violated, is surrounded on the one hand by the theological terror of Joanna Burden and Doc Hines, and on the other by its twentieth-century machinery of execution, the hysterical, overbearing violence of Percy Grimm. Christmas's death is as much a "lynching" as he is a "Negro"; that is, technical details do not count here. What counts is the fantasy Christmas embodies and exposes in others by appearing to act "like a nigger," by releasing formally and actually what Walter White called "the Frankenstein monster" of lynching, which puts its creators in fear of their own creation and threatens to bring about more violence than it can ever control.[84] It is thus significant that Faulkner agreed with Cowley that the Percy Grimm section should be anthologized in *The Portable Faulkner;* for as Faulkner remarked at that later date, he had "created a Nazi" before Hitler did, a "Fascist galahad who saved the white race by murdering Christmas."[85]

The power of the analogy between slavery and fascism, both productive of complex psychological infusions of overt hatred with infantalizing dependency, has been noted by historians and literary critics alike.[86] We need not accept it in detail here in order to see that the sacrifice of Joe Christmas by Percy Grimm — a sacrifice made in the name of a thorough denial, not just of the threat Christmas poses, but of the one he already *contains within him* as its requisite opposite — is exceeded in actual violence by the hallucinating specter that momentarily coalesces into a physical act. The physical violence of the sacrifice, like the sexual contagion it responds to, is enveloped in a violence that knows no tactile, containing bounds. One might well speak, then, of a *form* of violence that corresponds in part to the novel's displayed struggle with the *form* of Christmas's life and story; as his very existence sets in motion, but cannot be controlled by, the fantasies it arouses, so his murder cannot in any clear or final way, can with no catharsis or resolution, control or make meaningful their pattern. In this respect, Christmas's death is utterly opposed, for example, to that of Billy Budd, which conforms in measured, stately fashion to the mechanisms of justice that create and define Captain Vere's fatherly authority and reenforce the Christology of his victim.

Christmas's death is a sacrifice not because he sees it that way, or because Percy Grimm necessarily does, or even because the novel suggests that it is; rather, it is sacrificial in that it depends on the "mechanism of reciprocal violence," which René Girard has shown to be the origin of, and to be fully expressed by, ritual sacrifice. The reciprocal violence Girard describes is a "vicious circle" from which the community, once it has entered, in unable to extricate itself without selecting a surrogate victim who can contain the spread of violence by taking it upon himself. As such, the surrogate victim may be seen as a "monstrous double," a figure who is both inside and outside the community, who embodies all its possible differences, and thus "constitutes both a link and a barrier between the community and the sacred."[87] In designating Christmas a surrogate victim, we should be quick to note that he is no more carefully selected to die as a way of warding off further violence than he is, in his death, able to do so. The violence continues to spread — in the lives of the novel and in Faulkner's own novels of the next twenty years; in the agony of Jim Crow that Faulkner's novels and public declarations could do little to stop; and in the fantasies of violated blood that racial equality paradoxically resists and promotes. Like the contagion of sexual violence represented in the menstrual blood that horrifies Christmas by its monstrous significance, the contagion of violence that grows out of the fear of miscegenation represents a menace that has visible actualizations but invisible meaning.

Although Faulkner apparently never witnessed a lynching, his life was surrounded by them.[88] From at least two of them he drew the materials of *Light in August* and *Intruder in the Dust;* in the second he would temporarily resolve the crisis of blood, but in the first he gave way to the full horror it could release. Christmas is not a surrogate victim in the precise sense Girard describes, but as the "white nigger" he is very much, almost too much a monstrous double, for he contains — mask to mask, in mirroring images — the community's own projected desires and fears as well as their reciprocal realization. Like Twain's monstrous double, Tom Driscoll, who wears charcoal blackface when he murders his white "father," Joe Christmas embodies the twin acts of vengeance and sacrifice, neither of them within his control nor clearly ascribable to a conscious act of will; but unlike Tom and unlike Bigger Thomas, Melville's Babo, or Nat Turner, Joe is not "decently hung by a force, a principle" but, as his grandmother fears, is "hacked . . . dead by a Thing." That "thing" is not simply Percy Grimm (who is only its symbol, as Christmas himself is the symbolic embodiment of miscegenation) but an awesome power Faulkner can only account for by the mystic invocation of Fate — the "Player." Likewise, Christmas's castration, the mirroring affirmation and denial of sexuality, is a grotesque distortion of violent reciprocity. Occurring outside the sacrificial process of justice whose machinery may take the place of surrogate victimization in the control of contagious violence, the form of Christmas's death ensures, as White and Twain observed of lynching, that such violence will go on. The legitimized, legal violence with which *Native Son, Pudd'nhead Wilson, Benito Cereno,* and Nat Turner's rebellion all end serves to remind us that the shocking violence of *Light in August* depends in large part on its vitiating and overwhelming a system that cannot control it. As Faulkner put it quite appropriately in an episode that is otherwise humorous (the useless bloodhounds employed to track Christmas): "It was as if the very initial outrage of the murder carried in its wake and made of all subsequent actions something monstrous and paradoxical and wrong, in themselves against both reason and nature."[89]

This loss of control, this monstrous swelling of paradoxical actions is expressed, again, not just in the blasphemous character of Christmas himself, but also in the novel's form from beginning to end — most particularly, of course, from the moment the murder of Joanna Burden begins a third of the way into the novel. It is precisely at that point that the nearly uncontrollable fury of Faulkner's narrative is released. The threat of physical amalgamation, of the disintegration of racial distinctions, erupts into a violent assertion of distinctions — one that radically denies the physical amalgamation that already exists and the psychological amalgamation that follows from it; and one that leads Faulkner, in the face of such a blurring of emotions, to an equally violent and alienating narrative form. The attempt to unite the crisis of blood and the crisis of narrative form continues beyond *Light in August* in the more precisely probed and controlled violence of *Absalom, Absalom!* and *Go Down, Moses,* and it may be said to continue in the consciously measured and carefully worded rhythms of Faulkner's later public statements on the question of race. Like Twain's "imitation nigger," no less the "monstrous freak" than the Siamese twins his character grew from, and like Twain himself, Faulkner was haunted by an unanswerable question: "Why were niggers *and* whites made? What crime did the uncreated first nigger commit that the curse of birth was decreed for him? And why this awful difference made between white and black?" [90] *Light in August* begins Faulkner's stunning explorations of that question, explorations that would lead him deeper into his own past and into the past of his own first fiction; deeper into a history that came more visibly and paradoxically into focus as his career became more public and his native country more stridently recalcitrant on the question of race; and deeper into a moral and psychological problem that engulfs the promise of freedom. It would lead him next to an epic rendering of his country's epic trauma: the trauma of the house divided.

chapter 5

Absalom, Absalom!
and the House Divided

H ARRIET BEECHER STOWE missed her chance to preempt William Styron when the crazed rebel slave she modeled in part on Nat Turner (and also represented as the son of Denmark Vesey) ineffectually dies before he can bring about the great and murderous revolt he has been meditating in anticipation of a prophetic sign from heaven. Dred's death, of course, lets Stowe off the hook; she does not have to imagine clearly the deeper motives for, or the results of, organized insurrection, and she is free to lead her slaves and their white sympathizer north to freedom. Like *Uncle Tom's Cabin,* Stowe's *Dred* ends with sentimental rejoicing and reunion. Still, the distance between Uncle Tom and Dred is significant; for while Dred is largely portrayed as an insane animal, whose twisted understandings of biblical prophecy help make Uncle Tom by contrast the evangelistic minstrel he has often been taken to be, he represents a development in Stowe's thinking and literary powers that cannot be overlooked. Although most of the blacks in *Dred,* aside from its titular character, are in the emotional mold of the humble endurers of *Uncle Tom's Cabin,* and although the greater exceptions to this rule — those who can "pass" — are also in the mold of George and Eliza Harris, *Dred* brings Stowe closer to the intimate tragedy and psychological complexities of slavery than a reader of her most famous novel might expect.

She not only missed her chance to write *The Confessions of Nat Turner,* she also barely missed her chance to write *Absalom, Absalom!* For *Dred* is less concerned with the black rebel of the dismal swamp than with the explosive interlocking relationships among four brothers and sisters: Nina Gordon, daughter of Colonel Thomas Gordon, a deceased North Carolina planter, and now mistress of his estate; Tom Gordon, her brother, a hot-headed and dissipated Southern gentleman; Harry Gordon, their quadroon half-brother, who is overseer of the plantation and is saving money to buy his freedom in accordance with an agreement with his father; and Cora Gordon, their quadroon half-sister, who has been taken to Ohio and married by a white man, Colonel Gordon's nephew. Harry's wife, Lisette, the slave of a French woman and of mixed African and French blood herself, completes the main circle of characters. Despite obvious differences, what family in American fiction more resembles the "get" of Thomas Sutpen — Judith, Henry, Charles Bon, Clytie — and Bon's octoroon wife? Add Mrs. Nesbit, the fluttering aunt of Nina and Tom (their dead mother's sister) and the vague counterpart of Faulkner's Aunt Rosa, and the stage is set for *Absalom, Absalom!* Stowe, of course, does not write it, but she comes close enough to make *Dred* in many respects a more penetrating novel than the melodrama of Uncle Tom. Tom and Harry Gordon share that "rooted enmity between . . . brothers" which Stowe brings into yet harsher focus by making exceptionally affectionate the ties between Nina and Harry; [1] by having the spiteful Tom attempt to buy Lisette to satisfy his lust (Nina buys her instead to protect Harry); and by making Tom ultimately responsible, after the death of her husband, for disinheriting Cora and seizing her estate, after which she murders her children and is condemned to death. The plot reaches a crisis after Nina dies from cholera and the estate, Canema, comes under Tom's control. He declares Harry's manumission agreement with their father invalid, renews his attentions to Lisette, and completes his acquisition of Cora's property. After a violent quarrel with Tom, Harry and his wife flee to Dred's rebel outpost in the swamp; after further legal and mercenary skirmishing, the dead Nina's abolitionist fiancé, Edward Clayton, joins the renegades and, once Dred is killed, follows them north to Canada with his family and slaves.

The integration of Stowe's three main plots — the plight of the Gordons, Clayton's emancipation plans and his righteous legal career, and Dred's potential rebellion — is not entirely successful; and as in the case of Dred, so in the case of the Gordon brothers and sisters she cannot (certainly not in 1856) measure the full dimensions of blood intimacy and blood rivalry. Like Canema itself, however, the book is permeated by an aura of decay and failed magnificence — of a grand design gone wrong through the sins of the fathers. In this respect Tom is right, from the wrong point of view, to blame the "white niggers" (as he puts it) for the collapsing vision. "How often I've wished that I was a good, honest black nigger," Harry tells his wife in a passage prefiguring Joe Christmas and Charles Bon, "but, now, I'm neither one thing nor another." The contradictory love and shame of his father is itself a tragedy, Harry adds, but is nothing compared to his own: "We have all the family blood, and the family pride; and what to do with it? . . . I feel in my heart that I'm like Colonel Gordon — I know I am; and, sometimes, I know I look like him, and that's one reason why Tom Gordon always hated me." The greater hurt, and one whose complexity Stowe can only bring near the level of consciousness, is "to have a sister like Miss Nina; to feel she *is* my sister, and never dare to say a word of it!" [2] The suggestions of incestuous attraction in *Dred* are shadowy at best, but the threat of disintegration in a once stately social and psychological order is very real. The blame is not hard to fix: miscegenation — not, of course, as the single flaw in an otherwise noble design, but as a representation of its gravest disorder and most perplexing dilemma, a representation of that double bind which was made increasingly visible in the South just before the war and which, as we have seen in the case of

Light in August, would become even more monstrous and perplexing for Jim Crow in the next century. How, without intense moral and psychological convulsions, could the South keep slaves as beasts and lovers alike? And what, then, to do with the children who so vividly embodied these contradictory attitudes in one blasphemous image?

One of the most interesting and in some respects unresolvable standoffs between South and North before and after the war was the issue of miscegenation. Many abolitionists (including Stowe, after her fashion) pointed to Southern miscegenation as the ultimate tragedy of slavery; however, many Southerners accused the abolitionists (and the North in general, including Lincoln) of encouraging miscegenation and of precipitating the war in order to guarantee it as the ultimate freedom. Both sides were largely wrong. Southern miscegenation was not epidemic (though statistics, of course, are in this case difficult, if not impossible, to verify) and many slaveholders were quite vocally outraged by it;[3] most Northerners hardly looked forward to a mixing of the races but more often, as both Stowe and Lincoln did, advocated colonization to whatever degree it might be possible. But at the level of imagination, the level of fantasy at which we must measure the conflicting layers of intimacy and fear, the turbulent passions the war itself could never resolve but could only release into a century-long trauma, the level at which the fratricidal war that divided a country becomes superimposed upon forms of actual and psychological fratricide casting their shadows over South and North alike — at that level, both sides were undeniably right. Without slighting powerful political and economic explanations of both the Civil War and Jim Crow that may in the end be more factually convincing, it is not misleading to consider that, just as the war itself only came in progress to be a struggle for emancipation, so in the longer run and in retrospect, it came to be a struggle over the far-reaching, hopelessly complex and paradoxical issue of miscegenation, the one issue that visibly emblematized all others.

In describing the contours of racial hysteria that make Joe Christmas an object of requisite sacrifice, we took note of James Baldwin's contention that Stowe's apocalyptic exhortations in *Uncle Tom's Cabin* grow out of "theological terror" and as such are not wholly unlike the frenzy of a lynch mob. The deeper resemblances between *Dred* and *Absalom, Absalom!* (and whatever "racist" attitudes their authors share) may be measured in a similar way; for the gothic draining of emotions that Charles Bon's story necessitates, those furious transports of sympathy that Quentin and Shreve require to tell his story, are in their own way contemporary echoes of Stowe's emotional overflowings. The gothicism of *Absalom, Absalom!* grows out of that sentimentality which is the South's most singular tradition — the tradition of stupefying nostalgia, the painful and tender looking backward toward the ever-living dead dream. We have seen in earlier chapters how Faulkner at once embraces and savagely attacks that nostalgic dream (and particularly its representative embodiment, White Womanhood) and moreover how it may be said to engender his stylistic complexities. Both his own ambivalence and the complexity of his style reach a peak in the gothic tragedies of Charles Bon and Henry and Judith Sutpen, where the extremities of anxiety implicit in such nostalgia are fierce indeed. The gothicism of *Absalom, Absalom!* is not by any means the sentimentality of a minstrel show — not the benign dream in which "all coons look alike" — but the nightmare in which black *and* white begin all too hauntingly to look alike.

To see the sentimental dimensions of Faulkner's gothicism more clearly, we need to consider in a preliminary way the racial aspects of "the House Divided," a phrase in contemporary use even before Lincoln made it famous in his 1858 speech. The image of a nation divided against itself is apt in more ways than the obvious one of threatened union, for it also represents the dangerous, paradoxical ways in which North and South, each internally divided as well, were not simply opposed but in significant respects were almost mirrored images. Such a mirroring was revealed, to take a minor example, in the wake of *Uncle Tom's Cabin,* whose proslavery detractors pointed precisely to the book's heartwarming depictions of happy slaves as evidence that, on the whole, the peculiar institution was a noble one and a tyrant like Simon Legree the worst of exceptions.[4] Whether such arguments carry much weight is not completely relevant; as George Forgie points out, what Stowe (and Lincoln) understood was that the crisis of the House Divided "was not a conflict between one group that wanted to preserve a particular way of life or value and another group that wanted to destroy it," but rather was one in which different kinds of conservatives "sought to preserve cherished values and traditions."[5] To lose such a conflict after years of bloodshed and destruction could — and did — lead to the most frantic of nostalgias.

The nostalgic longing for a lost world served to conceal both the gradual recognition that the "happy slave" had largely been putting on an act and the fear that arose when, once that act was no longer necessary, the specter of equality assumed forbidding proportions. Because the preservation of either way of life seemed in the long run to entail destruction of the other, the war was inevitable (what else "might have been," to borrow a recurring phrase from *Absalom, Absalom!,* is now hard to imagine); what as a consequence was inevitable is something Melville saw clearly when he ironically reversed the points of view in *Benito Cereno.* It is the New Englander, Amasa Delano — with his sentimental visions of slaves as fawning mothers, lap-dogs, barbers, and entertainers — who is astonished and pained to see the "shadow of the Negro" descend upon the broken, spiritually wasted slaveholder, Benito Cereno. The slave Babo's "act" of rebellion, masked in this further, excruciating irony on Melville's part, not only reveals the utter fragility of the South's own vision of itself, but more strikingly, and with more terrifying depth, prefigures a problem that neither the South nor the North was entirely ready to face. The failed colonization plans of Stowe and Lincoln, as well as those advocated by the South, are only one sign of a sentimental ideal doomed in practice. Like both sides' visions of contented slaves, such plans were grand illusions that could not undo several hundred years of actuality. It needs to be pointed out, however, that the illusions of North and South alike represented the drastic repression of a fear that, though it had differing forms of public expression, was in essence one of merged, mirroring images. The North accused the South of condoning and practicing miscegenation, and the South accused the North of encouraging and facilitating it. It could hardly be seen at the time, since neither side was wholly justified, that the darker side of the threat to union, the side covered by the paternalistic masks of blind ignorance and willed sentimentality, would later appear to be the one that the struggle to reunite the divided house had been about but could not control. On the contrary, the struggle could only make the threat — for the first time, perhaps — painfully evident.

Stowe's *Dred*, arguably a better novel than *Uncle Tom's Cabin*, is never likely to be accorded its proper status, for it did not have — could never have had — the same impact as the heart-rending effusions of Little Eva and Uncle Tom. Stowe is still trapped in *Dred* by her inability to portray convincingly black characters who are neither insane nor overly humble nor, most of all, essentially "white." But in the case of Harry Gordon and the family he does but cannot belong to, the dilemma of the "white nigger" receives one of its most significant treatments prior to Twain and Johnson. And in any event, is not Faulkner himself, nearly a century later, still caught in Stowe's trap? To recognize this neither excuses the sentimental racism of *Uncle Tom's Cabin* nor makes Faulkner's own racial fears less enigmatic or dramatically exacting. As he turned from *Light in August* to *Absalom, Absalom!* (1936) he turned from the tragedy of Jim Crow to the tragedy that made him possible — indeed, it seems, inevitable — and he did so by turning, as Stowe had, to the sins of the fathers that led necessarily to the violence of the brothers. He brings to a culmination, with an intensity only the war and its aftermath could make visible, the several fratricidal dimensions of America's national sin; and his novel ends, almost like Stowe's, in forged reunion and escape from the darkest past of the South. It ends in 1909 in an old abolitionist stronghold in New England, having precariously reunited its story to the unfulfilled vision of *The Sound and the Fury* by leading Quentin Compson through an agonizing rehearsal of Thomas Sutpen's flawed design, through the *might have been* that had to be, and bringing him to the threshold of his suicide.

THE "FLAW" in Thomas Sutpen's grand "design" is, of course, his first son's supposed black blood. Abandoning his wife and son in Haiti, Sutpen carries his dynastic scheme to frontier Mississippi, only to have that repressed son return as his second son's best friend and, apparently, his daughter's fiancé. Sutpen does not (according to Quentin, according to his father, according to his grandfather) call it "retribution, no sins of the fathers come home to roost," but just a "mistake," one that inescapably impedes his vision of "fine grandsons and great-grandsons springing as far as the eye could reach" and leaves him immobilized in attempting to fathom its meaning. He can either recognize Charles

Bon or not recognize him, he says, "either destroy my design with my own hand" or, letting the affair take its own course, "see my design complete itself quite normally and naturally and successfully to the public eye, yet to my own in such a fashion as to be a mockery and a betrayal." [6] This re-creation of Sutpen's dilemma by Quentin and Shreve occurs at a significant point in the "design" both of Faulkner's book and his career that we must consider; we must consider as well the question of whether or not Sutpen is a representative Southern planter, a point of some critical debate. That debate, however, is not necessarily relevant to the issue of miscegenation. The average planter did not rise from Tidewater poverty, conceive a grand design in answer to being turned away from the front door of a plantation by a "monkey nigger," sail to Haiti and participate in an ongoing racial revolution, and see his dreams of grandeur shattered when his white son murders the "black" brother who is going to marry his sister. Still, the contours of Sutpen's mythic career are certainly more accurately revealing than the equally mythic magnolia-scented portraits by Thomas Nelson Page, Thomas Dixon, and Margaret Mitchell, which enjoyed, in complete contrast, such extraordinary popularity in Jim Crow's South. It is in the context of such rampantly nostalgic versions of slavery that Faulkner's novel becomes most powerful and Sutpen's resolute "innocence" most meaningful. For that "innocence" — the last barrier to Sutpen's tragic recognition and the last threat holding Faulkner's lost dream in place — is the strangling center of Southern nostalgia. Without it, even the remembered design falls into ruins.

There is no doubt that the paradoxically lost, but defiantly maintained, innocence of the South has numerous motives and outcroppings, many of them practically necessary and others anxiously fantastic. One might trace them, for example, to the "flaw" Cash detects in antebellum pretensions to aristocracy, which were "not an emanation from the proper substance of the men who wore it, but only a fine garment put on from the outside." [7] For Cash, the planters could not have been properly aristocratic because they were often violent and acquisitive, and their origins in frontier vulgarity were too recent and obvious. But, we might ask, as Eugene Genovese has, "What aristocracy ever arose from any other kind men?" [8] The economic and political aspects of those two points of view are important; but in the case of Thomas Sutpen, who would appear to support either contention, the major "flaw" in his aristocratic design overwhelms his vulgarity and renders visibly specious the veneer of innocent grandeur that most every design for slavery depended on and to which the South, at least through Faulkner's career and life, tenaciously clung. And in any event, as Cash later notes, the most vocal pretensions to aristocracy were retrospective. The defensive posture of the South after the war and into the next century created, among other peculiarities, the strange situation in which, "while the actuality of aristocracy was drawing away toward the limbo of aborted and unrealized things," the claim of its possession as an "indefeasible heritage" was "reasserted with a kind of frenzied intensity." [9]

Because not only the South but the entire nation may be said to have lost its innocence in the Civil War, its most fratricidal conflict, that flaw is larger than Sutpen himself can reveal. Both North and South appealed to the revolutionary fathers throughout the war, just as they had prior to it in arguments over the place of slavery in the Constitution and the founding fathers' grand "design" for America itself; it is therefore not at all fortuitous that Sutpen's first mistake occurs on an island that, in Faulkner's description, might be a mythic replica of American history itself, "a theater for violence and injustice and bloodshed and all the satanic lusts of human greed and cruelty," a country located

> halfway between the dark inscrutable continent from which the black blood, the black bones and flesh and thinking and remembering and hopes and desires, was ravished by violence, and the cold land to which it was doomed, the civilized land and people which had expelled some of its own blood and thinking and desires that had become too crass to be faced and borne any longer, and set it homeless and desperate on the lonely ocean — a little lost island in a latitude which would require ten thousand years of equatorial heritage to bear its climate, [its] soil manured with black blood from two hundred years of oppression and exploitation.[10]

As in the telescoped history of slavery in the Americas Melville presents in *Benito Cereno,* Faulkner's description of Haiti indicates that, though the crisis was long in coming, the flaw was there all along. To this extent, Sutpen's crisis of innocence, as well as the flaw that engenders it, is the nation's. That *Absalom, Absalom!* was even written is perhaps the best evidence that the flaw was deep.

It is nonetheless striking how close the Civil War came to circumventing the question of slavery, to postponing it, as Lincoln hoped to do, until a later date. One factor in Lincoln's attitude, though certainly not the only one, may be found in his continually having to defend himself against charges of fostering (in crueler moments, of practicing or being the product of) miscegenation. Almost as often as he spoke against the Dred Scott decision, he was called upon, or felt compelled, to make this defense. "There is a natural disgust in the minds of nearly all white people at the idea of an indiscriminate amalgamation of the white and black races," Lincoln remarked in an important 1857 speech that echoed Jefferson's beliefs. As usual, the charges had come from Stephen Douglas, who argued (as Lincoln summarized it) that those who contended that the Declaration of Independence included Negroes did so "only because they want to vote, and eat, and sleep, and marry with Negroes!" Here, as he would throughout the 1858 debates with Douglas, Lincoln protested the "counterfeit logic which concludes that, because I do not want a black woman for a slave I must necessarily want her for a wife." He adds that he too is horrified ("Agreed for once — a thousand times agreed") by "the mixing of blood by the white and black races," and goes on to note that, because nearly all the mulattoes in the United States "have sprung from black slaves and white masters," a "separation of the races is the only perfect preventive of amalgamation."[11]

Lincoln's most famous speech on the House Divided, delivered the following year, would make no clear mention of the miscegenation issue; by then he was Douglas's official opponent for the Senate, and it may be that he thought it best to leave tacit his defense of one of the Republican party's thornier issues. In the 1857 speech, however, Dred Scott's family itself is rallied as "an illustration only" of Lincoln's basic position. Had the court's decision gone the other way, Lincoln pointed out,

> the chances of these black girls ever mixing their blood with that of white people would have been diminished at least to the extent that it could not have been without their consent. But Judge Douglas is delighted to have them decided to be slaves, and not human enough to have a hearing, even if they were free, and thus left subject to the forced concubinage of their masters, and liable to become the mothers of mulattoes in spite of themselves: the very state of case that produces nine-tenths of all the mulattoes — all the mixing of blood in the nation.

Given this situation, separation of the races — "if ever effected at all, [it] must be effected by colonization," Lincoln remarked — is the only ultimate answer. But because "an immediate separation is impossible, the next best thing is to keep them apart where they are not already together. If white and black people never get together in Kansas," for example, "they will never mix blood in Kansas. That is at least one self-evident truth." [12]

The New Testament image of the House Divided that Lincoln invoked the following year in his most famous speech on slavery not only prefigured the fratricidal conflict he maintained would *not* be necessary but also, as Forgie has demonstrated, included for Lincoln his own fraternal rivalry with Douglas, who in Lincoln's view had been engineering an attack on the House of the founding fathers ever since the Kansas-Nebraska Act in 1854. [13] It would be two years before Lincoln would defeat the rival brother and, then, enter the White House resolved to save the Union by restoring the vision of the founding fathers, a vision that in his opinion held slavery repugnant and implicitly called for its *eventual* elimination, but one whose ambiguity, of course, had never ceased to provide evidence for either (or any) point of view. Although "a husband and wife may be divorced," Lincoln said in his first inaugural address (4 March 1861), we "cannot remove our respective sections from one another, nor build an impassable barrier between them." Instead, we must take our time, let passions cool, until "the mystic chords of memory, stretching from every battlefield and patriot grave to every living heart," are "again touched, as surely they will be, by the better angels of our nature." A little over a month later, Fort Sumter fell, and Lincoln called forth an army to protect the nation — as he would later phrase it in appointing McClellan to command the army — from "parricidal rebellion." [14] The crisis Lincoln feared had come — not exactly as, and much faster than, he had expected.

The tendency toward legalizing slavery in all states — the inevitable result, as Lincoln saw it, of the Kansas-Nebraska Act and the Dred Scott decision — had been exacerbated rather than lessened in recent years. Lincoln's remarks on the occasion of his House Divided speech in 1858 held this possibility at a point of perilous balance, which in retrospect would seem to articulate as well a crisis and division stretching beyond that of sectional conflict alone:

> In my opinion, [slavery agitation] will not cease until a crisis shall have been reached and passed. "A house divided against itself cannot stand." I believe this government cannot endure permanently half slave and half free. I do not expect the union to be dissolved — I do not expect the house to fall — but I do expect it will cease to be divided. It will become all one thing, or all the other.

Lincoln saw the tendency toward extending slavery as a conspiracy — or, as he put it, a "design," a "concert of action among its chief architects." [15] Lincoln's theory of a conspiracy has been much debated; but whether or not there was such a "design," Lincoln's theory virtually brought it into being. Like the figure of the House Divided itself, and like the fraternal conflict with Douglas it promoted, the conspiracy theory fed into the increasingly melodramatic structure of the national debate over slavery. It was a structure Lincoln at once resisted and rose to prominence in, and one in which, by the end of the 1850s, Forgie writes, "the crisis of the Union not only imitated, but had become, a work of art, with the paradoxical result that as the crisis grew more serious its seriousness grew more difficult to measure." Whether or not Lincoln may then be seen to have helped create "a situation that [would] put the house in danger, thereby permitting him to act not only defensively but also heroically to save and restore it," [16] it is true that Lincoln's beautiful rhetoric helped create the heroic drama of the crisis — even though it was only in the middle of the war that he abandoned his hope for postponing abolition and issued the Emancipation Proclamation; and apparently only by the end of the war, as in his second inaugural address (4 March 1865), that he came to see slavery as a national sin and the war in terms of a divine plan for its end.

The further Christological significance of Lincoln's assassination on Good Friday, 1865, at the time obscured the fact that the resonant House Divided speech had *not* predicted, much less advocated, war and that it expressed Lincoln's essential belief that preserving the Union *did not* require the abolition of slavery. He did not expect "the Union to be dissolved . . . the house to fall," but he did expect it would "cease to be divided" into "half slave and half free" — not immediately, but sometime. I have suggested that Lincoln's avoidance of the miscegenation charge in the House Divided speech is significant; and it does not seem misleading to suggest that it is conscious and intentional, that its introduction would have rendered more problematic than ever Lincoln's desire to postpone the question of abolition. One might say instead that it made Lincoln's stand positively necessary. As in the years before his election, so as the war began Lincoln had to appeal to abolitionists and racists alike (often, of course, they were the same), had to mobilize the sentiments of a melodramatic conflict and at the same time, as Woodward points out, recognize that "unless he fought that war with the support of racists and in the name of white supremacy it would be *his* lost cause and not Jefferson Davis's." [17]

There is reason to think that what Lincoln had in mind — in the back of his mind — when he said that slavery agitation would "not cease until a crisis shall have been reached and passed" thus included in supressed form the one crisis he could not face, the crisis of amalgamation that abolition seemed to entail. This more vexing aspect of the House Divided, one that divided each section of the House as it fell, cannot alone fully explain either the war or Lincoln's attitudes toward slavery. But it brings into perspective, with an urgency that would only be apparent as the war developed and concluded, a paradoxical aspect of Lincoln's career. His opinion about the conspiratorial "design" on behalf of an extension of slavery must necessarily be seen to contain a fear that miscegenation — up to now largely restricted to the slaveholding South, he said — would also spread. Yet by the same token, how could slavery eventually be abolished without creating potentially more rampant, if less inhumane, forms of amalgamation? As Lincoln's 1857 speech indicated, he thought the second less likely and in any event preferable in the long run to the first; but he also thought its complete prevention, by separation of the races, the best and most natural solution of all. That solution was colonization in Haiti, among other places; he died without finding a better one. The House divided between North and South concealed a further division between white and black, one that was paradoxically evident in their literal, physical union and one that, far from being dissolved by a reunion of the warring sections and an abolition of slavery, could only be made more prominently explosive. Insofar as the Emancipation Proclamation was more a military and technically political decision than an embracing act of human liberation, it is probably to the advantage of Lincoln's mythic career that he did not live to struggle with the further crisis it precipitated. In short, his own design for restoring the Union, not to say his original design for preserving it, was flawed.

I am suggesting, of course, that there is an analogy between Lincoln and Sutpen, each of whom labors heroically to build or preserve a magnificent "house" symbolic of his national and personal dream, and both of whom, at about the same time, face a crisis in the house and try desperately to postpone it. In each case, the Civil War itself forces a resolution of the crisis — though not in either case without violent consequences. It is not by any means an analogy in which they or their designs are exactly duplicated but, rather, one in which they are mirror images in the sense that a mirror image reverses the figure to which it corresponds. To the extent that Lincoln and Sutpen both derive their visions of perpetuated design from that of the founding fathers — the Declaration of Independence and the Constitution — their careers and public pronouncements (Lincoln's speeches and Sutpen's rehearsed story) embody the essential American dream and its fundamental "mistake." In remarkable counterpoint to his prominent statements of white supremacy, Lincoln's troubled devotion to equality is everywhere evident in his speeches, and his rise from humble origins to heroic magnificence, like Sutpen's rise, dramatizes the dream denied to an entire race of Americans for close to a century after the signing of those documents — a dream redeemed into a promise by Lincoln and others but broken and betrayed, for nearly another century, by those judiciously read in the thought of the fathers and devoted to perpetuating their visionary design.

In the previous chapter we took note of Faulkner's contention in 1958 that blacks, currently "second-class citizens," must one day be assimilated into white society. It would not happen quickly, he said, but it must happen *eventually*. He went on to note, in the wake of *Brown* v. *Board of Education*, that "all the laws in the world are not going to make the two races mix if they don't want to, just as all the laws in the world won't keep them apart if they do want to." Even though things had "gone backward" since the Supreme Court decision, Faulkner maintained, racial equality had "advanced gradually and steadily" since 1865. Faulkner's essential belief in "separate but equal" is only brought into proper perspective, however, when we note that he opened this session at the University of Virginia by stating that "a hundred years ago Abraham Lincoln said, 'This nation cannot endure half slave and half free.'" Today, Faulkner said, Lincoln would amend this to respond to the problem of second-class versus first-class citizenship.[18] There is certainly little doubt of that; what is also no doubt striking, not to mention intolerable, is that it could take so long — and appear to take longer yet — to find and correct the flaw in Lincoln's design.

Not only did the nation lose its "innocence" in the Civil War, it also spent the next hundred years, one might say, in protesting that loss through a series of grand expressions of paternalism that, however inevitable or necessary they seemed at the time, were often no less remarkable or extravagant than those of Thomas Sutpen. Faulkner was reading from the House Divided speech in light of the war Lincoln hoped to avoid, and more particularly in light of the now visible problem Lincoln seemed dramatically to suppress in that speech. In this respect, however, Faulkner may have been reading it correctly, for just as *Light in August* reveals its greater resonance when it is placed in the larger historical context of *Absalom, Absalom!* and *Go Down, Moses,* so too the ironies of Lincoln's position would not be fully apparent until, say, 1896 (*Plessy* v. *Ferguson*) or 1954 (*Brown* v. *Board of Education*). We do not, I think, have to torture Lincoln's position too much to make it resemble Sutpen's dilemma over the recognition of his "black" son, Charles Bon: if Lincoln had let the abolition of slavery take its own eventual course, his restoration of the Union would indeed, to some observers then and perhaps to all in retrospect, have been "a mockery and a betrayal"; by abolishing slavery "with [his] own hand," he necessarily destroyed the design — for saving the Union without interfering with slavery where it already existed — that he had insisted on time and again. Lincoln was ready to assume the role of the founding fathers and preserve their design (ambiguous though it was on this issue), but he was often — and by necessity — as paternalistic as most of his contemporaries, slaveholders included, in his attitudes toward blacks. (It is not for nothing that many liberated slaves unavoidably and gratefully saw him in the role not just of Moses or Christ but more simply of a father.) Likewise, Thomas

Sutpen is determined to continue to enhance the Southern design of slavehold-ing paternalism, but he is not ready to accept a "Negro" son into that design. (It is not for nothing in this case either than Bon wants not a piece of that design but simply his father's recognition of him as a son.) As Quentin and his father, and *his* father, put it, "Sutpen's trouble was innocence." [19]

Such innocence is obviously tormenting. The frenzy of *Absalom, Absalom!* reveals this again and again — and then again. If we are still in doubt, let us add Woodward's observation that, though it resembled other American dreams of opulence, the dream of the South has seldom been so convincing. Because the South for half of its history "lived intimately with a great social evil and [for] the other half with its aftermath," its preoccupation is "with guilt, not with inno-cence, with the reality of evil, not with the dream of perfection." If it "plunged into catastrophe" to escape "the torments of its own conscience," however, the escape was not very successful. [20] And yet, in its still peculiar fashion, it was: how else explain the long procession of grandiloquent myths? As Faulkner saw quite clearly, the razor's edge dividing repressed guilt and ostentatious inno-cence was painfully sharp. It still divided the mind as it had once divided the nation. In the case of *Absalom, Absalom!* it divides nearly everything in view — every pair of characters and every pair of narrators, every possible resolution of Charles Bon's tragedy and Quentin Compson's reliving of it, every physical and psychological body, every one of its many real and mythic houses (of Sutpen, of Compson, of David, of Oedipus, of Atreus, the House Divided), every mar-riage in fact and fantasy, blood and memory — everything, even the form of the novel itself.

The correlative pressure of such division is *union* — the reforged and redeemed innocence that includes but overcomes guilt, the resurrected, undead might-have-been, the *"world filled with living marriage"* that Miss Rosa Coldfield, for example, inhabits one *"summer of wistaria"* in 1860. [21] There is no way to overesti-mate the stupendous, tortuous effort Faulkner makes in *Absalom, Absalom!* to force into crisis and overcome the tragic divisions his novel is built upon; the repeated metaphor of that effort, and its perfect formal analogy, is marriage and its implied recognitions and responsibilities. It operates throughout the book in ways we must account for, but it derives its power quite simply from expressing, at its deepest, potentially most tragic and threatening level, one central issue that the Civil War would in retrospect seem to be about and the issue *Absalom, Absalom!* is so outrageously about: amalgamation — or rather, miscegenation. It is worth making this distinction, for *miscegenation* first came into being as a term in 1863, almost on the heels of the Emancipation Proclamation. *Amalgamation* meant simply a mixing, but *miscegenation* quite clearly meant interracial *sexual* mixing, and the term therefore quickly acquired a contagious and derisive force, one that expressed the nation's most visceral fears, paradoxical or not, about emancipation.

As we have seen, Lincoln's 1857 defense against charges that the Republican party encouraged miscegenation took the logical form of pointing out that his not wishing to own a black woman did not entail his wishing to marry one. Clearly, miscegenation was not the only point of conflict between the sections, and the charges against Lincoln were not taken overly seriously by anyone in the North; indeed, they largely subsided until emancipation became probable and, finally, actual. In late December 1863, they exploded again in the form of an anonymous pamphlet entitled "Miscegenation: The Theory of the Blending of the Races, Applied to the American White Man and Negro." [22] The proslavery authors coined the term *miscegenation* (from *miscere*, to mix, and *genus*, race) and represented the pamphlet as the work of an abolitionist, in hopes of discrediting the Republican party in the upcoming elections. Only miscegenation, the pamphlet claimed, could insure the progress and prosperity of the country; the war would guarantee not only physical freedom for blacks but also sexual freedom for both races, particularly in the South, where organized interracial breeding would be carried out on a massive scale and white women would at last be free to give expression to their secret passions. Eventually the pamphlet was recognized as a hoax, but not before it unleashed a barrage of attacks and a strong response from J. H. Van Evrie, whose "Subjenation: The Theory of the Normal Relation of the Races" exactly imitated the style and format of "Miscegenation" but argued violently against its doctrines. As the 1864 campaign progressed, the charges against the Republicans and Lincoln grew more hysterical. One pamphleteer claimed, for example, that the Republicans were plotting to kill or castrate all Southern white men and apportion their women for the use of "Black Ourang-Outangs." Others spoke of Lincoln's "Miscegenation Proclamation" or depicted him in political cartoons and prints as the sponsor of miscegenation, while one leaflet offered a "Black Republican Prayer," which parodied the Lord's Prayer and called upon "the spirit of amalgamation" to shine forth and flourish, "that we may become a regenerated nation of half-breeds, and mongrels" and "live in bonds of fraternal love, union, and equality with the Almighty Nigger, henceforward, now and forever. Amen."

Such charges, again, were not taken seriously by a very large number of people in the North; but they became widely, if not universally, credible in the South — if only at a profound emotional and rhetorical level. In the case of Van Evrie, the refutation of the ameliorating theory of miscegenation was a passion; he had already written *Negroes and Negro "Slavery"* (1861), and, when the book was reissued in 1868 as *White Supremacy and Negro Subordination*, its claims seemed more vehement and relevant than ever. It has to be noted, however, that since Van Evrie argued against *all* miscegenation, throughout the world and in the slaveholding South, as well as against what he thought to be the most serious menace posed by emancipation, he is in important respects emblematic of the schizophrenic position of the South in particular and the nation in general. In the "awful perversion of the instincts of reproduction" that we see around us daily in the South, Van Evrie wrote, God's design is transformed into "the most loathsome and most hideous of social miseries." Abolition will only further this degeneration; once it is accomplished, we will be left for years "to struggle with the load of sin and disease thus brought upon ourselves by our crimes against reason and the ordinances of the Eternal," and will require a span of time that "cannot be estimated with any certainty" in order finally "to recover from the foul and horrible contamination of admixture with the blood of the negro." Like his Jim Crow counterpart, Charles Carroll, Van Evrie held mulattoes responsible for nearly all crimes and racial disorder, and he attacked the "strange and disgusting delusion," the "diseased sentimentality" of the North, which casts "an air of romance" over mongrel women while the terrible miseries of "their own white sisters falling every hour from the ranks of pure womanhood" are totally disregarded.[23]

Because he anticipated, among other things, the hysterical defense of Southern womanhood that would become and remain the touchstone of white racism, it is no wonder that Van Evrie's book seemed more to the point after the war than it had upon initial publication. That anticipation is significant, however, for it serves to enact the mechanism of repression that the war revealed — a mechanism that had certainly been at work in the antebellum South all along but became necessarily more and more extravagant in its aftermath. Such repression inevitably entangled an outcry against threatened sexual violence by blacks and a vehement denial of similar violence by whites (or, if not its denial, its fanatically righteous justification), a denial that Van Evrie's own protests could not reduce and one, as we will see, that took a logical and tragic form. Even *Gone with the Wind* (1936), that rarified epic fantasia of the Jim Crow South, would manage to suggest that the many "ignominies and dangers" brought upon the South by Reconstruction "were as nothing compared with the peril of white women." Such a particular fear amid a more general anarchy leads Scarlett O'Hara to feel for the first time "a kinship with the people around her."[24] Because it held the invading Yankees most responsible for miscegenation in the South, Mitchell's novel of hot-blooded gynealotry and patriotic fervor could, of course, make little allusion to the requisite counterpoint of this hysteria, the absolute perversion of "kinship" that Mary Chesnut recorded in her notorious diary entry of 1861:

> We live surrounded by prostitutes. An abandoned woman is sent out of any decent house elsewhere. Who thinks any worse of a negro or a mulatto woman for being a thing we can't name? God forgive us, but ours is a *monstrous* system and wrong and iniquity. Perhaps the rest of the world is as bad — this *only* I see. Like the patriarchs of old our men live all in one house with their wives and their concubines, and the mulattoes one sees in every family exactly resemble the white children — and every lady tells you who is the father of all the mulatto children in everybody's household, but those in her own she seems to think drop from the clouds, or pretends to think so.[25]

Chesnut might certainly have endorsed Van Evrie's contention that "*mulattoism is to the South what prostitution is to the North*," but she could have agreed only in figurative terms with his insistence that, just as in cases of prostitution and incest, so in the case of mulattoism Nature opposes this "monstrous violation of the physical integrity of the races," this "'original sin,' as it may well be termed," by physiologically punishing the children it produces "to the third and fourth generations for the sins of the fathers." [26]

Van Evrie's theory of degeneration depended on detecting a "similarity of species" between the *mulatto* and the *mule* (they have the same etymology), one that results in a "diminishing vitality," a "tendency to disease and disorganization," and an eventual sterility among the "mongrel" element, and therefore insures that it will never be "of sufficient amount to threaten the safety or even disturb the peace of Southern society." [27] This rather striking conclusion is only unsurprising when it is recognized to contain (or sublimate) one threat by dismissing another. When the book was first published before the war, the theory of degeneration (with its biblical sanction of punishment unto the fourth generation) was a scathing critique of slaveholding miscegenation; after the war, it could only appear to express as well an ironic rationalization of the counter-threat abolition seemed to entail. Van Evrie was not whistling in the dark, however, for at a social and psychological level the punishment of the third and fourth generations (of all generations) was real indeed — so real that Faulkner himself would seek recourse in the figure of physiological degeneration in order to describe the dilemma of Jim Bond, the fourth-generation descendant in *Absalom, Absalom!* of his family's "original sin," whose unintelligible howling unites the novel's disparate voices and engulfs their frantic attempts to salvage the Sutpen dynasty in a single anguished cry. As Shreve says to Quentin Compson on the last page of the book, there is still "one nigger Sutpen left. Of course you can't catch him and you don't even always see him and you never will be able to use him. But you've got him there still." [28]

This is the conclusion of the novel, however, and to reach it Faulkner had first to create a design and, it seems, destroy it with his own hand. To see clearly how he did so, we must see clearly how central the facts and metaphors of marriage are in *Absalom, Absalom!* Van Evrie was certainly not alone in thinking that marriage among slaves, because they are governed by "capricious affections" and characterized by a "feeble moral nature," would be "obviously unnatural, monstrous, and wicked." [29] By situating his observations on this subject within the context of a romantic tribute to the sacred institution of white marriage, Van Evrie once more made painfully explicit the reason why miscegenation was the gravest threat to slavery in the South (and would seem the even graver result of abolition). It made a mockery of white marriage in a particular and terrifying way — by making the races indistinguishable (in theory and sometimes eventually in fact) and by making them, therefore, *equal.* The South was destroying its own design by sinning against God's design. The precarious balance between these points of view — between slavery itself as sin and miscegenation alone as sin — is one that would drive both the South and the nation into fantastic forms of refutation and denial for the next hundred years, forms as utterly deranged and precious (and immensely popular) as *Gone with the Wind,* and as penetrating and tragic (and widely ignored) as *Absalom, Absalom!*

That these two books — both obsessed with marriage and family to the point of obscuring the political crisis of civil war to which they refer — could appear in the same year at first seems almost irrational.[30] Mitchell's novel, of course, sold millions of copies and became America's favorite movie; Faulkner's novel was greeted with perplexity, disbelief, and outrage. The one made clear to some observers how strange Jim Crow's career was, while the other measured the length and complexity of that career by exposing the enervating intimacies within the grand design that made it possible. Both in their complementary ways continued to measure the physical and emotional entanglements between white and black in the South, the one by denying the sins of the fathers altogether, the other by expressing their intimate, intolerable actuality. Yet it is only when we see how much of *Gone with the Wind* Faulkner had, as it were, internalized in *Absalom, Absalom!* that its full significance is made clear. Scarlett O'Hara descends not only (ironically enough) from Stowe's Nina Gordon and from countless white heroines in the novels of Dixon, Page, and others, but she is also much the antecedent of the sister Quentin Compson could never truly possess, the one Faulkner could never clearly portray. The one impossible marriage *Absalom, Absalom!* refers to continually is the one that divides the house of Compson and the house of Sutpen alike, brings the two into momentary union before tearing them apart, and creates the extraordinary psychological and stylistic turbulence in Faulkner's reimagining of Quentin's dilemma. It also, we shall see, raises from the detritus of eccentric observation to the dignity of acute psychological truth a passage from Mississippian Henry Hughes's *Treatise on Sociology* (1854), whose seeming burlesque of syllogistic argument is a perfect index of the tormenting issue of miscegenation:

> Hybridism is heinous. Impurity of races is against the law of nature. Mulattoes are monsters. The law of nature is the law of God. The same law which forbids consanguinous amalgamation forbids ethnical amalgamation. Both are incestuous. Amalgamation is incest.[31]

ALTHOUGH it obviously played no part in Faulkner's writing of *Absalom, Absalom!* and though he amusingly claimed in 1937 that he had not read it because it was "entirely too long for any story," *Gone with the Wind* provides an interesting emotional context for Faulkner's novel insofar as it represents the version of the Civil War Faulkner claimed he got from "the maiden spinster aunts which had never surrendered." One of them, Faulkner reported in 1958, went to see the film version, "and as soon as Sherman came on the screen she got up and left."[32] Miss Rosa Coldfield might have done just that. While she does not finally dominate the novel, Rosa's obsessive rehearsals for Quentin of Sutpen's failed dynasty, the murder of Bon, and her own tortured courtship by the "ogre" generate the atmosphere of spent dreams and feverishly maintained innocence in and against which subsequent versions of the tragedy are played out. The novel's magnificent opening scene between Rosa and Quentin is itself a kind of courtship, a ritual immersion of Quentin into the gothic convulsions of Rosa's fading by hyperdistilled erotic memories. The turning rhythms of Faulkner's prose here, as elsewhere, create a strained communion in which Quentin and Rosa, breathing and memory, body and house and voice, are fused in a sensation of calm that is poised nevertheless on the extreme edge of violence.

The extraordinary balance between nostalgia and rage, in which the solid present — the dust, the screens, the heated air, the twice-bloomed wisteria — breaks down into the resurrected ghost of past grandeur, the stillborn lust of Rosa's "impotent yet indomitable frustration," creates an eroticism not simply of the flesh but of memory — creates of Rosa herself the demon she accuses Sutpen of being and (as Mr. Compson later expresses it) an "instrument of retribution" rising "bloodless and without dimension from the sacrificial stone of the marriage-bed." The exact purpose of that retribution is made no clearer to us than Rosa is able to make it to herself; and it is not clearly retribution at all, for as she tells Quentin of Sutpen's proposal that they breed on trial before getting married, "*I forgave him. . . . Why shouldn't I? I had nothing to forgive.*" Rosa's balked courtship and marriage to Sutpen do, as Shreve will suggest, leave her "irrevocably husbanded" to an "abstract carcass of outrage and revenge" [33] — but not in her version of the courtship, which is less a smoldering desire for revenge than an excessively melodramatic lament over the denial of desire itself. Rosa is neither wife nor mother; in one respect she is for Faulkner emblematic of those war widows who were never brides at all, the many undefeated for whom the war took not only their land, their slaves, their golden dream but also the men they would never have. And in the nervously exposed contours of her passion Rosa also betrays, as the novel restrains her sister, Ellen, and her niece, Judith, from doing, a further aspect of the crisis of union the war would release into the hysteria of racism for a century to come.

Rosa's "demonizing," as nearly every reader of *Absalom, Absalom!* has characterized it, is certainly conspicuous, but it only becomes significant when it is seen within the context of her now brittle but still tender passion and grief for her first "nothusband," "*Charles Bon, Charles Good, Charles Husband-soon-to-be.*" The "*shadow-realm of make-believe*" in which her passion lives, the "*fairy-tale*" she creates for herself and the young man she never sees, even in death, brings Rosa closer to incest than her later courtship by Sutpen will, and it brings her close to an act of miscegenation she does not recognize as such. Or so it seems. There is no direct evidence in the novel that Rosa ever knows Bon is a "Negro," but then there is no direct evidence that Quentin does either, and his peculiar testimony is assumed to be conclusive, at least to the extent that nearly all readers of the novel take it for granted. He finds out the truth about Bon when he visits Sutpen's Hundred with Rosa — not, apparently, from Henry but from Clytie. As Shreve puts it: "She didn't tell you in so many words because she was still keeping that secret for the sake of the man who had been her father too . . . she didn't tell you, it just came out of the terror and the fear after she turned you loose and caught the Aunt Rosa's arm and the Aunt Rosa turned and struck her hand away."[34]

The 1909 scene repeats the 1865 scene Rosa has already described to Quentin, in which Clytie attempts to stop her from mounting the stairs to Judith's room after Bon is murdered. It is worth reproducing a portion of this scene, for it is the heart of Rosa's chapter and brings into focus the conflicting passions and stunned recognitions of consanguinity that compel the entire novel. Approaching the stairs to see at last the dead Bon she would never see, Rosa is stopped first by the "*immobile antagonism*" of Clytie's face, by her body, which seems to "*project upward something . . . inherited from an older and a purer race than mine*" and shapes in the air between them "*that bedroom long-closed and musty, that sheetless bed*" and its "*pale and bloody corpse.*" When her commands to Rosa fail to stop her, Clytie grasps her arm:

> *Then she touched me, and then I did stop dead. . . . my entire being seemed to run at blind full tilt into something monstrous and immobile, with a shocking impact too soon and too quick to be mere amazement and outrage at that black arresting and untimorous hand on my white woman's flesh. Because there is something in the touch of flesh with flesh which abrogates, cuts sharp and straight across the devious intricate channels of decorous ordering, which enemies as well as lovers know because it makes them both. . . . We just stood there — I motionless in the attitude and action of running, she rigid in that furious immobility, the two of us joined by that hand and arm which held us, like a fierce rigid umbilical cord, twin sistered to the fell darkness which had produced her. . . . And then suddenly it was not outrage that I waited for, out of which I had instinctively cried; it was not terror: it was some cumulative over-reach of despair itself. . . . I cried — perhaps not aloud, not with words (and not to Judith, mind: perhaps I knew already, on the instant I entered the house and saw that face which was at once both more and less than Sutpen, perhaps I knew even then what I could not, would not, must not believe) — I cried "And you too? And you too, sister, sister?"*

Like so many passages in the novel, this one (if not at first, certainly in retrospect) intimates the secret of Bon's blood, but it does so in a fashion charged with ambiguous power. Rosa's shocked exclamation, "you too, sister, sister?" suggests not only that Clytie is clearly Judith's sister (Sutpen's daughter), and not only that Clytie, like Rosa, may be vicariously in love with Bon, but also that those possibilities reveal two further ones that constitute, in Faulkner's imagination if not her own, precisely what Rosa "could not, would not, must not believe" and what the novel holds in passionate suspense: that Bon is Clytie's "brother" and that Bon is "black." The scene does not spell out this recognition, but it certainly suggests it more pointedly than does Quentin's climactic visit to Sutpen's Hundred forty-five years later. When the three of them — Rosa, Judith, and Clytie, "*as though we were one being, interchangeable*" — await Sutpen's return after the war, Rosa speaks of Clytie as one who embodies the war's "*perverse and inscrutable paradox: free, yet incapable of freedom who had never once called herself a slave*" and, moreover, "*who in the very pigmentation of her flesh represented that debacle which had brought Judith and me to what we were.*"[35] In between this assertion of Clytie's tragedy and the earlier scene that so clarifies the "debacle" she represents, Rosa speaks passionately, with the rapture of fantasized violation and husbanding, of the *"world filled with living marriage"* that only imagination can create.

Rosa's failed courtships, one in imagination and one in fact, have often and quite rightly been read as the rhetorical highpoints of Faulkner's novel; but the psychological complexities of her expressed passion — complexities that the novel both reveals and buries at the same time — have for good reason resisted elaboration. In particular, the issue of miscegenation has been largely ignored because it is assumed that Rosa suspects nothing of Bon's parentage. Because it is the strategy of *Absalom, Absalom!* to intimate but suppress its critical information until the very end, and even then to reveal it only in the dramatic, self-reflexive mask of tacit recognition, however, the true torment of Rosa's courtship by Sutpen may only be explicable if we assume — as the scene between Rosa and Clytie suggests — that Rosa herself, perhaps vicariously, understands the full dimensions of Bon's tragedy as well as Sutpen's. The "debacle" represented by Clytie's "pigmentation" is purposely ambiguous: it is the debacle of slavery and the war itself that makes Judith and Rosa widows without having been brides; but it is also the debacle of miscegenation, which the novel so continually engages as the curse and sin that brings Sutpen's design, like that of the South itself, to collapse. It is the debacle that makes Clytie neither slave nor free (neither before nor after the war) and makes Charles Bon neither slave nor son and brother. Like the motive for Bon's murder, the psychological tragedy Rosa's failed dream represents must be seen to exist in the interstices of the novel's action and its assumptions about the crisis of consanguinity; for if it seems to gather together and swallow up the grief Ellen and Judith never express, and therefore to transfer into the atmosphere of volatile fantasy the one passion in actuality Faulkner seems unable or unwilling to articulate, it does so with a particular emotional urgency.

Although the language of Rosa's re-created courtship, its burgeoning moment of passion held forever on the brink of fulfillment, contains as clear an expression of the recognized truth about Bon as we may wish, there is no reason to insist on its actuality. What matters, rather, is that Faulkner, in creating this powerful scene, should invest so much deliberate energy in drawing the fated Bon toward recognition at all, a recognition the novel intimates again and again but that its events can actualize only in brutal denial. What else does Bon want but recognition — by his sister, his brother, his father? And why should not Rosa, the fever of her vicarious life driving her toward that recognition, see now in Clytie's darkened face what we are to imagine Quentin sees half a century later? Faulkner does not present that recognition clearly in either instance; his language is thoroughly charged with it, however, charged with a recognition wasted and betrayed year after year, beyond Quentin's death and well into Faulkner's life, but charged as well, Rosa's ecstatic memories tell us, with a recognition more vital and lasting — and threatening — than we may wish. In this book filled with shadows blurring into visions, with unliving marriage and passion consummated in death, it is entirely appropriate that this scene bring us to the verge of a recognition we are unwilling to make, that it vitalize the scene, the act, the moment that never *will be* in the certain tragic fullness of what *might have been.*

Southern gynealotry and, in this instance, the fanatic undefeat of the maidens and spinsters whose "nothusbands" never came home, include and themselves express an acute psychological division that makes dramatically immediate the other forms of divided sensibility *Absalom, Absalom!* explores. The "monstrous" antagonism that Rosa confronts in the form of Clytie is nothing less than that which Mary Chesnut found "monstrous" about slavery — its sexual crimes, not simply their physical violence but even more so, perhaps, the emotional violence that miscegenation entailed. That violence enclosed both black and white, parents and children, husbands and wives in a cage of paradoxical feelings. To the extent that "sexual intimacy strikingly symbolized a union he wished to avoid," Winthrop Jordan writes, the slaveholder could indeed deny the fruits of his passion by not recognizing them. Because they confused the essential distinction between the races, mulattoes threatened to "undermine the logic of the racial slavery upon which his society was based," and by classifying them as Negroes, the slaveholder-father "was in effect denying that intermixture had occurred at all." But that inevitably put his wife, and Southern white women in general, in a peculiar position, for it heightened the mythic melodrama of gallantry and courtesy that almost every account, fictional or not, makes characteristic of the slaveholding South. The confusing atmosphere in which the white woman was asked to live, Jordan remarks, "warped her affective life in two directions at once." As she was made to feel "that sensual involvement with the opposite sex burned bright and hot with unquenchable passion and at the same time that any such involvement was utterly repulsive," she may well have approached her prospective partners "as if she were picking up a live coal in one hand and a dead rat in the other."[36]

One need not take Jordan's analogy beyond the figurative dimensions it is meant to encompass to see the distortions of passion miscegenation could produce in whites as well as blacks — distortions that entirely depended upon one another and, as we have seen in the case of *Light in August,* eventually produced a hysterical climate of racial fantasy that would make the repression and denial of miscegenation more necessary than ever. The distinctions that have to be made between Joanna Burden and Rosa Coldfield are no doubt important, but they depend less on psychology than temporality; that is, the movement back from the tragedy of Jim Crow to the tragedy of slavery that Faulkner's extending of the theme of miscegenation necessitated is one that required him to dramatize the initial crisis of blood and identity out of which its later manifestations had grown. The *"unravished nuptial"* in which Rosa lives along with Judith (and, it seems, Clytie), the *"one constant and perpetual instant when the arras-veil before what-is-to-be"* awaits *"the lightest naked thrust,"* the *"cocoon-casket marriage-bed of youth and grief"* she lies down in once and forever in 1860, the long relived and remembered *"might-have-been which is more than truth"* [37] — these singular moments of a marriage that was never to be acquire their energizing power from the fact that, leaving aside altogether the question of Rosa's knowledge of Bon's blood, we have to read them as revealing a desire for Bon the novel itself must express, even if it can do so only indirectly or unconsciously. Exactly because these moments are offered up in the realm of remembered fantasy, Rosa's gothic eroticism contains a virulent nostalgia and willful innocence that betray the dark underside of slaveholding marriage: that white women often lived in the face of a monstrous affront and — more alarming indeed — may well have had passions of their own. The children of miscegenation not only threatened to blur the distinctions that made slavery possible, but the unions that produced them threatened to distort sexual relations and marriage itself, for black and white alike, into peculiar and tragic forms.

In the year before the war, Rosa says, *"Ellen talked to me of trousseau (and it my trousseau), of all the dreamy panoply of surrender which was my surrender"*; when the news of Lincoln's election and the fall of Sumter comes, Rosa is sewing "for her own vicarious bridal" the garments that she "would never wear and never remove for a man whom she was not even to see," still sewing when Mississippi secedes and the regiment commanded by Sutpen and Sartoris appears in town beneath regimental colors "sewed together out of silk dresses." [38] The superimposing of these actions is a symbolic expression of their relentless entanglement in *Absalom, Absalom!* Still sewing those marital garments in memory, and still unable to put them on or take them off forty-five years later — later still when Faulkner writes the book we read — Rosa lives in a world of tortured innocence that is only conceivable because it is, in this case more than ever, the product of a superannuated guilt. That guilt is not necessarily Rosa's, but it is Faulkner's (as author) and it is the South's. The fevered moment of union she lives in still, distended by the ruinous divisions that bring it into being, is haunting in extremity: it is a moment in which she cannot, will not, will never "surrender." For reasons absolutely dependent upon the tragic realities of miscegenation, Rosa's marriage to Bon that never was is a crucial part of the failure of Sutpen's design — crucial because it illuminates the mockery of Sutpen's actual marriages to Eulalia Bon and Ellen Coldfield and the one he proposes to Rosa.

No tragedy is greater than Bon's or Clytie's or that of their mothers, but Rosa's brings them into perspective, not only by uniting them but also by diffusing their shadows through and into the intimate heart of the slaveholding South and its unsurrendering memories. The greater passions Rosa and Faulkner express in her extraordinary disembodied meditation on the world of lost love are nearly unaccountable unless we take seriously the unsettling dimensions of sexual union to which they refer, dimensions in which sexuality became split between love and lust, and in which familial and affectionate relations of every kind could be torn from their natural paths of development and turned into grotesque reflections of the institution they supported. As Frederick Douglass reported in 1845, the slaveholder, in sustaining "to his slaves the double relation of master and father," at once indulged his wicked desires, increased his property, inspired the contempt and cruelty of his wife, and left himself subject to acts of extreme emotional estrangement. Cruel as it may seem "for a man to sell his own children to human flesh-mongers," wrote Douglass, he must otherwise "not only whip them himself, but must stand by and see one white son tie up his brother, of but a few shades darker complexion than himself, and ply the gory lash to his naked back." [39] One can measure the achievement of *Absalom, Absalom!* no more clearly than by noting with what inspired passion, and without capitulating either to sentimentality or to bitterness, it works against the violent limitations such a situation placed on human love.

Faulkner's novel can express that love only by remarkable indirection — most significantly, as we will see, in the re-creations of Quentin and Shreve, but most passionately (and therefore most indirectly) in the pressures that culminate in Rosa's unravished nuptial, the mock marriage that in its reciprocal affirmation and denial of love most ably characterizes the central emotional tragedies of slavery. As Rosa sews her trousseau, the conflict that will suspend all actions and decisions for four years begins. The murder and the design it will at once preserve and destroy are held in suspense while the South seeks, in magnificent fashion, to deny its union with the nation and the North seeks, in fashions devised by Lincoln, to restore union without abolishing slavery. Neither plan will work; the price for both the South and the North is the story Faulkner will still tell more than half a century later when, dividing his novel in half, he shifts its burden from Rosa Coldfield, widow, to Quentin Compson, suicide, one of the characters he "had to get out of the attic to tell the story of Sutpen." [40]

W HEN Cash comes to speak of contemporary Southern writers in *The Mind of the South* he notes that they are, Faulkner included, "romantics of the appalling" who only hate the South "with the exasperated hate of a lover who cannot persuade the object of his affections to his desire," much as "Narcissus, growing at length analytical, might have suddenly begun to hate his image reflected in a pool." [41] The Quentin Compson who claims rapturously at the conclusion of *Absalom, Absalom!* that he does not hate the South certainly falls under Cash's definition, and there is every reason to see the later book as a lengthy, analytic exploration of the narcissistic hatred of himself and his heritage that Quentin expresses, but Faulkner cannot fully explain, in *The Sound and the Fury*. In the first book, Faulkner had clearly shown his house to be divided, but he had not made entirely clear the psychological complexities of that division and the gothic collapse of sensibilities it could produce. At that point, the horror remained essentially unnameable; at best it was focused in a term that had immediate emotional and formal significance but little psychological depth — incest. It is now difficult, if not impossible, to read *The Sound and the Fury* outside the context of *Absalom, Absalom!* but it is worth bearing in mind the purposeful ambiguity of that context, despite its more literal phrasing of the horror — *miscegenation.*

The attempts readers have made from time to time to divorce the two books, to claim none but coincidental connections in either formal or psychological terms, can only seem more incredible than ever after John Irwin's splendid reading to the contrary.[42] Irwin's elucidation of the mirroring, antagonistic psychological relationships among *Absalom, Absalom!*'s principal actors and narrators, involved as they are in a dramatic reconstruction of events that may have taken place in the form they devise but cannot be said undoubtedly to have done so, makes conspicuous their necessary interchangeability; that is, it makes them "family." The energizing power of Sutpen's design and its collapse drives into union with him and his family all of those who try to "tell" his story — Rosa, Mr. Compson, Quentin, and Shreve. As though imbued with "gaunt and tireless driving" by "sheer association with him" and enclosed in the "aura of unregeneration" his "invoked ghost" continues to create, they engage vicariously in Sutpen's own "amazed recapitulation" of his design and participate once again in estimating its tragic flaw. What Mr. Compson speaks of as Rosa Coldfield's "vicarious bridal," as well as the "vicarious image" of himself in Bon with which he claims Henry Sutpen has seduced his own sister, describe the pervasive narcissism of the novel's relationships.[43] Such narcissism, as Irwin argues, makes every character the potential or implied double of others and brings them all into positions of intimate emotional involvement in which what is only vicarious, only *imagined,* takes on a psychological immediacy and tangibility that overrides and engulfs what might have been actual.

Faulkner's own tortured effort to measure Sutpen's design through "a rhetoric strained almost to the breaking point by an agony of identification"[44] is the medium of that vicarious involvement — a medium that fully conforms to the pressures it seeks out and fabricates by dissolving the barriers between fact and fantasy, fathers and sons, brothers and sisters, brother and brother, white and black. As in the contradictory case of Quentin's incestuous (that is, "impure") obsession with Caddy's "purity" in *The Sound and the Fury,* one might speak of that mediation, forced into action by the greater cultural strain it seeks to identify, as a formal realization that the imposed structures of containment that make moral action meaningful and powerful do so only in reaction to implied violations of those limiting structures. Only the approach toward, and transgression of, such limits fixes their meaning, just as the desire, in Quentin's case, to commit incest is exactly what defines it; it becomes incest when the taboo remains in place, even in violation, or more significantly when the *act* cannot be actualized at all but only expressed as *desire;* that is, as an imaginary or vicarious possibility. Because it nearly repeats his remarks to Quentin in *The Sound and the Fury,* Mr. Compson's description of Henry Sutpen's discovery of "the pure and perfect incest" — "the brother realizing that the sister's virginity must be destroyed in order to have existed at all, taking that virginity in the person of the brother-in-law" [45] — represents both his understanding of those limits and his inability to explain the Sutpen tragedy. His explanation here makes Henry into Quentin as Mr. Compson understands him; but because it apparently occurs before he has received the crucial information that Quentin's visit to Sutpen's Hundred with Rosa reveals, Mr. Compson's version cannot account for the more tragic extenuation of the limits incestuous desire responds to in this instance. That further structure of limitation, which is paradoxically more fixed and more resolutely dissolved both in fact and in the entangling reciprocities of the novel's own imaginative design, is miscegenation.

In this chapter, as elsewhere in the novel, Faulkner's narrative covertly reveals what it strives to hold in suspense, for Mr. Compson goes on to speak of Bon's "effluvium of Sutpen blood and character" even as he elaborates a theory for the murder based on the "morganatic ceremony" between Bon and his octoroon mistress. As he himself recognizes at this point, however, such a theory "just does not explain." "You re-read" the story of the Sutpen family, "the paper old and falling to pieces, the writing faded, almost undecipherable," he remarks, "you bring them together again and again and nothing happens." Even so, Mr. Compson's dwelling on the "ceremony" between Bon and his "wife" provides a significant context for the unraveling of Bon's tragedy eventually undertaken by Quentin and Shreve, for it is at the climax of his recapitulation of Bon's gradual exposure of Henry to the peculiar sexual conventions of New Orleans that the ultimate barrier of the novel is preliminarily revealed. Unable to convince Henry that the mulatto mistresses of New Orleans are neither whores nor wives but part of a doomed race who are perhaps "the only truly chaste women, not to say virgins, in America," Bon plays his "trump" card: "Have you forgotten that this woman, this child are niggers? You, Henry Sutpen of Sutpen's Hundred in Mississippi? You, talking of marriage, a wedding, here?" [46]

The barrier of Bon's marriage to the octoroon is ultimately overwhelmed by the barrier of incest and, later still, the barrier of miscegenation. But as the etymology of *incest* (*in* + *castus*) suggests, it is the superimposition of these barriers, which are themselves opposed, mirroring figures, that expresses the tragic depth of *Absalom, Absalom!* by making exceedingly "monstrous" the love Quentin and Shreve try desperately to account for by creating. They do so in a series of compelling inventions that, as they progress, more and more deviate from the simpler but less conclusive explanations of the tragedy offered by Rosa and Mr. Compson virtually in order to create a barrier that can be, that *must be* passed in imaginative violation and union. The novel's extreme exertions of kinship — notably among Henry and Bon, Quentin and Shreve, "not two of them but four, the two who breathed not individuals now yet something both more and less than twins" — struggle to rehearse once again the disintegration of Sutpen's design by accepting its "flaw" as irreducible but redeeming the passions that force it to tragic culmination. Nowhere is this more evident than in the narrative scene that follows Shreve's reconstruction of the relationship between Bon and Henry at college, Bon recognizing his brother and Henry asserting that, if he had a brother, he "would want him to be just like you." [47] The scene grows out of the novel's most precarious invention, the New Orleans lawyer engaged by Eulalia Bon to blackmail Sutpen (first with the threat of bigamy, then with the threat of incest), and as such it presents the gravest crisis, the potentially most damaging flaw in Faulkner's own design.

Because it is the burden of Quentin and Shreve to save from wasted effort the previous struggles of Rosa and Mr. Compson to bring Sutpen's story into coherent focus, the lawyer's role, knitting together a series of unlikely incidents, is necessarily perilous and seemingly fortuitous. But the crisis this produces in Faulkner's own design perfectly matches, and by analogy forces to an agonizing pitch, the reciprocal relationships of Bon and Henry, Shreve and Quentin. More than anything, perhaps, it grows out of the novel's expressed need to suggest, to intimate, to wrest from doubt while leaving all doubts in place, a motive for Bon's actions that is more than simple revenge. "And now," Shreve says, "we're going to talk about love":

> But he didn't need to say that either, any more than he had needed to specify which he meant by he, since neither of them had been thinking about anything else; all that had gone before just so much that had to be overpassed and none else present to overpass it but them . . . it did not matter to either of them which one did the talking, since it was not the talking alone which did it, performed and accomplished the overpassing, but some happy marriage of speaking and hearing wherein each before the demand, the requirement, forgave condoned and forgot the faulting of the other — faultings both in the creating of this shade whom they discussed (rather, existed in) and in the hearing and sifting and discarding the false and conserving what seemed true, or fit the preconceived — in order to overpass to love, where there might be paradox and inconsistency but nothing fault nor false. [48]

The "marriage of speaking and hearing," so gracefully elaborated in the probing rhythms of Quentin's and Shreve's shared rehearsal of the Sutpen story, constitutes the reaching and passing of the novel's greatest emotional and imaginative crisis. The act of "overpassing" expresses the danger of this crisis and its manifest resolution, for the love between Bon and Judith, and most particularly the love between Bon and Henry, that Shreve and Quentin go on to design, itself extended in their own fraternal intimacy, is one that must "overpass" momentarily, and hold in passionate suspense for the duration of the Civil War, the single barrier that will at last lead to fratricide. In order to achieve this union, the novel's own design must engage in a risk equal to that of Bon and Henry, must pass over possibilities and likelihoods that run counter to that forged union; most significantly, it must continue to suppress the very information (which Quentin has possessed ever since the events that occur between chapters five and three — but are not revealed until the last pages of the novel — and which Shreve too now possesses) that makes the "overpass to love" dramatically necessary: that Bon is Henry's brother and a "Negro."

Quentin and Shreve are probably correct in thinking that to Henry the "ceremony" between Bon and the octoroon would have been irrelevant, "only something else about Bon to be, not envied but aped if that had been possible." [49] So far as the novel is capable of revealing it, the incest as well would have the same repulsive attraction; for as Quentin and Shreve reconstruct it, even incest can be overpassed by love. The one thing Henry cannot pass over is Sutpen's own "trump," that Bon is "black." Instead, he kills his brother. It is worth emphasizing the brutal immediacy of this act, for the novel strives heroically to delay it, obscure it, render it unfathomable or mysterious, hide it from view — and yet makes murderously apparent the overriding reason for it. The entanglement between Bon's "passing" as white and the "overpass to love" between Henry and Bon it first makes necessary and then impossible is a thoroughly tormenting one; it circumscribes the crisis of blood that would be the very crisis of the South now and for the next hundred years. Henry kills Bon approximately a month after the end of the war, some three weeks after Lincoln's assassination, and one day before Lincoln's burial following the ritual journey home of his coffin. The crisis of union that Lincoln presaged had been "reached and passed" but, as suggested earlier, at the cost of a further crisis with which Lincoln was not clearly prepared to deal. In *Absalom, Absalom!* the one crisis holds the other in abeyance for four years and then resolves it, destroying in a further, nearly unnameable act of fratricide the momentary union that has been achieved.

From the point of view of the South, of course, the restoration of the Union was obviously no victory. One can lay the two crises upon each other only to the extent of recognizing that the retrospective acts of imagination Quentin and Shreve engage in to restore a union between brothers, even to the point of condoning incest, must inevitably lead — as the events of both the novel and history dictate — to a last crisis in which brothers are, more than ever, not brothers at all; in which freedom either makes continued affection between master and slave largely impossible or, as was more usually the case, exposes that affection as an utter fabrication; and in which the actualities of kinship that miscegenation produced appear more intolerable than ever. Leslie Fiedler is certainly right to point out that *Absalom, Absalom!* is remarkable in the genre of American gothic fiction "for having first joined to the theme of slavery and black revenge, which is the essential sociological theme of the American tale of terror, that of incest, which is its essential erotic theme." [50] That union is indeed a remarkable one, but we need to note as well that the one barrier that Faulkner's novel cannot pass, even as it tries in desperation to repair Sutpen's design with its own, is both fused with and yet absolutely opposed to the other. Miscegenation and incest, here in fiction as elsewhere in fact, create a drama of intimate merger and extreme alienation that both doubles and divides husband and wife, father and son, brother and brother. More to the point, however, the potential miscegenation between Bon and Judith cancels out the potential incest. No one fact more characterizes the schizophrenic nature of slaveholding miscegenation. In killing for the first, Henry denies the latter: Bon is not his brother but, as he himself puts it to Henry, *"the nigger that's going to sleep with your sister."* [51]

These potential sins cannot, of course, be so neatly separated — no more so here than in the history of slavery, where "sons" were and were not sons and "brothers" were and were not brothers, and where the successive mingling of masters and slaves, white and black, therefore could not possibly be the incest it unavoidably might be in fact. One need only think ahead to the rival McCaslin lines of descent in *Go Down, Moses* to understand how accurate Henry Hughes's seemingly irrational exclamation that "amalgamation is incest" might be. The paradoxical tragedy and promise of such mixing only becomes evident, however, in the aftermath of the war — ten years, twenty years, fifty years later — in, say, 1909 or 1910 when Quentin Compson probes the Sutpen tragedy and kills himself, or in 1936 when William Faulkner writes a novel about incest and miscegenation. Slavery controlled miscegenation and whatever incest accompanied it by denying that they had any meaning, by denying, in effect, that any limits had actually been violated. Emancipation not only released a convulsive hysteria about potential miscegenation in the form of black violence against white, then, it may also be said to have destroyed the mechanisms of control that were a barrier to incest and to have made possible, if not entirely likely, a further mixing, a "monstrous" violation of blood in which, because both black and white strains could be hidden from view, miscegenation and incest could indeed occur at once.

Although it is not the most explicit part of his argument, Irwin's reading of Quentin's dilemma continually suggests that it grows out of a possibility he only comes to understand (and we only recognize retrospectively) in *Absalom, Absalom!* — that his frantic obsession with Caddy's purity, as well as his inability to insure it or preserve it for himself, are motivated by the contagious threat of miscegenation. For Quentin, incest insures not only emotional and moral purity but also purity of blood; what the Sutpen tragedy reveals to him, however, is that incest *may not* insure such genealogical purity, or that even if it does, can do so only by mocking reference to a dream long dead and long since turned nightmare. The reunion of the House Divided dissolved the barrier between North and South, between free and slave, and gradually defined a new social and political self for blacks; but by making acts of miscegenation legitimately (if not yet legally) meaningful, it necessarily introduced a new barrier, a suddenly unthinkable and more frightening form of "impurity" that whites in particular thought there was good reason to fear. As courts, legislatures, and the history of American race relations would prove for years to come, the miscegenation taboo was as strong as, even stronger than, the incest taboo — strong enough, at times, to justify the utmost violence. In this respect, *Absalom, Absalom!* can perhaps only be seen to "explain" *The Sound and the Fury* by means of *Light in August*, the novel in which Faulkner can first be said to have extended his major theme and brought to fruition his explorations of novelistic form.

When Faulkner later remarked that "Quentin was still trying to get God to tell

him why, in *Absalom, Absalom!* as he was in *The Sound and the Fury,*" the question
he referred to, of course, was the one that occurs to Quentin as he begins to
listen to Rosa: "*Why God let us lose the War.*" [52] Without exception, the answer
throughout Faulkner's works is "slavery." More particularly, it is "miscegenation," which is both the curse of slavery (as observers in such contrasting positions as Lincoln and Van Evrie maintained) and the curse of emancipation (as
generations of Southerners and Northerners would maintain). Irwin's powerful
arguments about the conflict between, and reversal of, generations that the two
novels dramatize require this additional emphasis; for Quentin's rereading of his
own life in the context of Henry Sutpen's reveals his own incestuous gynealotry
as the contemporary expression of denied paternal responsibility, an expression
whose manifest twentieth-century form Faulkner explored in *Light in August.*
Quentin's obsession with Caddy certainly has Oedipal contours, and his imagined sequestering and protection of her virginity does in retrospect resemble
Henry's protection of Judith. Yet the shadow self of Bon that Quentin both identifies with and slays is not only a psychological projection but also a deeply
sociological one; that is, the Oedipal reading of Quentin's desire for paternal
revenge only makes complete sense in the larger context of Southern paternalism, which as slavery ended took new, more perplexing and tragic forms.

THE RELATIONSHIP between paternalism and literary form has
dimensions that exceed the purpose of this essay. Let us simply note that
Faulkner saw *Absalom, Absalom!* as the preliminary culmination of his own fictional design of Yoknapatawpha. It is his most ambitious, detailed, and complex
novel, and he felt compelled to add to it not only a genealogy and chronology
but also a map of Yoknapatawpha, which summarized his work to date in visual
form. The struggle to bring into focus the contours of his mythical kingdom is
not, in this respect, entirely unlike the challenge that faces Sutpen throughout
the novel but arises most particularly, as Rosa describes it, once he returns from
the war, his one son having murdered his other: the challenge to encompass "*as
though in a prolonged and unbroken instant of tremendous effort embracing and holding intact
that ten-mile square while he faced from the brink of disaster, invincible and unafraid, what
he must have known would be the final defeat.*" [53] The failure to achieve perfect coherence in his work and to experience the ecstasy that accompanies it was a problem
Faulkner spoke of almost obsessively in interviews and classrooms. His point of
reference, as we have seen earlier, was always *The Sound and the Fury,* in which
his writing produced the ecstasy even though he considered the novel it produced a magnificent failure. The introduction he wrote for that book in 1933
(which was never published as such) speaks of his having learned to read his own
literary masters as though "in a series of delayed repercussions like summer
thunder" and having experienced in *The Sound and the Fury* an "emotion definite
and physical and yet nebulous" that was never recaptured in *Sanctuary, As I Lay
Dying,* or *Light in August.* [54]

One way in which to consider *Absalom, Absalom!* and its grand design, then, is as an act of formal recuperation on Faulkner's part, an act that both probes the origins of the twentieth-century configurations of the South he had dwelt on up to that point and strives to bring into focus the design uniting past and present, fiction and fact. The numerous analogies and metaphors of design and reconstruction that pervade the novel refer at once to Sutpen's and to Faulkner's, each of them the "sole owner and proprietor" and, more significantly, the "father" of a vast domain on the edge of collapse. In Faulkner's case, the "final defeat" represents both the agony of literary composition and the historical trauma with which it is intimately involved. As Faulkner reread the story of Quentin Compson in the light of the Sutpen tragedy, he was searching out Quentin's own tragedy; he was reaching back toward the ecstasy of composition that had eluded him ever since *The Sound and the Fury;* and he was struggling, along with all the narrators of *Absalom, Absalom!*, to set in place a lost dream whose precise nature is that it has already collapsed. He was "reading by repercussion" his own work and the tragedy, the original sin, that set it in motion, knowing full well, as Rosa once again puts it, that *"there is no all, no finish; it is not the blow we suffer from but the tedious repercussive anti-climax of it, the rubbishy aftermath to clear away from off the very threshold of despair."* [55]

Rosa's assertion here appears in the context of the "echoed shot" that was all she ever heard of Bon's murder and the closed door of Judith's bedroom she could not enter. It is the same door that Quentin, throughout the novel, cannot pass through; and it is the door Faulkner himself refuses to enter, perhaps because for him, as for Quentin, it hides the ultimate intimacy of incest, whether between Quentin and Caddy or between Bon and Judith. In this respect, the most important mysteries, the crucial points of obscured or undelivered information in *Absalom, Absalom!*, as in *The Sound and the Fury,* revolve around moments of unfulfilled and nearly unnameable love and around Quentin's Oedipal battle with his father to fulfill and articulate that love. If one were to assert that there is a formal relationship between the two books that is itself incestuous or marital, one might measure the powerful ecstasy Faulkner's reworking of Quentin's dilemma sought, successfully or not, to recapture. We do not need to do so, however, in order to see that the two novels' formal relationship, like those of the characters involved, is one of merged intimacy and antagonism, and that the crisis of family identity each involves depends upon the exact crisis that incest and miscegenation bring into being: a crisis of blood in which sons are not sons and brothers are not brothers, and in which the distinctions between them that must be maintained, however fantastically, are also the ones that keep the lost dream in place long after it has collapsed.

Drawing on René Girard's theory of sacrificial crisis, I suggested earlier that Joe Christmas is a "monstrous double" because he embodies the crisis of blood in one horrifying image and must, therefore and paradoxically, be killed as a way of warding off, of containing, the reciprocal violence that accompanies a disintegration of distinctions within the cultural order. Since Girard's observations about the nature of that reciprocal violence derive from his understanding of the formal doublings and reciprocities of action and dialogue in Greek tragedy, they are perhaps even more relevant in the case of *Absalom, Absalom!* As Faulkner later remarked, and as the multiple allusions to Aeschylus, Sophocles, and Euripides make clear, it is "the old Greek concept of tragedy" that destroys Sutpen. "He wanted a son which symbolized [his] ideal, and he got too many sons — his sons destroyed one another and then him. He was left with — the only son he had left was a Negro."[56] Faulkner's explication is a little hazy, but the crisis of Sutpen's cultural order, which is also that of the South at large, is clearly one that results from an effacement of necessary racial and familial differences. Such a "destruction of differences is particularly spectacular," Girard notes, "when the hierarchical distance between the characters, the amount of respect due from one to the other, is great — between father and son, for instance." When the conflict is prolonged over the course of time or the course of genera-tions, "the resemblance between the combatants grows even stronger until each presents a mirror image of the other," and at extremity, "the whole cultural structure seems on the verge of collapse." The potentially most disruptive and paradoxical form of such conflict and disintegration appears in the reciprocal violence of twins or brothers, who in their very nature contain such discord and, when that discord is actualized, represent the violent crisis of reciprocity in its utmost configuration. Precisely because "symmetry and identity are represented in extraordinarily explicit terms" in the case of twins or brothers, Girard adds, this formal mirroring, in its singular state of nondifferentiation, "ultimately becomes the very exemplar of difference, a classic monstrosity that plays a vital role in sacred ritual." At a further reach of the crisis is the threat posed by incest, which "leads to formless duplications, sinister repetitions, a dark mixture of unnameable things."[57]

The bearing of Girard's theory upon the doubling and "twinning" of characters and narrators in *Absalom, Absalom!* is readily apparent. And though he does not discuss it, the last remark I have quoted suggests an even more critical extenuation of the reciprocal crisis — that which appears in the admixture of blood and identity when incest is involved with, and ultimately paired with, miscegenation. It is exactly the nature of the crisis that leads the South into Civil War (and the entire nation into a prolonged act of fratricide) that it grows out of a "monstrous" system in which, at the simplest level, slaves both were and were not human beings, and in which, at a more significant level for our purposes, sexual violence could issue in a state of simultaneous differentiation and nondif-ferentiation between father and son or brother and brother. (One should add that the same crisis prevails and, as we have seen, is furthered in the paradoxical relationships among husbands, wives, mothers, and daughters.) The slave father whose "son" was not his son and particularly the slave son who had, therefore, no father at all stand in the most painful roles in this recipocal tragedy. To the extent that Charles Bon embodies the dilemma of the latter with a particularly violent and ironic power, what Genovese points out about the potential emotional dilemma of the slave is exceedingly relevant here. The pressured relationship between master and slave could create a situation in which the master seemed at times to embody not only cruelty and injustice but also strength and virtue, and therefore could create in the slave a "longing for the master, understood as absolute other." But once this "act of love" is frustrated, as it usually was, it "collapses into hatred, and generates, at least potentially, great violence."[58] *Absalom, Absalom!* includes this dimension of the crisis but engages its most volatile configuration by representing as well the other, more reprehensible aspect of the parental conflict — that between the white father and the son who *is* and *is not* his son.

It is this mirroring conflict — "mirroring," in that brother and brother, son and son, are completely alienated yet nearly interchangeable — that Faulkner drives to a hallucinating pitch in the fraternal entanglements among Henry, Bon, Quentin, and Shreve, the first two resembling each other and their father, the second two resembling each other and mutually assuming, as their re-creation of the tragedy progresses, a voice that sounds just like Mr. Compson's. The attempts many readers have made to separate the voices into distinct genres (the gothic, the Greek tragedy, the romantic, and so on) are certainly warranted, but only because such attempts reflect an inevitable anxiety that the voices, effacing necessary narrative distinctions just as the action of the novel effaces cultural distinctions, *will* begin to be indistinguishable. As the crisis of the book is prolonged and held in abeyance in parallel with the suspension of the Sutpen crisis over the course of the Civil War, each of the storytellers and actors wears the "mask" of Greek tragedy Mr. Compson alludes to early on, "interchangeable not only from scene to scene, but from actor to actor and behind which events and occasions [take] place without chronology or sequence"; and they do indeed, to borrow a prophetic passage from *The Sound and the Fury*, seem to talk all at once, "their voices insistent and contradictory and impatient, making of unreality a possibility, then a probability, then an incontrovertible fact, as people will when their desires become words."[59] As in Poe's tales of incest and Melville's *Pierre*, the distinctions between narrators (or authors) and characters dissolve in a frenzy of nondifferentiation in which identity collapses along with almost every vestige of plot, chronology, and order.

Yet this collapse, like that of Sutpen's design, does not quite take place — and for good reason. At a narrative level, we are left with enough clues, enough fragile threads of evidence to reconstruct the novel's design; and at the level of action, where the two designs merge and separate, we are met with a violent reassertion of order and chronology. That violence is Henry's murder of Bon, which, despite its tragic consequences for all involved, saves Sutpen's design in theory by vigorously asserting distinctions that have threatened to become obliterated. It does so in a peculiar way, however, for as we noted earlier, the murder has extremely ambiguous motivations, ones that extend the reciprocal crisis to a more complex level. In murdering Bon not as the "brother" but as the "nigger" who is going to sleep with his sister, Henry in effect asserts that Bon is not his brother and not his father's son (that is, he "overpasses" the incest); if he had killed him as "brother" rather than as "nigger" (had "overpassed" the miscegenation) he would have had to recognize the legitimacy of a paternity his allegiance to his father, and to the South, finally will not permit. If Henry had not killed Bon at all (or if Bon had killed Henry), the crisis of reciprocity — what "might have been" — would have become unbearable: the design would have become a "mockery and a betrayal" (as Sutpen puts it), and incest and miscegenation would have become more than ever the "monstrous double" whose existence the Southern slaveholding design must deny.

Because the burden of the novel is to assert the possibility of love in spite of the brutal requirements of convention, the reconstruction by Quentin and Shreve of a fraternal love that *must* be violated is the only ceremony that *can* be accomplished. As Melville found in his own reconstruction of a loving act of sacrificial violence in *Billy Budd*, "the *might-have-been* is but boggy ground to build on,"[60] and the actions of responsive love can be more agonizing, and require more circumventive plotting, than the ritualized violence that makes them necessary. The proper analogy here is not the mysterious fraternal rivalry and stately paternal ceremonies of *Billy Budd*, however, but the perilous intimacies that break down racial barriers in *Huckleberry Finn*. Like the fraternal bonds between Huck and Jim, and like Huck's "lie" that tells the truth of conscience, the intimacies of Henry and Bon, Quentin and Shreve, are eventually shattered by violence and betrayal. As Twain and Faulkner clearly saw, the present crisis could only be measured by the drifting dream of the past, the betrayed promise redeemed by the one lasting, fictional act of imaginative sympathy. Twain's own ambivalent contention in 1890 that his literary methods "begot themselves, in which case I am only their proprietor, not their father,"[61] describes with haunting exactness the breakdown of paternal roles that *Huckleberry Finn* initiates and *Pudd'nhead Wilson* makes outrageously complete — a breakdown that Faulkner also spoke of in numerous remarks about his own methods and style, and one that he implicitly endorsed when he described himself as "proprietor" of a vast fictional design and created a new and, as it seems, completely necessary and logical narrative form in which to gauge the crisis of the South. For both Twain and Faulkner, as for Melville, the paternal responsibility of authorship both determined and, because they saw the tragedy so clearly, also destroyed the forms of fiction in which that sympathy had to be — could only be — expressed.

The scintillating merger of characters and voices that *Absalom, Absalom!* creates as it drives toward its climax thus reflects, but at the same time stands in opposition to, the narrative form of *Light in August*. The earlier novel depends upon suggesting dramatic entanglements that cannot take place and upon alienating the story of Joe Christmas, in both formal and actual terms, from those that surround it. The story that revolves around Charles Bon, however, does indeed sacrifice him, and just as violently; but it does so only after thoroughly fusing his story with those of the characters who struggle to accept him as "brother," who recognize, as it were, that his blood is their blood and that his tragedy is undeniably theirs as well. The crisis of novelistic form in both *Light in August* and *Absalom, Absalom!* — the one creating extremities of separation and alienation, the other creating extremities of merger and imitation — matches the crisis of blood, in the second instance making intimately visible the contours of the tragedy that would propel the South, and the nation with which it had ostensibly been reunited, into the further tragedy of Jim Crow. At that point both the design of the South and the design of the country, after provisional separation, seemed to come together again.

Faulkner's own design comes together as well, for *Absalom, Absalom!* incorporates aspects of all his previous fiction and reveals both the origins of Joe Christmas's tragedy and the obscure motives for Quentin's. As they merge in the intimacies of kinship, the voices of the novel perhaps most resemble — "just like father's" — that of Sutpen, which, though he is long dead, is strangely clarified by their re-creations. The clarity of Sutpen's voice as he tries with calm desperation to fathom his "mistake" reveals to Quentin and to Shreve everything Quentin's own father cannot, and at last — at long last in the novel's final recollection — brings Quentin face to face with the self he will kill six months later as he confronts the act of fratricide that the novel can reveal only in a dramatically sharpened, self-reflexive form:

> *And you are — ?*
> *Henry Sutpen.*
> *And you have been here — ?*
> *Four years.*
> *And you came home — ?*
> *To die. Yes.*
> *To die?*
> *Yes. To die.*
> *And you have been here — ?*
> *Four years.*
> *And you are — ?*
> *Henry Sutpen.*

The urgently restrained moment of union between Quentin and Henry brings into perspective the other moments of perilous and violent communion that define that novel's own flawed design: the "touch of flesh with flesh" that unites and divides Rosa and Clytie; the vicarious intimacy that Quentin and Shreve create for Henry as he contemplates Bon ("I used to think that I would hate the man . . . whose every move and action and speech would say to me, I have seen and touched parts of your sister's body that you will never see and touch"); the exchanged warning and cry of outraged fraternity that accompanies the vengeance of Wash Jones ("Stand back Wash. Don't you touch me." . . . "I'm going to tech you, Kernel"); and most of all the extraordinary passion that infuses Quentin's and Shreve's re-creation of Bon, Sutpen, and Henry on the battlefield in the spring of 1865, Bon seeking only to "*touch flesh*" with his father, Sutpen refusing, and Henry forced in the utmost agony of intimacy to face the crisis for him. The language of the encounter between Henry and Quentin, withholding virtually everything that burgeons within it, mirrors the crisis joining 1865 to 1909 and entwining their respectively fated chronologies — Henry at last revealed as the murderer of his own "brother," and Quentin now more than ever, as Rosa says of Henry, "almost a fratricide." [62]

THE SUTPEN HOUSE, as Judith archly puts it on the occasion when she hands over Bon's letter to Quentin's grandmother, is "like a bed already too full," and its story like that of "five or six people all trying to make a rug on the same loom." [63] The novel's endless repetition and repercussion of images and actions certainly bears this out — to such an extent that any full account of the layering patterns is forbidding. They all lead toward and fall away from that which cannot be expressed: first, the bedroom of his sister in which the dead Bon lies; and second, the bedroom in which the dying Henry lies. Those beds, in figure and in fact, hide to the end the secret they appear to reveal, the secret that the whole burden of Faulkner's novel rests upon. The "overpass to love" that Quentin and Shreve create in order to force the fraternal rivalry between Henry and Bon to its ultimate crisis fails, as it must, to prevent the act of fratricide; but it succeeds, to the only extent that it can, in preserving at a point of precarious union the love that must paradoxically be expressed and denied in an act of violence. The novel's refusal to reveal fully its ultimate secret is in perfect keeping with the perilous, indirect admissions of paternity and fraternity that the scenes between Sutpen and Henry, and between Henry and Bon, on the eve of the collapse of the South can reveal: for how else express the agony of Bon, Henry, and Sutpen alike, how else intimate the "monstrous" thing at the heart of the defeat that the South now faces? The passion consumed in that moment of wasted intimacy is as close as they, and Faulkner, can come to discovering the reason "why God let us lose the War."

"The only clean thing about War is losing it," Faulkner once wrote to Malcolm Cowley, for "as regards material, the South was the fortunate side." [64] This may well be true, in more ways than one, but at a cost that has turned out to be just as peculiar as the institution that war abolished. The ratio between fortune and cost is the haunting depth and complex immediacy, the potent nostalgia and the troubling contemporary relevance, of Faulkner's fiction, whose own design, like that of Lincoln, struggles yet with a "flaw" insistently present, insistently fratricidal. The long act of retrospection — delaying, postponing, meeting only indirectly its critical question — that Faulkner undertakes in *Absalom, Absalom!* and *Go Down, Moses* is one that brings the twentieth and nineteenth centuries together in fiction and in fact, inevitably entangling white and black, curse and revenge, promise and betrayal. The "overreach of despair" that Rosa's touching of flesh with Clytie produces, and the "overpass to love" that Quentin and Shreve require to culminate their own involvement in the Sutpen tragedy, are themselves mirroring images that merge and divide Faulkner's characters and his country with all the virulent contagion that actual or imagined mixing of blood can create.

In the end, that contagion spreads to a bedroom in Cambridge, Massachusetts, 1910. Donald Kartiganer is certainly correct to point out that the last chapter of *Absalom, Absalom!* represents a "painful disintegration of [the] communion"[65] created between Quentin and Shreve in their reimagining of Bon's own anguish, for it is essential at this level, as at every other, that the momentarily created union, the passionate fraternity, give way to violent ambivalence — Quentin frantically denying that he hates the South and Shreve taunting him about the Jim Bonds that are going to take over the world, so that "in a few thousand years, I who regard you will also have sprung from the loins of African kings."[66] The brutal antagonism of Bon's son, Valery, so reminiscent of Joe Christmas, and the howling idiot produced by his marriage to an animalistic black woman, are impossible to "overpass"; but they must be seen to represent not only Faulkner's deepest fears and prejudice, but also his most painful and sympathetic understanding of the South that he, like Quentin, claimed not to hate. They are the remaining fragments of Sutpen's nightmarish design, and as such they continue to express the long trauma that outlived the design. "As a social factor," George Washington Cable once observed, the slave was "purely zero," no better than "the brute at the other end of his plow-line." The mingling of white blood with black made little difference: "One, two, four, eight, multiplied upon or divided into zero, still gave zero for the result."[67] Jim Bond is a concentrated emblem of the sins of the fathers to the same extent that *Absalom, Absalom!* is, as Faulkner would later say, a "condensed and concentrated" version of the "general racial system in the South."[68]

Nothing could more severely betray Faulkner's own ambivalence or make any clearer that his novel has virtually nothing to say about the horrors of slavery as a labor system, but rather revolves around the flaw that, far from abrogating those other horrors, only made them more prominent. The heroic stature of Sutpen and his willed "innocence" are no more denied by his sons than are David's by Absalom and Amnon; and in the biblical account, David's cry — the novel's title — is prompted not by Absalom's murder of Amnon, who has raped their sister, but by the later death of Absalom, the son who has risen up in rebellion against his father. It might well have been Lincoln's cry, and it might, a hundred years later, have been Faulkner's. Like the fall of David's house, the fall of the South seemed more and more to Faulkner, in myth and in fact, an extended fulfillment of prophecy or, more exactly, a lasting curse for original sins. By the time he wrote *Absalom, Absalom!* the House Divided had long been restored in name, on paper; but the South and the fictions it lived by, and the nation and the policies it tacitly or legally endorsed, were as nearly divided as ever. In his next major novel, *Go Down, Moses,* Faulkner would compose a serial history of the South that contained from one end to the other the long, halting progress of the design for freedom that was constructed, collapsed, and reconstructed again over that period and then beyond it. In several stories that went into the novel in revised form, the character who finally became Ike McCaslin was first represented as — who else? — Quentin Compson. He was still not dead.

chapter 6

Half Slave, Half Free:
Go Down, Moses

To snatch in a moment of courage, from the remorseless rush of time, a passing phase of life, is only the beginning of the task. The task approached in tenderness and faith is to hold up unquestioningly, without choice and without fear, the rescued fragment before all eyes in the light of a sincere mood. It is to show its vibration, its color, its form; and through its movement, its form, and its color, reveal the substance of its truth — disclose its inspiring secret: the stress and passion within the core of each convincing moment.

— CONRAD, preface to *The Nigger of the Narcissus*

IT SEEMS nothing short of madness: the black character executed for murdering an Illinois policeman in the title story of *Go Down, Moses* (1942) was originally named Henry Coldfield Sutpen, the grandson of Rosa Sutpen, one of Thomas Sutpen's slaves. Before settling on Samuel Worsham Beauchamp, Faulkner first tried Carothers Edmonds Beauchamp,[1] a solution that at least had the advantage of freeing his character — with the few tangible rewards such freedom could offer — from the strangling contagion of one family's two strains of blood, even though it may ultimately have made that of the McCaslin-Beauchamp family seem unbearably involuted. The second change is significant for reasons that must be examined; but the first is compelling evidence that the tragedy of *Absalom, Absalom!* was, in Faulkner's mind, far from finished either in 1909 or in 1936. Was "Rosa Sutpen" simply a slave, or was she, like Clytie, also Sutpen's daughter? Or was she his mistress or, like Tomasina in *Go Down, Moses*, both his daughter *and* his mistress? Or, more startling yet, was the black blood slave and the white blood Coldfield — and if so, was it Ellen's, Judith's, Rosa's? Why "Henry"? Was Henry Sutpen part black *too*, or was the murderer's name a mocking indictment of Sutpen's design?

Although there is no solution to this mystery and no reason to render it so hopelessly confused, the questions it raises bear evidently on *Go Down, Moses*, in which the conjunction of incest and miscegenation that the earlier novel had violently repudiated is once more revealed, in figure and in fact, as the heart of the South's long, continuing catastrophe. Indeed, "tragedy" hardly seems to describe the sins of the father or the tormentingly complex relationships among his descendants in this case; unlike *Absalom, Absalom!*, which is extremely complex as a narrative but, once certain assumptions or decisions are made, relatively simple in action, *Go Down, Moses* is nearly suffocating in its crossing and recrossing of plots and symbolic action. Aside from the fourth section of "The Bear," the stories are straightforward enough, but their chronological entanglement and superimposition in the form of a novel creates purposely shocking tensions and ambiguities. As the strains of action and the strains of blood wind in and out of the narrative from story to story, the novel more and more resembles the biblical saga it constantly alludes to, and the curse under which the South labors seems less and less likely to be lifted. Clearly, it is not lifted by Ike McCaslin's repudiation of his patrimony — no more than it had been by Quentin Compson's suicide. Since the character of Ike evolved out of Quentin, who was Faulkner's original protagonist in "Lion," "The Old People," "A Bear Hunt," and the earlier story "A Justice," all of which fed into *Go Down, Moses* in less or greater part,[2] we must assume Faulkner was fully satisfied neither with the explication of Quentin's suicide that Henry's murder of Bon afforded nor with the act of fratricide itself.

The abrupt, overbearing violence of that act and Henry's later immolation in the fire seemed to close the door on the Sutpen tragedy and its potential contagion with resolute finality; but Faulkner was soon opening the door again, searching for new clues, new strands of missing action, new ways to confront the act of miscegenation that might be, could be, had to be an act of incest. To this extent, the initial representation of Samuel Beauchamp as Henry Coldfield Sutpen is something of an excursion into authorial fantasia, revealing that the contagion in blood has become a compositional contagion as well. The mixing of characters and plots that this strategy and the preliminary figuring of Ike as Quentin would have entailed reflects the precarious extremity of Faulkner's own design, posed on the brink of collapse but at the same time taking risks in every way equal to the emotional strain it is meant to express. The "action" that takes place, as it were, between *Absalom, Absalom!* and *Go Down, Moses* is the disintegration of the barrier — against an actualization of miscegenation as incest — that Henry's murder of Bon holds in place: as though struggling ever more insistently to unify the fictional domain of Yoknapatawpha, Faulkner crossed the threshold that unites two distinct castes in one family of violated blood in *Go Down, Moses*. But because the resolution of *Absalom, Absalom!* could be taken back no more easily than Quentin's suicide in *The Sound and the Fury*, Faulkner was forced to rearrange the plots that were developing — almost beyond control, it seems — in the stories that became *Go Down, Moses* and eliminate the loose ends that bound it so urgently to the flawed design and divided house of Thomas Sutpen.

Such a reconstruction of Faulkner's intentions is admittedly speculative, and it is likely that, far from planning another complex reworking of the Sutpen and Compson stories, he was simply casting about for something to write. The three novels that appeared between *Absalom, Absalom!* and *Go Down, Moses* — *The Unvanquished* (1938), *The Wild Palms* (1939), *The Hamlet* (1940) — were also composed of shorter stories; while they generally reflect an ease of style that is a new departure for Faulkner, they also reflect the mundane fact that he was working feverishly to make money by selling the stories to magazines before turning them into novels. Each is successful in its own way, but the structure of *Go Down, Moses*, since the links between its stories are often perilous and at times seemingly invisible, may be seen to express in renewed complexity the crisis of form in which Faulkner's major novels represent the continuing crisis of blood in the South. If Samuel Beauchamp had remained Henry Coldfield Sutpen, if Quentin had usurped the role of Ike, if — but as Melville writes of "manhood's pondering repose of If," "our souls are like those orphans whose unwedded mothers die in bearing them: the secret of our paternity lies in their grave, and we must there to learn it."[3]

O NE would not need Faulkner's report that he was reading *Moby-Dick* to his daughter in 1940 in order to assert its importance as an influence on "The Bear."[4] Melville's hunting ritual, his exploration of white imperialism in conflict with alien races, his brooding meditations on the revealed and unrevealed powers of paternity, his agonized salute to the god of Nature who must be lovingly challenged and slain — all of these conspicuously American themes reappear in Faulkner's story, and in doing so they remind us that, as in *Absalom, Absalom!*, Faulkner is moving further away from his own early "modernism" and placing himself, deliberately or not, more clearly in the tradition of classic nineteenth-century American fiction. Part of the power of *Go Down, Moses* derives from the tradition of frontier humor Faulkner had already employed so successfully in *As I Lay Dying* and more recently in *The Hamlet*, whose stories coalesced into a novel at roughly the same time as those of *Go Down, Moses*. But the tall-tale comedy of the Snopes family gives way in *Go Down, Moses*, and more particularly "The Bear," to the same darker side, the same inscrutable mystery, of totemic sacrifice that ultimately overpowers Melville's moments of frontier comedy in *Moby-Dick*. One might well view *The Unvanquished, The Wild Palms,* and especially *The Hamlet* as necessary relief and comic escape from the nightmare vision of *Absalom, Absalom!* and, in turn, see all the gothic horror return — first in bits and pieces in "Was" and "The Fire and the Hearth," and then in all its tragic complexity in the remaining stories — as *Go Down, Moses* formed itself into a novel. In both instances, the transition between comedy and tragedy, far from altogether distinguishing them, instead holds them in suspended antagonism, defining one and the other by their curious proximity; and in both instances as well, that antagonism is often defined by the varying perspectives taken toward questions of sexual power or legitimacy.

It is nearly as difficult to imagine *Go Down, Moses* without its bear as it is to imagine *Moby-Dick* without its whale. And Ike discovers, as Ishmael asserts, that the secret of his "paternity" lies in the grave of an unwedded mother — not his own mother, of course, but the slave mother who carries the white McCaslin blood into the black Beauchamp family. But there is this difference among others: it is not immediately clear what relation the ritual of the hunt has to the stories concerned with racial conflict and intimacy in the old and new South. To be sure, there are two explicit points of contact — first, Ike's reading about incest and miscegenation in the family ledgers, which coincides with the deaths of old Ben and Sam Fathers in 1883; and second, Ike's later discovery of Roth Edmonds's contemporary act of miscegenation and incest with a "doe . . . that walks on two legs," which coincides with the stage of degradation the annual hunt has reached in 1941. Beyond that, the metaphor of the ritual hunt appears in all the stories, ranging from simple burlesque in "Was" (where Uncle Buck enters "bear-country" when he unwittingly lies down beside Sophonsiba Beauchamp) to ceremonial violence in "Go Down, Moses" (where the catafalque of the executed Samuel Beauchamp would be "the slain wolf"). In "Pantaloon in Black," Rider is one of "them damn niggers," the deputy says, who "look like a man and . . . walk on their hind legs like a man" but, when it comes to "normal human feelings," might as well be "a damn herd of wild buffaloes"; when Lucas faces down Zack Edmonds in "The Fire and the Hearth," his eyes are "like the eyes of a bayed animal — a bear, a fox."[5] Beyond all of this, of course, Ike's repudiation of his patrimony is linked — by all the desperation of style and extrapolated theme Faulkner can summon — to the rites of initiation that the hunt and the surrogate paternity of Sam Fathers represent. Even so, the connections seem as tenuous as Ike's own repudiation, which is significantly paradoxical and certainly fails to lift the McCaslin curse.

Like virtually all of Faulkner's novels, *Go Down, Moses* proceeds by "a method of implication, working as metaphor works,"[6] and the implications in this case are vexing to the same degree that they grow out of, and respond to, the precarious form of the novel itself. The metaphors of game, ritual, and pursuit that pervade the stories reveal their related strategies by referring, in almost every instance, to the struggles between hunter and beast or white and black. The proximity of these two contests is never far out of view once it is first defined, in "Was," in the ritual pursuit of Tomey's Turl, "that damn white half-McCaslin," who is bayed, flushed, baited, treed, and run to den every time he escapes to court Tennie Beauchamp. The full century that falls between the hunt of Tomey's Turl, who is the son of Carothers McCaslin and his own mulatto daughter, and the "doe hunting" of Turl's unnamed descendant in "Delta Autumn," who bears the illegitimate son of Roth Edmonds, comprises the contest for freedom that Ike McCaslin thinks he has won by renouncing his patrimony at age twenty-one, but which reappears to him more than fifty years later in all its tragic consequences. When Ike touches the hand of Roth's "nigger" mistress — "the gnarled, bloodless, bone-light, bone-dry old man's fingers touching for a second the smooth young flesh where the strong old blood ran after its long journey back to home" — the terrible futility of that renunciation is realized.[7] Ike's encounter with Roth's lover is indeed, as Michael Millgate remarks, "the point at which all the threads of the novel seem to cross, at which the whole pattern of the book emerges with final and absolute clarity."[8] Ike's gift to her of the hunting horn he has inherited from General Compson accomplishes nothing and seems patently repugnant alongside his advice that she go back North and marry a black man. And yet it is the one symbolic act, the one futile but generous gesture, of which Ike is capable; it continues to define the paradox of revulsion in guilt and generosity in shame that characterizes Ike's life from the moment Sam Fathers sets him free.

Ike's momentary touching of the woman's hand re-creates the charged moments of flesh touching flesh in *Absalom, Absalom!* and, for the moment it lasts, reconnects Ike to the paternal blood that will die with him but live on in the monstrous contagion of the Beauchamp line. The futility of Ike's renunciation has several dimensions, but the one the novel revolves around is his failure, not unlike that of Henry Sutpen, to legitimize the McCaslin blood by passing it on and accepting his patrimony. His own marriage fails when his wife demands that he accept his inheritance, when he refuses, and when she in turn, after this "first and last time he ever saw her naked body," refuses to sleep with him again. In "saving and freeing his son" from the "wrong and shame" that is also his inheritance, Ike loses him.[9] Like the marriages that never happen in *Absalom, Absalom!*, the son that is never born to Ike defines a state of possibility that seems both the best solution and at the same time its horrible contrary. Ike's repudiation depends on this paradox; for while his refusal to assume control of the land and freed slaves that are his due saves neither of them from the continuing curse, it does insure that the white McCaslin blood will descend only through the distaff Edmonds line or through the black Beauchamp line. It is this act that makes possible the slight but powerful ascendancy Lucas Beauchamp has over the Edmonds men, who are nominally his "masters," and it is that ascendancy, along with Ike's own tortured repudiation, that expresses the South's and Faulkner's lingering obsession with the legitimizing power of paternal "blood."

Ike's argument with Cass in 1888 at first depends on his contention that the land belongs to no one, that on the instant Ikkemotubbe realized he could sell it, the land "ceased even to have been his forever, father to father to father." When that argument goes nowhere, Ike enlarges his strategy by invoking the plan of God, who "saw that only by voiding the land for a time of Ikkemotubbe's blood and substituting for it another blood, could He accomplish His purpose," and therefore chose Carothers McCaslin, "the seed progenitive of the three generations He saw it would take to set at least some of His lowly people free." At length, after the reading of the ledgers, interspersed among a long rehearsal of the war, of Reconstruction, and of events that have not yet taken place, Ike and Cass are simply back where they started, Cass asserting that Ike is the only legitimate heir, even — and especially — if the land is seen to belong to Sam Fathers, and Ike declaring, "Yes. Sam Fathers set me free." Far from clarifying Ike's repudiation, the context of Sam Fathers's surrogate paternity only makes it more elusive. The problem cannot be resolved by any simple opposition between wilderness and civilization (for Ike does not clearly choose one over the other, and the hunt itself quite deliberately entangles them) or between pure and "mongrel" blood (for Sam Fathers embodies strains of black, white, and Indian blood, and is thus "the scene of his own vanquishment and the mausoleum of his defeat").[10] It can only be resolved in any fashion whatsoever by recognizing how thoroughly it depends on an act that occurs throughout the novel in various forms and reaches an agonizing but perilously diffused pitch in the last story — the act of grief.

What Ike discovers in the commissary is the same haunting thing Roth later discovers when, reaching the white maturity that is also his inheritance, he refuses to sleep beside Henry Beauchamp: "He knew it was grief and was ready to admit it was shame also, wanted to admit it only it was too late then, forever and forever too late." The accomplished act, suspended forever in the unchangeable moment of its occurrence, divides the two boys as irrevocably as it has their fathers and families before them. Such grief, the true measure of Faulkner's own sympathy and shame, as it would be of Charles Mallison's in *Intruder in the Dust,* is the one expression that unites the lost innocence of the hunting ritual and the assumed manhood of Ike's repudiation: it is not shame alone that Ike discovers when he reads the ledgers at age sixteen (because he has lived side by side with the children of Tomey's Turl, "he knew what he was going to find before he found it") but grief — his own grief, which grows directly out of the suicide of Eunice, who walked into an icy creek one "Christmas day six months before her daughter's and lover's . . . child was born, solitary, inflexible, griefless, ceremonial, in formal and succinct repudiation of grief and despair who had already had to repudiate belief and hope." It is the very nature of Ike's grief that it has no solution; shame alone could be assuaged by his acceptance of his patrimonial responsibility and the generosity toward the Beauchamps it might afford, but grief — like the sin itself and like the deaths of old Ben and Sam Fathers — cannot be undone. Although it is Cass who speaks, it is Ike who remembers, on the day of his repudiation, how seven years earlier Cass had read to him from Keats's "Ode on a Grecian Urn" the lines *"She cannot fade, though thou hast not thy bliss, / Forever wilt thou love, and she be fair."* The "truth" of the bear hunt that Cass insists Keats's poem illuminates at that time seems to Ike *"simpler than somebody talking in a book about a young man and a girl he would never need to grieve over because he could never approach any nearer and would never have to get any further away."*[11] But as he recalls Cass's reading of the poem seven years later, he is recalling the preceding phrase that Cass omits — "yet, do not grieve"[12] — and recalling as well what the text of the ledgers and Carothers McCaslin's legacy must also reveal: *"So I reckon that was cheaper than saying My son to a nigger* he thought. *Even if My son wasn't but just two words. But there still must have been love* he thought. *Some sort of love."*[13] That love — doubtful at best, a mockery at worst, and in any event fruitless beside the agony it entails — defines both the limits and the ramifying contours of Ike's repudiation, the one act in which he can enact the grief that is his true inheritance.

One must simply assert this, for the willful complexity of the fourth section of "The Bear" can express only the tangled acts of memory that are, for Faulkner, Southern history and are for Ike the utterly precarious justification of the repudiation he makes to the baffled Cass. The fourth section is the heart of the novel not simply because it contains Ike's repudiation but also because its fragmented form, visibly enacting Ike's own spiritual disembodiment, as well as the chronological disjunctions that characterize the story his repudiation dominates, offers a magnified example of the structural complexities of the entire novel. In a fashion reminiscent of the disembodied utterances of grief that constitute the fragmented story of Addie Bundren in *As I Lay Dying,* the tangentially connected stories that surround "The Bear" on all sides and define the shifting burden of Ike's repudiation are focused in the pages that read into and out of the family ledgers; and the ledgers, like Benjy's section in *The Sound and the Fury,* are a concentrated representation, a mysterious and seemingly sacred account, of acts and passions whose symbolic value draws into itself and envelops the interpretations it necessitates. As though converging upon the fourth section of "The Bear" from the perspectives of past and present, the stories drive toward, and fall away from, the revelation of grief in the act of incest and miscegenation that coincides with the sacrificial death of the totem animal. Those two acts have a relationship charged with paradoxical significance, but it is worth noting at the outset that the complexities of style that the enactment of Ike's repudiation involves quite deliberately obscure, in a cloud of loose ends and illogical argument, the meaning of that repudiation.

The fourth section's collapse of narrative and chronological distinctions accords in every respect with the potential collapse of racial distinctions, and therefore of the cultural hierarchy, that the ledgers record. To judge the power of the simultaneous collapse and preservation of those distinctions, we need to borrow a phrase from one of the novel's most dramatic and important scenes. Immediately preceding the flashback in "The Fire and the Hearth" to the ritual combat between Lucas and Zack, Faulkner speaks of Lucas and Cass as "coevals in more than spirit even, the analogy only the closer for the paradox." [14] The analogy is blood, and the paradox is that, though Cass's McCaslin blood is distaff and Lucas's McCaslin blood is paternal, this fact is legally voided by the caste of race. The figures of analogy and paradox culminate here in the recollected struggle of Lucas and Zack, which we must return to, but they serve as well to define the peculiarities of Ike's repudiation. For the analogy between the ritual hunt and Ike's refusal of his patrimony, linked as they are by the fragile lines from Keats's ode, can only be described as a full flowering of paradox, one in which forms of opposition are intimately merged in proportion to their necessary separation and near contradiction.

Keats's ode describes this paradoxical intimacy as an event that never *can* but always *will* take place; as it continually eventuates in imagination, the poem's act of love is generated in conjoined nostalgia and anticipation, existing both in the timeless world of art and the projected world of unfulfilled fantasy. Just as the "wild ecstasy" here defined as perpetual pursuit is, paradoxically, one that never takes place at all but at the same time takes place in every imagined reading of the poem, the event itself, and the analogy between poem and event, are themselves closer for the paradox. Likewise, Ike's creation of an act of "love" out of the cryptic lines of the ledger, although it can hardly be said to be exactly analogous to the Keats ode, also depends on the powers of paradox: first, it must have existed even though there is every reason to doubt it; second, even as he asserts the necessity of love, Ike's repudiation seems to deny all possibility of honoring that love; and third, even though the figures of immortality that define the ritual hunting of deer and bear may be seen to correspond to the sexual pursuit of Keats's "unravish'd bride," they define the corresponding relationship between master and slave only by a more agonizing paradox: the ravishment has taken place, and the whole history of Ike's family is its evidence. The incest and miscegenation of Carothers McCaslin is not, like Rosa's in *Absalom, Absalom!,* an "unravished nuptial," but an accomplished fact. To this extent, it *is* like the ritual hunt: it has happened, it is past, it cannot be undone but can only be made the subject of grief. Whatever love it once entailed, and whatever love the contemporary mixing of the races could now provide, are left suspended at a point of imminence that, it seems, will never be capable of realization.

Faulkner had invoked Keats's ode in *Sartoris* and *Light in August,* but in those instances it served to express an ideal of feminine beauty or artistic excellence, and had never been subject (except by the most extreme implication in the case of Lena Grove) to the pressures of racial conflict. Here, however, the "mad pursuit," the "struggle to escape" Keats speaks of is forced to bear a heavy burden, for the pastoral "sacrifice" that Keats's urn and poem render immortally unfulfilled form the very burden of Ike's tormented conscience. The concluding lines from which Cass draws his observations on the "truth" that "covers all things which touch the heart — honor and pride and pity and justice and courage and love" — are preceded by ones that more appropriately characterize Ike's dilemma: "When old age shall this generation waste, / Thou shalt remain, in the midst of other woe / Than ours . . ." What remains in this instance is the immortal moment of the death of old Ben — his "loverlike" embrace of Lion and his ritual death dance with Boon, in which they momentarily resemble "a piece of statuary" [15] — and an irrevocable act of human blood violation in which Ike insists there must have been "some sort of love." Both moments hang suspended in memory, forced by the exertions of Faulkner's hazardous analogy to encompass a timeless truth in which, it seems, the agony and suffering of consequent generations is overborne by the beauty of the sacrifice.

The timelessness of the sacrifice is very much to the point, however, for what Ike's repudiation most reveals is that it is incapable of translating into a realm of timelessness events that have everywhere the temporally visible and tragic actuality that the text of the ledgers codifies: "all there, not only the general and condoned injustice and its slow amortization but the specific tragedy which had not been condoned and could never be amortized." Both the renunciation of his patrimony and the timeless beauty of the remembered wilderness sacrifice fail to arrest the long agony of racial conflict and, when it occurs once again more than a century later, the horror of miscegenation. It is well to emphasize this, for the moments of greatest achievement in *Go Down, Moses* depend on the tensions of this paradox — depend, that is, on Faulkner's attempts to translate into terms of ritual remembrance and celebration acts that resist the translation at every point, as well they might. That resistance is abundantly evident in "Delta Autumn," where Ike and the wilderness are "coevals," "two spans running out together, not toward oblivion, nothingness, but into a dimension free of both time and space," but where Ike's vision of "wild strong immortal game [running] forever . . . falling and rising phoenix-like to the soundless guns," is abruptly shattered by the appearance of Roth's "white" doe: *"Maybe in a thousand years or two thousand years in America,* he thought. *But not now! Not now!* He cried, not loud, in a voice of amazement, pity, and outrage: 'You're a nigger!'"[16]

IN *Light in August* Faulkner brought his work conspicuously into an American tradition by joining the tragedy of race with the Calvinistic rhetoric of damnation; in *Absalom, Absalom!* he set his story in the middle of the nation's most traumatic internal conflict and joined the violence of race hatred to the terror of incest; in *Go Down, Moses* those themes are joined to a third American theme, the sacrifice of the totem animal. That conjunction itself proves paradoxical, but it depends initially on a psychological development that is everywhere evident in the history and literature of American racial violence from its beginnings in slavery to its most recent manifestations in the tragedy of Jim Crow. It depends, in short, on the continued insistence of commentators both more and less "racist" in their points of view that the Negro is a "beast" — physiologically, emotionally, socially, or in every conceivable way. That such assumptions and assertions often, perhaps always, reveal more about whites than blacks is something Faulkner saw with as much penetrating engagement as anyone; what he also saw more clearly than many is that this hardly makes the force and consequences of those perceptions any less real.

The racist fiction and sociological literature of the late nineteenth and early twentieth centuries understandably reflected the current vogue of scientific naturalism; but its arguments for the "bestiality" of blacks were in many ways secular versions of theories that in earlier years had derived either from the biblical curse of the sons of Ham or from the transposition of that curse into a rationalistic chain of being that situated alien and mixed races at levels below the pure and "white."[17] As we have seen in the cases of J. H. Van Evrie and Charles Carroll, however, those arguments were often superimposed in the Southern mind, so that the purported plans of God and Nature circularly supported each other — though not without contradiction; mulattoes, for instance, were often held to be the most degenerate of the black "species" at the same time they were, because of their white blood, seen to be most capable of social and intellectual development. The war made such contradiction inevitable, however, for the destruction of Southern slavery entailed the replacement of failed theories of providential design with physiological theories that would keep blacks in their social and economic place, and defend against the threat of racial mixing that, in a shocking reversal, now came from the freed slaves rather than their masters. This reversal, with all the rhetorical power of repression such a psychic apocalypse could produce, made the Negro more than ever a "beast" and made the mulatto more than ever an emblem of the return and revenge of the repressed. It made "the Negro," as person and particularly as self-projected white image, something always to be feared and kept at bay, often to be hunted down and killed, at times to be made the object of ritual public sacrifice.

We have already noted how the metaphors of ritual hunting radiate out of "The Bear" into all the stories of *Go Down, Moses* but that, even so, there seems no obvious justification for this aside from Faulkner's desire to give his collection the appearance of thematic continuity. This is certainly the case, yet it is also the case that such continuity rests upon assumptions of thorough intimacy and dependence between master and slave, white and black, or — in this further case — between hunter and beast. The analogous relationship of hunter and beast clarifies the process of inversion that is potential or actual in the other relationships, for the hunt, as it approaches its most vitalized configurations and particularly as it reaches its culminating act, entails a form of ritual intimacy in which the ascendancy of slayer and slain fluctuates, equalizing the respect for, and power over, the other that each has and prolonging the moment of resolution to a degree that defines both the purpose and the success of the hunt. In its perfected form, the hunt, like the "wild ecstasy" of ravishing elaborated on Keats's urn, would last forever. It does not last forever, of course, and the pressure of that realization is what Ike McCaslin feels after he kills his first buck and, in "loving the life he spills," ceases "forever to be the child he was yesterday." What he remembers is not the shot, the kill, but the ritual initiation, "the touch" of Sam Fathers's hands that, with "the hot smoking blood" of the buck, "consecrated him to that which . . . he had already accepted," joining the two of them in the ever-suspended moment in which "still out of his instant of immortality the buck sprang, forever immortal." [18]

As it does throughout *Go Down, Moses* in larger and more significant ways, the fluid narrative chronology of "The Old People," mixing act and memory, anticipation and grief, perfectly complements the immortal moment of the hunt and acts out the paradox it depends on: the immortality of the buck in its moment of death depends completely on that death; it has no meaning apart from it and, in fact, reveals that the entire purpose of the hunt is to preserve the moment it necessarily destroys. This act of transfiguring violence signifies the reality of the hunt and expresses its requisite chronological inversion, for as Ortega points out, "one does not hunt in order to kill; on the contrary, one kills in order to have hunted." [19] The context of Keats's ode in which Faulkner places such a moment asks us to recall that its paradox is not unlike that of Caddy Compson's virginity, which as Quentin discovers must be destroyed to have existed at all.

The explicit sexual overtones of Ike's hunting of both deer and bear support this analogy, just as the blood consecration, which links Ike to animal mother and surrogate father alike, represents in its own right the paradoxical violence in which the act of love may be expressed. There is, moreover, no other way to account for Ike's assertion that there must have been "some sort of love" between Carothers McCaslin and the daughter whose child he fathers than to see it as desperately attached to the ritual of the hunt: that love, particularly that love, must for Ike have been destroyed in order to have existed at all.

The celibate marriage of hunter and beast in "The Bear," as in Cooper's *The Deerslayer* or in *Moby-Dick*, for example, collapses the sexual identities of each in order to express an androgynous, self-generating and self-consuming union in which either may be lover or mistress, father or mother, in which the hunter, like Ike, loses his "innocence" by taking Nature as "his mistress and his wife," and the animal, like old Ben, is both "the man" and the hunter's "alma mater." The touch, the consummation of the kill brings into actuality "the existence of love and passion" that Ike, as though prematurely entering "the bedroom of a woman who has loved and been loved by many men," recognizes at this point prior to Ben's death "is his heritage but not yet his patrimony."[20] The charged passion of hunter and beast in their act of celibate eroticism resembles, then, the ungenerative "pure and perfect incest" that Quentin's father speaks of in *The Sound and the Fury* and again in *Absalom, Absalom!* But in the same way that the act of incest is there overwhelmed and, indeed, denied its intimate meaning by the act of miscegenation it threatens to become, the two substitutions of blood that Ike's repudiation depends on here (the first, in the ritual consecration that weds him to beast and mentor; the second, in what Ike sees as God's exchange of Indian blood for white and white blood for black) are simply contradictory. The ritual hunt sublimates sexuality and isolates the act of love as immortal, forever unconsumated and still possible; yet unlike the fantasized incest of Quentin or Henry Sutpen, the act of miscegenation on which Ike's repudiation turns does no such thing, despite his rhetorical efforts to the contrary, but continues to reveal its sexual violation as obstinately real, irrevocable, and — it seems — unredeemable.

The difference is not difficult to locate. In the one case the blood substitution in purely figurative (though its symbolic enactment is real), while in the other it is very real (though its symbolic manifestations are, if monstrously so, figurative). No forays into biblical prophecy or romantic imagination can undo it; they can only, as "The Bear" attests, make it more prominent. This does not mean, however, that the mediating function of the hunt has no relevance to Ike's repudiation of his patrimony — far from it. It makes the analogy, once more, all the closer for the paradox. Here again, Ortega's observations are to the point. The essential resemblance between hunter and beast, and the mirroring postures and actions they engage in as the hunt progresses toward its moment of visionary transfiguration, culminate in the violent "spilling of blood." It is in this act that "the essential 'within' comes outside," Ortega remarks, "as if the most radical absurdity had been committed: that which is purely internal made external."[21] The violation of the kill, like the sexual violation it strives to transcend by imitating, exposes the very secret of existence, which can only be made manifest by violence against it. There may be every reason to find that violence repelling, even to consider it a pointless exercise of mastery. By the same token, what act could be more paradoxical, could more proceed out of physical and emotional violence that makes a mockery of love, than miscegenation, or especially incest *and* miscegenation? What "spilling of blood" could more imitate love but reveal in its excess of sexual violence a further ritual of mastery in which identities are collapsed only to be asserted more brutally than ever?

That act, as we have seen in the cases of *Light in August* and *Absalom, Absalom!* is nothing but — to borrow Ortega's phrase — a "radical absurdity," one in which sexual and familial identities are strained into distorted shape and in which the essential "within" is made blasphemously external. There is no way, and no reason, to draw an exact parallel between the ritual kill and miscegenation, and Ike's repudiation, precisely because it links them, proves the futility of doing so. As I have already suggested, however, there is a further way to approach the problem, one that clarifies the figurative significance of miscegenation as both the South's original sin and its more contemporary horror as they are exemplified, respectively, in *Absalom, Absalom!* and *Light in August.*

Because the hallucinating fear of the Negro as "beast" that characterized many theoretical justifications of American slavery and became particularly fierce in postbellum racial hysteria undeniably grew in part out of repressed guilt over the visible actualities of slaveholding miscegenation, the language in which such fears were expressed, both before and after the war, reveals a psychological instability that makes the analogy between repressed white lust and projected black threat acute by frantically denying it, closer for the paradox. In the apt words of Winthrop Jordan, white men attempted "to destroy the living image of primitive aggressions which they said was the Negro but was really their own." The threat comes not from *within* but from *without:* "We are not great black bucks of the fields. But a buck *is* loose, his great horns menacing to gore into us with life and destruction. Chain him, either chain him or expel his black shape from our midst, before we realize that he is ourselves."[22]

When Faulkner later spoke of the "hunting" of Tomey's Turl in the context of Uncle Buck's and Uncle Buddy's strange manumission arrangement, he struck the point rather exactly. Because Buck and Buddy knew by instinct that slavery was wrong but did not know quite what to do about it, Faulkner said, Turl "became quarry . . . that received the same respect that the bear or the deer would." The pursuit of Turl, himself the very product of Carothers McCaslin's incestuous miscegenation, is mostly comic in "Was," though, as Faulkner noted, this hunt is "of a deadlier purpose than simple pleasure."[23] Even though the full significance of the ritual hunt assumes it, that deadlier purpose is largely hidden from view in *Go Down, Moses.* Largely, but not entirely, for the story that seems most out of place in the collection, "Pantaloon in Black," has virtually none of the comedy its title implies and stands at an important turning point in the novel. The murder Rider commits in the wake of his profound grief and his consequent lynching, far from being irrelevant to the McCaslin saga, function as a transition between the restrained ritual violence of "The Fire and the Hearth" and the ritual hunting of the beast by Ike McCaslin in the next three stories. Divided between the thoroughly passionate depiction of Rider as he moves toward the act of murder and the white deputy's baffled account of Rider's motives and his lynching, the story expresses utterly contradictory understandings of grief. Although it does not depend on the stock accusation of black sexual violence, Rider's lynching results, in the deputy's account, from an irrational madness that appears to have nothing to do with grief. Of course it has everything to do with it; and like Lucas's ritual challenge of Zack and like Ike's repudiation, it has everything to do with love. Although one of the Beauchamps may have been a better transitional figure, the story of Rider exposes the painful gulf between black and white emotions that is displayed in all the stories and that Ike — or perhaps we should say Faulkner — strives paradoxically to bridge in the grief-stricken repudiation of his patrimony.

Both the hunt and the hysteria of racial fears displace the lust and violence of the subject onto the object of sacrifice. Jordan's observations and the deliberate inversion of sexual desires Faulkner depicts explicitly in *Light in August* and implicitly in *Absalom, Absalom!* support such a theory of displacement, but we may find further confirmation in the strangest of testimonies, one that is all the more strange for accepting and overriding the very paradox it exposes. The plot of Thomas Dixon's *The Sins of the Father* (1912) suggests a development in his romances of race that is not unlike Faulkner's. Daniel Norton's gubernatorial aspirations and his reputation as a leading white supremacist are vexed when his illegitimate mulatto daughter, through the vengeful plotting of her "white" mother, Norton's maid, returns home and, unbeknownst to all, secretly marries Norton's white son. When the truth is revealed, Norton and his son form a murder and suicide pact; Norton shoots his son and then himself, and though Norton dies, the son lives to discover that the girl is not his sister. The plot is slightly more interesting than this, but the point worth noting here is Dixon's characterization of the affair between the stalwart Norton and the seductive Cleo that sets it in motion. The threat originates with her, a "young leopardess from an African jungle" concealed within "the lithe, graceful form of a Southern woman." The more obvious her advances, the more he weakens. However, once Norton proves to be "defenseless against the silent and deadly purpose that had already shaped itself in the soul of this sleek, sensuous young animal," Dixon shifts the ground in a significant way. Norton struggles not simply against the relentless lust of the mulatto, but also against the Beast within himself — "the Beast with a thousand heads and a thousand legs; the Beast that had bred in the bone and sinew of generations of ancestors, wilful, cruel, courageous conquerers of the world." Carrying "in his blood the inheritance of hundreds of years of lawless passion," Norton exemplifies the sins of the fathers he is doomed to repeat.[24]

Although its final message is not essentially different, *The Sins of the Father* is more penetrating than *The Leopard's Spots* or *The Clansman* because Dixon's central metaphor — the Negro as "beast" — is here revealed, at least provisionally, as the frantic psychological projection that it is. Since Cleo's own lust presumably results from both her physiological "degeneration" and her warped expectations of "equality," the beast within Norton meets itself without as though in a mirror image. It is the more than tacit recognition on Norton's part that the beast is within, however, that makes urgent, in the postbellum South, its renewed mastery — the mastery now of the *self* it is and the *other* it has created. Norton's obsessive campaign theme is sexual segregation of the races, a theme that in all the splendid power of its development between the Civil War and Faulkner's own century marks the ambiguous status of the freed slaves. White lust can no longer be released with impunity, for such an act now adds not to the value of one's property but to the visible threat against it. The "beast" has indeed been loosed, set free; the internal has by a radical act been made external.

It is important to take note of this transition, for Norton's inherited lust, and the language of the new naturalism in which he expresses it, magnifies at a particular level the South's general inheritance of guilt, whose continuing expression throughout Faulkner's life and in his work is a suffocating nostalgia, an innocence frantically remembered and maintained, and one whose manifestation in forms of social proscription and regulation reflect in every instance the psychological division within the white mind. Ike McCaslin seeks to resolve this dilemma by refusing to participate in it, choosing to dwell, as he knows he cannot, in "those old times" that are perpetually present, "not only as if they had happened yesterday but as if they were still happening," as if "none of his race nor the other subject race which his people had brought with them into the land had come here yet." By repudiating his patrimony, Ike removes himself as mediating term and leaves the families of Edmonds and Beauchamp utterly divided, descending in a parallel as neatly separated but intimately dependent as the accounts of the ledger, "two threads frail as truth and impalpable as equators yet cable-strong to bind for life them who made the cotton to the land their sweat fell on."[25] If *Go Down, Moses* is evidence, it would seem that manumission and abolition, far from vitiating the intimate dependence of masters and slaves, on the contrary served to increase it in more comprehensive, more ambiguous forms. Certainly, the South and the nation were no longer half slave, half free, but Lincoln's prophetic phrase, for reasons he himself had feared and partially foreseen, had taken on new meanings that could have been anticipated, but could not be fully controlled, by anyone.

Although Ike grew out of the character of Quentin Compson, who lives in a similar impossible world, he might rather be said to resemble Henry Sutpen, who repudiates his own patrimony yet, in the end, kills his brother not as "brother" but as "nigger." He kills him not as incestuous lover but as bestial lover, and this fratricidal act more than any other — more than Quentin's suicide, more than Joe Christmas's execution — illuminates the function of Ike's repudiation as it depends on the ritual hunt. The strategy of the hunt is to obliterate distinctions between hunter and beast, hold them posed in reflected postures as the ritual dance, the loving communion approaches its climax, and then to reassert those distinctions in an act of murderous violence. Like the violent act that reaffirms the purpose — even if it fails to actualize the potential — of Sutpen's design, the violent act that culminates the hunt necessarily destroys the loving intimacy that precedes it and upon which its sacrificial significance depends. The totem animal must be killed in order for that intimacy to have existed at all and in order for his sacred status to be made manifest. Likewise, Charles Bon must be killed, as Quentin and Shreve see quite clearly in the hallucinating reciprocities their reconstruction of the act requires, in order for the loving intimacy between him and Henry to have existed and in order for the act to assume the tragic significance it ultimately has.

Henry, in his agonized identification with the monstrous double he kills, and Ike, in his ritual consecration and patrimonial repudiation, embody in distinct but related forms the division between "innocence and lust" that D. H. Lawrence claimed is characteristic of the "white psyche" in America. The country itself, Lawrence contended, "has a powerful disintegrative influence upon the white psyche. It is full of grinning, unappeased aboriginal demons [and] ghosts, and it persecutes the white men, like some Eumenides, until the white men give up their absolute whiteness." [26] Lawrence was writing of Cooper's *Deerslayer*, but the disintegration of the white psyche the nation's long trauma of slavery entailed is more threatening than the disintegration that necessitated the killing and removal of Indians. They are related, as Faulkner sensed when he joined the two in *Go Down, Moses*, but the resemblances between Natty Bumppo and Ike McCaslin are elementary at best. The hunt for Cooper, at whatever level we might want to examine it, and despite the relevance of its ritual elaborations to Cooper's own political vision, is largely pastoral fantasy, while for Faulkner it is, as he remarked of the pursuit of Tomey's Turl, deadly serious. The virtues of the hunt in "The Bear" and *Go Down, Moses* in general occupy the same troubled position that "innocence" does in the South's many myths of itself: they arise from the ruins of the dream they are meant to substantiate. Such virtues, as R.W.B. Lewis has argued, have "nothing to do with 'primitivism,' or with noble savagery, or even the American Adamic dream of unspoiled original innocence in the New World — nothing except this," that in Faulkner's version of the myth honor and virtue emerge from "a 'transvaluation' of that dream and that innocence: at the instant the falsehood is exposed and the existence of evil is acknowledged." [27]

One may rightly contend, as Lawrence's subtle irony makes particularly clear, and as Lewis would acknowledge, that this is true of many American myths. Cooper, Melville, and Hemingway, for instance, certainly recognized as much; but Faulkner's version differs in that it perseveres in the face of odds that become greater by the moment, more and more insure the futility of the accomplishment, and therefore bring it to the verge of hallucination as he substitutes one blood sacrifice for another. He does so in order to bring into view a dimension of the lost New World of which Cooper, for example, was rather painfully innocent, one which the entire nation, for that matter, successfully suppressed or virtually ignored until 1863, but which Jonathan Edwards the younger had articulated with haunting and prophetic precision in 1792, about the time Carothers McCaslin moves his family and slaves to Mississippi and buys his land from Ikkemotubbe. Echoing Jefferson's, and prefiguring Lincoln's, concerns over miscegenation, Edwards told the Connecticut Abolition Society that white Americans confronting their Negro slaves had two choices: either "raising their color to a partial whiteness" or "leaving to them all their real estates." If slaveholders wish to

> balance their accounts with their Negro slaves at the cheapest possible rate, they will doubtless judge it prudent to leave the country, with all their houses, lands and improvements, to their quiet possession and dominion; as otherwise Providence will compel them to much dearer settlement, and one attended with a circumstance inconceivably more mortifying than the loss of their real estates, I mean the mixture of their blood with that of the Negroes into one common posterity.[28]

Such a choice between miscegenation and patrimonial repudiation would appear zealously schematic if it did not correspond so closely to Ike McCaslin's dilemma and predict in more complex configurations the history of black emancipation from the Civil War through Faulkner's life. With an irony one can only consider vengeful, it anticipates the fear that would lead Lincoln and others to their utopian plans for colonization and lead the South and the nation to perilous contemporary justifications of the flawed designs of Thomas Sutpen and Carothers McCaslin for decades to come.*

---

* Such sentiments have reappeared generation after generation. During Faulkner's lifetime they were embodied in Theodore Bilbo, longtime United States senator and governor of Mississippi, and staunch advocate of African colonization for American blacks, who insisted that he "would rather see his race and civilization blotted out with the atomic bomb than to see it slowly but surely destroyed in the maelstrom of miscegenation, interbreeding, and mongrelization." The day was coming, Bilbo prophesied, when there would no longer be any chance for redemption. "Once the [white] blood is corrupted, there is no power on earth, neither armed might, nor wealth, nor science, nor religion itself, that can restore its purity. Then there will be no Negro problem because the blood of that race will be commingled with the blood of the white race, and a mongrel America would have no reason to worry over the race issue. . . . Shall our generation possess the vision, foresight, and courage to solve forever the race problem so that ours will be the heritage of all the generations of Americans yet unborn? Or shall we pass the problem on and on to grow in magnitude with the passing years until our posterity sinks into the mire of mongrelism?" See *Take Your Choice: Separation or Mongrelization* (Poplarville, Miss.: Dream House Publishing Co., 1947), pp. ii, 10. The "Dream House" was Bilbo's private mansion; the volume also contains a copy of his colonization bill, the "Greater Liberia Act," introduced in the United States Senate in 1939.

Ike, of course, does not turn over his inheritance to the Beauchamps, who have already been raised to a "partial whiteness," but his act of repudiation comes as unthinkably (though paradoxically) close to doing so as anyone, South or North, might imagine. He sees, as Edwards did, that the choice is not between innocence and sin; he sees, rather, that it is too late, forever too late, that the choice is between the abandonment of a myth and the sacrifice of the integrity of the white psyche. The stories of the hunt in *Go Down, Moses* preserve the myth of lost innocence even as the argument between Ike and Cass exposes its endless regression, reaching probably back beyond the sons of Ham, beyond Canaan and Eden itself, and certainly back beyond the sons and fathers of Carothers McCaslin to the "old world's corrupt and worthless twilight [carried to America] as though in the sailfuls of the old world's tainted wind which drove the ships." [29] The hunting stories preserve, at the irrevocable moment of its mythical fall, that innocence which must be destroyed to have existed at all and which therefore was doomed and damned to begin with. This, though, is also the history of the South, for whom that moment appeared with startling suddenness in 1865; by superimposing the central myth of the South upon the central myth of America, Faulkner extends one of its essential features, the narcissistic relationship between man and Nature, hunter and beast — or, in this case, between master and slave — to a further level that is capable of expressing, in figures of real and often physical intimacy, the entanglement between projected fantasy and repressed violence such myths require. Ortega's remark that "the past is a voluptuous siren," [30] as it characterizes the nostalgic lure in hunting of a simpler pastoral life, also describes the lure in the South of a lost world of Confederate grandeur and innocence. Insofar as Faulkner both penetrated that myth with excruciating irony and, with further irony, revealed himself the victim of all its powerful charms, he might have taken his example not from Keats's ode but from Allen Tate's "Ode to the Confederate Dead," which speaks not of urns but of tombstones, not of wild ecstasy but of

> the patient curse
> That stones the eyes, or like the jaguar leaps
> For his own image in the jungle pool, his victim. [31]

In the context of *Go Down, Moses* the hunting stories bridge the incipient and actualized violence between black and white in "The Fire and the Hearth" and "Pantaloon in Black" on the one hand, and "Go Down, Moses" on the other, with necessarily marginal success. In this respect they have a therapeutic value not unlike Nick Adams's fishing in "Big Two-Hearted River," for to the extent that the wilderness stories of Faulkner and Hemingway alike are autobiographical projections, [32] they reveal with greater power the psychological collapse they preserve at the brink of actuality. In Faulkner's case, because the resonant dimensions of that collapse are so much larger, the risk is more pointed; and Ike's repudiation, as it appears to be a veiled projection of Faulkner's own, only preserves honor and virtue at a terrible cost. Even as he asserts that there was "some sort of love" in Carothers McCaslin's incest and miscegenation, Ike's repudiation of his patrimony denies the contemporary significance of that love. The translation from myth to actuality is the one that Ike, despite Faulkner's heroic insistence that it be possible, does not make. Like that of Henry Sutpen, Ike's repudiation becomes fratricidal by asserting that racial distinctions cannot be overcome, that the responsibility for them can only be renounced; like that of Quentin Compson, its argument devours itself by assuming responsibility for a grief that is ultimately as abstract and irrevocable as time itself. *Go Down, Moses* writhes and strains under the moral agony of connecting the spilt blood of the hunt to the split blood — and, moreover, the violently disseminated blood — of slavery. While it surpasses Sutpen's resolute innocence, the virtue Ike acquires by losing his innocence is ever more paradoxical as its expresses the tormenting forms, the extremities of spiritual wasting such virtue may entail.

W E must resist the North," Gavin Stevens contends in *Intruder in the Dust* (1948), "not just to preserve ourselves nor even the two of us as one to remain one nation because that will be the inescapable by-product of what we will preserve . . . the postulate that Sambo is a human being living in a free country and hence must be free." The six-year lapse between *Go Down, Moses* and *Intruder in the Dust* corresponds more or less to the remainder of Ike McCaslin's life as it is projected in *Go Down, Moses*. Although the identification should not be understood to be in any way complete, Stevens has rightly been seen to articulate a number of Faulkner's own beliefs, ones that Ike begins to express in "Delta Autumn" and that Faulkner's own public statements on race and desegregation in the 1950s amply bear out. The good intentions of Faulkner and Stevens cannot be doubted, but there is no ignoring the moral strain they also express. "That's what we are really defending," Stevens continues, "the privilege of setting [Sambo] free ourselves." [33] But as Twain had brutally put it in *Huckleberry Finn* (whose publication in 1885, by interesting coincidence, corresponds closely to Ike's act of repudiation), Tom Sawyer "gone and took all that trouble to set a free nigger free!" [34]

Twain's novel is a haunting critique of *Intruder in the Dust*, whose apologists (including Faulkner himself on many occasions) have been attracted to the Huck Finnish virtues of Charles Mallison, have defended or explained away the crude Tom Sawyerish propaganda of Gavin Stevens, and have generally refused to recognize that the novel represents a decline in moral vision and a lamentable failure of literary execution. The same accusations have been wrongly leveled against *Huckleberry Finn* — quite wrongly, for the collapse into a melodrama of enslavement and liberation that Twain's novel enacts, some sixty years before *Intruder in the Dust*, reveals with all the irony Twain could bring to bear upon the emerging moral failure of his nation's own vision the utter necessity — *again, still, once more* — of setting free a people who had ostensibly been free for twenty years. In 1948 they had been free for eighty years, but Gavin Stevens, in the best Jim Crow tradition, still wants to preserve that privilege for himself and the South.

This posture, so close to Faulkner's own, is one thing among others that wrecks *Intruder in the Dust*, which begins as a powerful examination of the paradoxical relationship between a young white boy and an old black man but turns into a burlesque morality play of Faulkner's alter egos, half farcical detective story and half platform for Gavin Stevens's ceremonial pronouncements on "Sambo" and world politics. Charles Mallison's rescue of Lucas Beauchamp from charges of murder, precisely because of the pointlessly extravagant plot it requires, makes the humiliating and painfully convoluted rescue of Jim by Twain's boys as tragically exacting as Twain, in his ironic vision, saw it had to be. In Faulkner's new version there is almost no irony at all, and the burden of shame that is lifted from Charles's shoulders therefore leaves too little of the resonant ambiguity and fully realized moral complicity of Huck Finn's struggle with his conscience.

In one blinding flash — in the moment Lucas Beauchamp refuses Chick's payment for a meal, and Chick realizes it is now "forever too late, forever beyond recall" — Faulkner creates the very moment he needs to extend the complex tragedy of *Go Down, Moses* into a more contemporary setting and then proceeds to waste its magnificent potential, as the themes of ritual pursuit and potential lynching veer off into the genre of the detective story Faulkner never mastered and the righteous new Southern paternalism of Gavin Stevens. Lucas's conceived role as a contemporary "Nigger Jim" is all the more unsettling in view of the psychological complexity with which Faulkner had drawn him in "The Fire and the Hearth," where his subtle ascendancy over his white masters is rich and powerful. Even though that story is often divided between minstrel comedy and explosive tragedy, the juxtaposition of the two holds at a point of integrating tension the simultaneous enslavement and liberation that is Lucas's own peculiar patrimony. But in *Intruder in the Dust* it almost appears that *Light in August, Absalom, Absalom!,* and *Go Down, Moses* have been discredited as mere flights of fancy; since this is obviously not the case, we may wonder instead if Faulkner did not finally despair of making relevant to the contemporary South the turbulent passions of the past that had produced it. The concluding stories of *Go Down, Moses,* "Delta Autumn" and "Go Down, Moses," suggest as much, but they do so with differing strategies of deliberate pathos and irony. Not so *Intruder in the Dust:* though he speaks not of master and slave, but of savior and saved, Stevens is unnervingly right to say of "Lucas-Sambo" that he was "once the slave of any white man within range of whose notice he happened to come" but is "now tyrant over the whole county's white conscience." [35]

Although it is generally a ludicrous novel and a depressing social document, *Intruder in the Dust* reveals how close *Go Down, Moses* had come to a similar collapse of moral sensibility. The claustrophobic entanglement of plot and chronology that characterizes most of the earlier novel when it is viewed as a continuous family saga is one reflection of the intimate involvements of white and black, master and slave that converge in, and radiate out of, the family ledgers, "as one by one the slaves which Carothers McCaslin had inherited and purchased" and their descendants take "substance and even a sort of shadowy life" on the pages we read.[36] As it enacts the formal crisis of Carothers McCaslin's original sin, the fourth section of "The Bear" reaches out beyond the hunting episodes that enclose and contain it, reaches even beyond the limits of the novel, as it were, to define again, on the one hand, the convulsive passions of *Absalom, Absalom!* and to prefigure, on the other, the shocking superficiality of *Intruder in the Dust.*

Go Down, Moses works by a process of analogy and juxtaposition that is nowhere as successful as it is in *Absalom, Absalom!* and may be seen to represent a decay in Faulkner's ability to hold his design of tragic involvement in place. The problem stems in part from Faulkner's motives and strategies of composition. He had begun working on *Intruder in the Dust,* with an eye toward the commercial success such a "blood-and-thunder mystery novel" might (and would) eventually produce, as early as 1940; at the same time he was wrestling with different versions of the hunting stories and the "four stories about niggers" he thought could be fashioned into a novel along the lines of *The Unvanquished* in about six months.[37] Aside from *A Fable* (1954), the allegorical World War I novel that he also worked on fitfully throughout the 1940s, most of Faulkner's fiction after *Absalom, Absalom!* fills in, extends, and rearranges the map of Yoknapatawpha. Both *Requiem for a Nun* (1951) and the appendix he wrote for *The Sound and the Fury* in 1945, for example, are strained attempts to join the contemporary world to the distant past of the South; and even though such exercises may well be justified, they often have the effect of scattering Faulkner's design rather than consolidating it. What Elizabeth Hardwick once observed of the brief excursions into the romantic Confederate past in *Intruder in the Dust* is true in a larger sense as well of many of Faulkner's efforts over this period: they are "literary, flamboyant, historically ridiculous in terms of America today. . . . Faulkner has caught up with the confusion of the country today, and with bitterness he finds that it cannot be controlled and ordered or even thought about in the intimate, vitalizing way in which he knew and used the past." [38]

While it puts the case against Faulkner's career during and after *Go Down, Moses* too strongly, this is the rough judgment that must be made about *Intruder in the Dust;* and while one could argue that the seemingly inevitable collapse of Faulkner's envisioned design is, on the contrary, a measure of the strained sensibilities of the South in the 1940s as it approached, with mounting hysteria, the stimulating reality of desegregation, such an argument only makes more apparent the precarious strategy of *Go Down, Moses.* More and more Faulkner's country, like his novel itself, had become a chaos of fragments in which economic and political realities clashed with tired dreams and absurd pretensions, in which time variously raced and stood still, stranding whole families and fine minds in the nowhere of thunderous rhetoric and spent ideals. Faulkner's career in fiction is no doubt the record of such social and psychological fragmentation, and may well be its best expression; but the danger of such an argument, like the danger of the strategy it seeks to define, is that it can go either way. *Go Down, Moses* is surely a case in point, and in important respects it represents a return to the differing formal strategies of *As I Lay Dying* and *Light in August,* holding its stories in the suspended tension of alienating involvement that may be seen to issue on the one hand in a sustained meditation on grief, and on the other in a broad historical saga of racial conflict that concludes with the execution of a black murderer.

The title story of the volume is in this way perfectly expressive of Faulkner's ambivalence. Its relationship to the rest of the stories is enormously distended, almost to the point of breaking; its function as an index of social estrangement is nearly overwhelmed by its leaving unexplained and unexplored the life of Samuel Beauchamp. The impassioned family grief that Gavin Stevens can in no way share, but can only mechanically respond to by arranging for Beauchamp's funeral, is left side by side, for reasons precariously elusive, with Aunt Mollie's confused version of the slave spiritual from which the book and story take their title: "Roth Edmonds sold my Benjamin. Sold him in Egypt. Pharoah got him — ." [39] Faulkner, once again, has come face to face with the mask of "Negro" that cannot be penetrated; and though Gavin Stevens is in this instance the perfect reflector of the alienation of Mollie Beauchamp, and though it is evident here, as it was in *Light in August,* that Faulkner's attitude toward Stevens is one of jaded irony, his continued fascination with him in *Intruder in the Dust* (and later in *Requiem for a Nun, The Town,* and *The Mansion*) is difficult to fathom. Like the change of the murderer's name from Carothers Edmonds Beauchamp to Samuel Beauchamp, the shifting of the white burden of grief from the Edmonds and McCaslin families to the Worshams and Gavin Stevens seems not to actualize the ironies the story's title offers but to reflect Faulkner's own hasty flight from a tragedy that, as Ike discovers and as *Intruder in the Dust* makes embarrassingly obvious, would admit of no actual or dramatic resolution.

The parabolic form of *Go Down, Moses,* like the ledgers Ike reads (and like the ledger account of sold and unsold stories Faulkner kept throughout his career), offers the chronicle of "a whole land in miniature," but insofar as it begins to resemble Faulkner's complete fictional record, it is also a "continuation of that record which two hundred years had not been enough to complete and another hundred would not be enough to discharge." The magnitude of that debt, in all its ancient and contemporary extenuations, is expressed with remarkable precision in the novel, which seems itself to be one interpretation of the ledgers, one reading of a text whose whole strategy is to fold in upon itself and resist coherence and stability. The metaphor of translation that appears throughout the stories (we are even told, for instance, that Gavin Stevens has been engaged for twenty-two years in a "translation of the Old Testament back into classic Greek," a project not unlike Faulkner's career) [40] defines the act of interpretation the novel requires in order to be a novel at all. It defines as well, with extreme pressures, the concomitant transpositions of historical event into symbolic act and primitive ritual into social sacrifice that the novel, like Ike's repudiation, depends on. As it works to break down barriers between the stories and to define the various agonized forms of human freedom that emancipation and, later, "passing" would bring into focus, the figure of translation ultimately carries the whole precarious burden of Faulkner's novel. It does so by emerging from the very center of the book, like the sacred animal emerging from the tangle of Faulkner's visionary prose, in the ritual hunt and the consecration of blood that, we are told, sets Ike McCaslin free.

But free from what? Like the refrain "he was free" that pursues Charles Mallison through *Intruder in the Dust*,[41] proving beyond all doubt that he is *not* free, that it is forever too late, Ike's insistence that he has been emancipated carries Faulkner's imagined agony to the very edge of a moral abyss. To the extent that Sam Fathers's hunting camp is "a modern equivalent of Nigger Jim's island," as Irving Howe suggests, Faulkner's embedding of the theme of freedom within the pastoral myth may seem to be "the culmination of a shift in social allegiance, a shift that cannot and should not be transposed into political terms."[42] Howe's criticism is just, but two qualifying points must be made: first, that aside from its strategic devaluation in "Delta Autumn," there is nothing "modern" about the hunting ritual, for its essential value lies in the fact that it is lost, is mythic; and second, that the impossibility of transposing the one event into the other domain is the only way in which Faulkner can measure either one. Life on the river (for Huck) or aboard the *Pequod* (for Ishmael) or in the woods (for Ike) is already eminently "politicized" to the extent that such an *evasion* — to borrow one of Twain's potent terms — expresses with all the concealed or restrained power of moral urgency public commitments to action that will not or cannot be made, or that have already been violently betrayed.

In Ike, Faulkner re-created that version of himself which, like Huck, was also a version of his section and his nation as it clung transparently to an innocence that was resolutely lost. As they variously retain for themselves the privilege, in all its impassioned conscience, of setting Sambo free, the characters of Huck Finn, Ike McCaslin, and Chick Mallison are increasingly unsuccessful in exact proportion to the escalating challenge of their task. The difficulty for Faulkner's vision lay in draining away the reckless power of that conscience as it appeared in Ike McCaslin in the further effort, the comic melodrama of *Intruder in the Dust* and parts of "The Fire and the Hearth," to modernize it. Lucas gets his tobacco and his candy, to be sure, but they are not, like Ike's offering of tobacco and candy at Sam Fathers's grave, "translated into the myriad life which print[s] the dark mold of . . . secret and sunless places with delicate fairy tracks."[43]

B OTH "Go Down, Moses" and *Intruder in the Dust* show Faulkner at the limits of his tragic imagination. Their problems are his, and they derive in part from his own increasing recalcitrance on contemporary questions of racial inequality and in part from his difficulty in translating past passions into present vision. When he makes those difficulties one and the same, as in the characters of Quentin Compson and Ike McCaslin, they are nothing but the heart of his fictional representation of the South's long trauma. What the stories dominated by Gavin Stevens reveal, however, is that the brilliant success of that expression seems to depend — has perhaps depended all along — on a further form of enslavement, one that is also Faulkner's necessary burden and that James Weldon Johnson had recognized thirty years earlier: "The Negro is in much the position of a great comedian who gives up the lighter roles to play tragedy. No matter how well he may portray the deeper passions, the public is loathe to give him up in his old character; they even conspire to make him a failure in serious work, in order to force him back into comedy."[44]

While few of them have had the penetrating intelligence of Johnson, critics have occasionally leveled such charges at Faulkner in claiming that his only successful black characters are, by blood or behavior, "white." This is neither entirely true nor to the point: for one thing, "Sambo" was often real enough during Faulkner's career, certainly in the white mind; and in any event, the passionate dependencies between white and black, hallucination or not, form the territory Faulkner recognized to be, not just the only one he *could* imagine, but also the one he *had to* imagine. It was the one that defined all others by making them possible and necessary. The real problem with *Intruder in the Dust* is not Lucas but nearly everyone and everything else; and the story, after a promising start, betrays an abrupt falling off in Faulkner's ability to hold those dependencies at a point of psychologically dramatic tension. The long fall of the South implicit in the irrevocable moment of secession was indeed, as Faulkner put it in *Requiem for a Nun,* a kind of "transubstantiation,"[45] one that created out of times that *were* times that could never, but *might,* have been, and made of forms of enslavement that were undeniably, brutally real other forms that were as brutal as they were unreal, fantastic. Such a disordering of sensibilities in both temporal and social or political terms lies behind each of Faulkner's explorations, in twisting, distorted forms, of the mind of the South. Faulkner's life corresponded in essence and in particulars to the life of Jim Crow, and his dramatic expressions of the intimate physical and psychological involvements that created the agony of the South (as in *Absalom, Absalom!*) or those that extended such involvements in all their contemporary tragedy (as in *Light in August*) can hardly be characterized as racist fulmination or glorified as revisionist celebration.

By appearing to polarize these tendencies, which are elsewhere merged in all their impassioned fever, *Go Down, Moses* may be Faulkner's most honest and personally revealing novel, even though it is clearly not his best. If one were interested in personal revelation alone, however, one would have to draw the line of descent from Quentin Compson (or Shreve) to Ike McCaslin to Gavin Stevens, each of them partially ironic characterizations to be sure, but each revealing as well the developing trauma that Faulkner's public record on segregation in the 1950s would make visible. Such an interpretation may be important and may, as we noted earlier, prove that an author's chosen materials or themes are never entirely within his control; but we are perhaps equally likely to find meaningful not what an author says in his fiction or in public, but what he does not or can no longer say. *Go Down, Moses* illustrates this in two powerful and telling instances — in Ike McCaslin and Lucas Beauchamp, the two characters on whom Faulkner seems to spend his best powers as they dwindle into two different, but intimately related, failed visions. Ike's relinquishing of his patrimony resembles, in authorial terms, Faulkner's own, for never again does his power to imagine the burden of that inheritance, transcending and entwining historically sequestered events, reappear with such expressive dignity. And never again does Faulkner — aside from the restless, mismanaged attempt in the case of Nancy Mannigoe in *Requiem for a Nun* — approach the tragic dignity of a "black" character he momentarily discovered in Lucas Beauchamp.

The extraordinary power of "The Fire and the Hearth" holds in taut juxtaposition the Sambo comedy of Lucas's hunt for buried treasure with his divining machine (an "object symbolical and sanctified for a ceremony, a ritual") and the explosive tragedy of his ritual combat with Zack Edmonds forty years earlier. That contest between a black man and a white man who "could have been brothers, almost twins too" is Faulkner's most exacting dramatization of the reciprocal powers and impending violence that miscegenation could produce. Having risked his own life to save Zack's son at childbirth, Lucas must endure, first, the humiliation of having his own wife set up for six months as Zack's housekeeper, wet nurse, and possible mistress; and second, the further humiliation of waiting for Zack to claim his own son once Mollie returns home to nurse both the black Henry and the white Roth. As Faulkner imagines it, however, the contest between Lucas and Zack has less to do with contemporary events and the potential act of adultery than with the rivalry between two strains of Carothers McCaslin's blood, as each of its heirs tries to bluff the other into violating the honor that descends with it. When the two men lock and embrace, "kneeling, their hands gripped, facing across the bed and the pistol," the strains of McCaslin blood meet in all the restrained violence that the original act of passion has set in motion. The momentary dispersal of tension that ensues in Lucas's argument (made more to himself than to Zack) that Zack has used old Carothers to beat him, just as Cass had used him "to make Isaac give up the land that was his because Cass Edmonds was the woman-made McCaslin, the woman-branch," affords an even greater ascendancy to Lucas; for his initial answer to that strategy is not to kill Zack (or both Zack and himself), but to kill only himself and thus "beat [Zack] and old Carothers both." We cannot be sure whether or not this is also a bluff, for at that moment Zack springs,

> hurling himself across the bed, grasping at the pistol and the hand which held it. Lucas sprang too; they met over the center of the bed where Lucas clasped the other with his left arm almost like an embrace and jammed the pistol against the white man's side and pulled the trigger and flung the white man from him all in one motion, hearing as he did so the light, dry, incredibly loud click of the missfire.[46]

Reminiscent though it is of the crisis scenes in the house and bedrooms of Sutpen, and more particularly of the scene of absolution leading up to Joanna

Burden's death and the misfire that saves Joe Christmas's life, this scene of balked murder has essentially different significance. As it grows out of the charged context of violated blood in those earlier novels, however, the episode adds a further dimension to Lucas's ascendancy that is troubling in the extreme. When he later examines the misfired cartridge — "the dull little brass cylinder less long than a match, not much larger than a pencil, not much heavier, yet large enough to contain two lives" — Lucas muses:

> Have contained, that is. *Because I wouldn't have used the second one,* he thought. *I would have paid. I would have waited for the rope, even the coal oil. I would have paid. So I reckon I ain't got old Carothers' blood for nothing, after all. Old Carothers,* he thought. *I needed him and he come and spoke for me.*

In retrospect, Lucas's threat does indeed seem to have been a bluff, one intended to force into more agonized configuration his suicidal act, but one that strangely enough derives its power, in Lucas's eyes, from the very contamination of blood it is meant to repudiate. One might well contend that Faulkner has destroyed the powerful tensions that the ritual combat brought to culmination by leaving Lucas in the end, like Joe Christmas, the victim of the myth he acts out even as he acts violently against it. But what greater tragedy could there be than that myth, what more potent realization — here again like Joe Christmas and even Charles Bon — that the one irrevocable act of love contaminates all others that devolve from it? "How to God," Lucas asks at the conclusion of the scene that lives with him for life and continues to determine the small power he has as a black man who is and is not a "Negro," "can a black man ask a white man to please not lay down with his black wife? And even if he could ask it, how to God can the white man promise he won't?" [47]

Against the background of this powerful scene, the contemporary contest between Lucas and Roth over the divining machine seems pale and powerless, even if we take seriously Roth's recognition in Lucas's "absolutely blank, impenetrable" face of the composite stalemate of two bloods, the one that was *"pure ten thousand years when my own anonymous beginnings became mixed enough to produce me,"* the other that "had heired and now produced with absolute and shocking fidelity the old ancestor's entire generation and thought." The second is the face Lucas shows Ike on the day he appears to collect his legacy, now not the face of Carothers McCaslin alone, but "the tintype face of ten thousand undefeated Confederate soldiers almost indistinguishably caricatured, composed, cold, colder than his, more ruthless than his." Or as Roth sees it again, forty-five years later, "a composite of a whole generation of fierce and undefeated young Confederate soldiers, embalmed and slightly mummified," the heir of everyone *"countless, faceless, even nameless now except himself who fathered himself, intact and complete, contemptuous, as old Carothers must have been, of all blood black white yellow or red, including his own."* [48] To the degree that these passages impinge upon utter contradiction and grow out of Faulkner's attempt to wrest tragic significance from scenes that otherwise hardly bear close scrutiny, they are bound to appear confusing at best, and at worst to drift toward the pompous theory about Joe Christmas's contest of bloods offered by Gavin Stevens. Such confusion is to the point, however, for it expresses the increasing complication of projected and self-projected masking images that define the reciprocal entanglements between master and slave Faulkner began exploring in *Light in August* and brought to a climax in Thomas Sutpen's house of mirrors. Beyond that, it reflects the extraordinary risks Faulkner takes in *Go Down, Moses* to unite the ritual hunt and the combative contests between black and white in the central act of Ike's repudiation of this patrimony.

The reciprocal threats and surmises, and the accompanying reversals of power, between Lucas and Zack as they twice struggle over the pistol enforce their identity as brothers or twins; and their mirroring posture, in its intimate antagonism, resembles that of Henry Sutpen and Charles Bon as they approach the crisis of fratricide that will violently reassert racial distinctions that have threatened to collapse. The violent confrontation between Lucas and Zack depends on a similar paradox; for the sexual intimacy over which they fight repeats the original violation of racial distinctions and family honor that has made them mirroring images to begin with. This further resemblance between generations is enhanced by the fact that Lucas combats the contemporary outrage by endorsing the first, by drawing on the marginal patrimony that Charles Bon is denied. Like Ike, he asserts that there was — there must have been — "some sort of love" in the miscegenation of old Carothers and his daughter; and in the contest with Zack, it is the totem father, old Carothers, whose blood and attributes he has internalized, who gives Lucas his courage and "speaks" for him. To suggest that Carothers McCaslin "sets Lucas free" would be misleading in every conceivable way but one: he frees him, as Sam Fathers does Ike, from the caste he belongs to; and though that freedom is ambiguous, even a mocking betrayal, it observes a ritual allegiance to the past that in each case converts an act of violence into an act of love. The psychological pressures of such conversion are themselves analogous but inverted, closer for the paradox, leading Ike to repudiate the patrimony that is undeniably his and allowing Lucas — even as he asserts that Ike has been cheated out of his inheritance by Cass — to exercise the marginal patrimonial power over the Edmonds family that belongs to him only by virtue of Ike's repudiation. Ike and Lucas, separated as they are in the stories they dominate, are in this respect fraternally united by the paternal blood that one denies (though he has every legal right to it) and the other embraces (though he has no legal right to it at all).

Ike's repudiation and Lucas's moral ascendancy, like the ritual hunt they both refer to, are charged with the reciprocal ambiguities that define for Faulkner the paradoxical contest between freedom and mixing of blood; and the ritual of freedom that the combative struggle is meant to play out issues in each case in a moral power whose most conspicuous feature is its enslavement to the past. Even though that enslavement appears to be in one case freely elected and in the other involuntary, they move toward each other, without merging, in such a way as to suggest proximity and dependence. Born Lucius Quintus Carothers McCaslin Beauchamp, grandson of Carothers McCaslin and son of Tomey's Turl, Lucas simply changes his name, "taking the name and changing, altering it, making it no longer the white man's but his own . . . himself selfprogenitive and nominate, by himself ancestored," repudiating what he can repudiate no more or less than Ike: "1874 the boy; 1888 the man, repudiated denied and free; 1895 and husband but no father, unwidowered but without a wife, and found long since that no man is ever free and probably could not bear it if he were." [49] Respectively "freed" from the ancestor and the patrimony they repudiate but can never escape, Lucas and Ike stand poised against each other, as incapable of dramatic involvement as Faulkner leaves them, divided forever by the act of the grandfather they share, the very act that made their respective repudiations necessary. Although they both live into old age, they are barely brought together in the book — except, perhaps, through the transitional grief and violence of "Pantaloon in Black" — and at last, they simply disappear from it, Ike dying some years later with no heirs but the half a county to which he is "uncle," and Lucas completely omitted from the story of his mysterious grandson's execution and funeral.

G*O DOWN, MOSES* is frustrating not because it is complex but because that complexity shows every sign of being wrenched into parabolic form by Faulkner's precipitous method of composition. It refuses to become coherent as a novel to the same extent that it refuses to make dramatically coherent its central tragic actions; it remains, as David Minter has pointed out, a novel that "defines every text as an ur-text and pre-text, and then requires us to begin making connections and patterns that we must then revise or even repudiate" just as stringently as the novel itself repudiates the solutions it offers to the moral problems it poses. [50] Still, Faulkner creates, willfully or not, a narrative strategy that might well be seen to generate its greatest power in an act of collapse that parallels the collapse into those continuing antagonisms and unfulfilled promises that are the legacy of black and white together in America. Faulkner's reluctance (or failure) to bring together the rituals of freedom Ike and Lucas engage in suffers in its own right from the "old curse of his fathers" that descends upon Roth forty years before he repeats the sin it arises from. The novel itself enacts the confrontation of that "new barrier, still impregnable," which appears the instant "the child realizes with both grief and outrage that the parent antedates it, has experienced things, shames and triumphs both, in which it can have no part." In that instance, Roth's own grief and shame over his repudiation of Henry Beauchamp is antedated by something between his "*father and a nigger, over a woman,*" [51] while Zack's shame is in turn antedated by the similar, the original act of Carothers McCaslin, against which, according to the ledgers, Thucydus — neither father to his daughter nor grandfather to his grandson — makes no protest. Ultimately, Ike's, and perhaps Faulkner's, allegiance belongs to that generation rather than his own, to those consumed by passions dead and gone rather than those whose burden is the contemporary issue of the passions of the dead.

Faulkner's allegiance belongs as well to the generations that Ike, a character in fiction, outlives and now lives into and beyond, to the generations for whom Faulkner, an author, left a troubled vision and portrayed legacy that has not yet been repudiated and probably could not be repudiated even if it should be. It is therefore fitting, perhaps, that the period of Faulkner's most significant work should culminate in a novel that holds itself poised on the brink of *dis*integration; for the passions of the decade *Go Down, Moses* and *Intruder in the Dust* most obviously reflect were again bringing the South into tragic conflict with the Union it was nearly ready to secede from once more. The eighty years of Ike's life are also the eighty years between the Civil War and the increasing agitation for black civil rights in the 1940s. Over that period, the two sections had not only been precariously reunited but had at times, in the stunning actuality of cable-strong judicial and legislative decisions, become intimately entangled. Like the Edmonds and Beauchamp families, "the two houses had become interchangeable," but with the tragic irony this passage makes clear that the races they housed were as nearly divided as ever — divided often because "one blood ran in them both." [52] Such division, carried to a final configuration in the divisive themes and form of *Go Down, Moses,* expresses the further ramifying divisions within the white mind that Faulkner, by exposing them as his own, made compellingly visible. The nation divided into "half slave, half free," which Lincoln warned against in 1858 and Faulkner invoked once again in 1958, had inevitably assumed more urgent forms as black and white, alike half slave, half free, faced the new intimate antagonisms, the new promises and betrayals, that 1954 would reveal and Faulkner himself would not outlive.

In facing those events, South and North, black and white, faced and stared into each other as though gazing into the deep mirror of history in which the sins of the Southern fathers and the sins of the American fathers appeared as inextricably entangled as they were and are. Neither the lost innocence of the South nor the lost innocence of America has ever been what they are often claimed to be; but that is not entirely to the point, for only the profession of such innocence, made in the agony of implicit or fully realized grief, can define the qualities of memory required to distinguish past from present, promise from betrayal. To claim such qualities are distinctively Southern is necessary, perhaps, but only to the extent that Faulkner's South must be understood as one repudiated part of the disintegrated white psyche Lawrence maintained was characteristic of America itself. Ike's advice to Roth's mistress that she go back North and marry a man of the race she belongs to only by law displays that memory — in Faulkner's fiction as it was in the actualities of American history — on the verge of being lost forever. At this point, however, it is Ike's loss, not Faulkner's. "Old man," she replies, "have you lived so long and forgotten so much that you don't remember anything you ever knew or felt or even heard about love?" [53] This is the most powerful moment in *Go Down, Moses* and perhaps, because of the moving achievement and perilous commitment it culminated, the most powerful in Faulkner's fiction. One might almost wish it were the last.

Notes

CHAPTER 1

1. Frederick L. Gwynn and Joseph L. Blotner, eds., *Faulkner in the University: Class Conferences at the University of Virginia, 1957–1958* (1959; reprint ed., New York: Vintage-Random, 1965), p. 61.

2. Malcolm Cowley, *The Faulkner-Cowley File: Letters and Memories, 1944–1962* (New York: Viking Press, 1966), pp. 36–37, 90.

3. *Selected Letters of William Faulkner*, ed. Joseph Blotner (New York: Random House, 1977), pp. 220–21, 228, 237. Hereafter referred to as *Selected Letters*.

4. Martin Green, *Re-Appraisals: Some Commonsense Readings in American Literature* (New York: W. W. Norton, 1965), p. 194.

5. Robert Penn Warren, "Faulkner: Past and Future," in *Faulkner: A Collection of Critical Essays*, ed. Robert Penn Warren (Englewood Cliffs, N.J.: Prentice-Hall, 1966), pp. 1, 5.

6. Joseph Blotner, "William Faulkner's Essay on the Composition of *Sartoris*," *Yale University Library Gazette* 47, no. 3 (January 1973): 124.

7. Gwynn and Blotner, eds., *Faulkner in the University*, p. 194.

8. W. J. Cash, *The Mind of the South* (1941; reprint ed., New York: Vintage-Random, 1960). At their most audacious, Cash's characterizations of the Southern "mind" seem the intellectual equivalent of the psychological outlands of Yoknapatawpha. At one point, for example, he speaks of the dominant mood of Southern memory as one "in which directed thinking is all but impossible, a mood in which the mind yields almost perforce to drift and in which the imagination holds unchecked sway, a mood in which nothing anymore seems improbable save the puny inadequateness of fact, nothing incredible save the bareness of truth" (p. 48); at another point he describes the emerging legend of the old South as it came to be known a century later: "Perpetually suspended in the great haze of memory, it hung, as it were, poised, somewhere between earth and sky, colossal, shining, and incomparably lovely — a Cloud-Cuckoo-Land wherein at last everybody who had ever laid claim to the title of planter would be metamorphosed with swift precision" (p. 127). See C. Vann Woodward, "The Elusive Mind of the South," in *American Counterpoint: Slavery and Racism in the North-South Dialogue* (Boston: Little, Brown, 1971), pp. 261–83; quote at p. 264. On the romantic strain in Southern history, see also William R. Taylor, *Cavalier and Yankee: The Old South and American National Character* (New York: George Braziller, 1961), pp. 145–341.

9. Gwynn and Blotner, eds., *Faulkner in the University*, p. 1. Faulkner recounted the composition of the novel as it sprang from this image on numerous occasions.

10. Faulkner, "An Introduction to *The Sound and the Fury*," ed. James B. Meriwether, *Mississippi Quarterly* 26, no. 3 (Summer 1973): 413; Faulkner, "An Introduction for *The Sound and the Fury*," ed. James B. Meriwether, *The Southern Review*, n.s. 8, no. 4 (Autumn 1972): 710.

11. *The Sound and the Fury* (New York: Vintage-Random, 1956), pp. 46–47.

12. Ibid., p. 100.

13. Ibid., p. 286.

14. Ibid., pp. 94, 218, 367.

15. Hugh Kenner, *A Homemade World: The American Modernist Writers* (New York: Alfred A. Knopf, 1975), p. 205.

16. Cowley, *Faulkner-Cowley File*, pp. 114, 121–22. Faulkner's second remark came in response to a profile of him in *Life* magazine that Cowley was contemplating (later written by Robert Coughlan; see pp. 125–37).

17. "An Introduction to *The Sound and the Fury*," p. 414. It is not unwise, however, to take note of Faulkner's 1946 letter thanking Robert Linscott for returning the lost introduction: "Bless you for finding the introduction and sending it back to me. Random House paid me for it and I remember writing one, but I had forgotten what smug false sentimental windy shit it was. I will return the money for it, I would be willing to return double the amount for the chance of getting it out of danger and destroyed" (*Selected Letters*, p. 235).

18. *The Sound and the Fury*, pp. 185–86, 210–11.

19. See Gwynn and Blotner, eds., *Faulkner in the University*, p. 262.

20. See Faulkner, "An Introduction to *The Sound and the Fury*," p. 415: "There is a story somewhere about an old Roman who kept at his bedside a Tyrrhenian vase which he loved and the rim of which he wore slowly away with kissing it. I had made myself a vase, but I suppose I knew all the time that I could not live forever inside of it, that perhaps to have it so that I could lie in bed and look at it would be better . . . It's fine to think that you will leave something behind you when you die, but its better to have made something you can die with. Much better the muddy bottom of the little doomed girl climbing a blooming pear tree in April to look in the window at the funeral."

21. Maxwell Geismar, *Writers in Crisis: The American Novel, 1925–1940* (1947; reprint ed., New York, E. P. Dutton, 1971), p. 159. Geismar's relatively early estimation is particularly instructive, because he praises *The Sound and the Fury's* "evocation of our infantile origins" but maintains that the problems of Faulkner's later novels derive from a transposition of those preoccupations into the realm of racial conflict, a correct premise from which Geismar draws misleading but valuable conclusions.

22. David Minter, *William Faulkner: His Life and Work* (Baltimore: Johns Hopkins University Press, 1980), p. 103. Minter's genetic reading of the novel, which draws on Faulkner's biography and early poetry and fiction, is the best discussion available along these lines.

23. Faulkner, "An Introduction to *The Sound and the Fury*," p. 411; Faulkner, "An Introduction for *The Sound and the Fury*," p. 708.

24. Faulkner, "An Introduction for *The Sound and the Fury*," p. 710.

25. John T. Irwin, *Doubling and Incest, Repetition and Revenge: A Speculative Reading of Faulkner* (Baltimore: Johns Hopkins University Press, 1975), pp. 25, 111–12.

26. As the pages and chapters that follow will suggest, my reading of the relationship between these two novels, as well as their relationship with Faulkner's other major fiction, is often indebted to Irwin's exciting and innovative study. I would, however, dispute the necessity of his insistence on the categorical terminology of the Oedipal complex and the allied philosophical theories of genealogical reversal and revenge drawn from Nietzsche, Freud, Ernest Jones, Otto Rank, and Guy Rosolato. Irwin's allusive structure, because it tends to pit all characters and their sexual identities (and all categories and their key terms) against one another, while at the same time making them reversible, narcissistic doubles of one another, risks overemphasizing sets of abstractions that are fascinating in their own right but tend to turn the novels themselves into studies in the theory of psychoanalysis. More importantly, however, his reading leaves out of account the novels in which the development from incest to miscegenation, and from private neurosis to public trauma, takes place and slights the telling social and historical contexts of American race relations that would give his thesis greater validity. For a recent study that extends Irwin's arguments into these contexts (but also neglects the intervening novels), see Richard H.

King, *A Southern Renaissance: The Cultural Awakening of the American South, 1930–1955* (New York: Oxford University Press, 1980), pp. 77–85, 112–29. King argues that "the historically specific taboo underlying the Southern family romance is the taboo against miscegenation, the inverse of the incest taboo." The violation of both taboos represents the threat of collapse in the cultural order, he notes, and their simultaneous appearance "reveals as well the subterranean identity of women and blacks in the family romance. Both are taken to be hostile to culture as it is patriarchally defined." In this way, according to King, the sexual threat residing in black males unites the double violation of taboos. "It is the son [the infantilized black] fulfilling the Oedipal desire to have the mother and abolish the father (principle) and thus it threatens the perverted patriarchal order of the South. The two taboos come to be identified in the specific historical context" (pp. 126–27). Here again, the specifically Oedipal dimensions of the threat, much as they may provide a model for such desire or aggression, seem rather to obscure the fact that white women and blacks are hardly identified in actuality; they seem less significant than the more pervasive problems of threatened cultural and psychic order, an order in which the emotional and the political are vitally entangled and one capable, I want to suggest, of encompassing and defining the equally fragile order embodied in Faulkner's novels themselves and his own involvement in the act of literary representation. A more extensive but generally less stimulating psychoanalytic reading of racial conflict in Faulkner's major novels may be found in Lee Jenkins, *Faulkner and Black-White Relations: A Psychoanalytic Approach* (New York: Columbia University Press, 1981).

27. Taylor, *Cavalier and Yankee*, p. 160; Cash, *Mind of the South*, p. 339. On Faulkner's gynealotry in general, see Elizabeth M. Kerr, *Yoknapatawpha: Faulkner's "Little Postage Stamp of Native Soil*,*"* rev. ed. (New York: Fordham University Press, 1976), pp. 155–73.

28. Irving Howe, *William Faulkner: A Critical Study*, 2nd ed. rev. (New York: Vintage-Random, 1960), p. 42.

29. *Absalom, Absalom!* (New York: Vintage-Random, 1972), p. 12.

30. *The Sound and the Fury*, p. 144.

31. For discussions of this theme, see Gary Lee Stonum, *Faulkner's Career: An Internal Literary History* (Ithaca: Cornell University Press, 1979), pp. 41–93, passim; and Minter, *William Faulkner: His Life and Work*, pp. 46–69, 99–103.

32. *The Sound and the Fury*, pp. 106, 412.

33. Ibid., pp. 143, 96.

34. Joel Williamson, *New People: Miscegenation and Mulattoes in the United States* (New York: The Free Press, 1980), p. 95.

35. *The Sound and the Fury*, p. 411; *Requiem for a Nun* (New York: Vintage-Random, 1975), p. 199.

36. Jean-Paul Sartre, "William Faulkner's *Sartoris*," *Yale French Studies* 10 (1953): 99.

37. For the best reading along these lines, see David Wyatt, *Prodigal Sons: A Study in Authorship and Authority* (Baltimore: Johns Hopkins University Press, 1980), pp. 72–100.

38. Joseph L. Fant III and Robert Ashley, eds., *Faulkner at West Point* (New York: Random House, 1964), p. 49.

39. Gwynn and Blotner, eds., *Faulkner in the University*, p. 6.

40. James B. Meriwether and Michael Millgate, eds., *Lion in the Garden: Interviews with William Faulkner, 1926–1962* (1968; reprint ed., Lincoln: University of Nebraska Press, 1980), p. 141.

CHAPTER 2

1. Jean Stein, "William Faulkner: An Interview" *Paris Review* (Spring 1956), reprinted in Frederick J. Hoffman and Olga W. Vickery, eds., *William Faulkner: Three Decades of Criticism* (New York: Harcourt, Brace & World, 1963), p. 72.

2. *As I Lay Dying* (New York: Vintage-Random, 1964), p. 55.

3. Martin Green, *Re-Appraisals: Some Commonsense Readings in American Literature* (New York: W. W. Norton), p. 174.

4. *As I Lay Dying,* p. 79.

5. Ibid., e.g., pp. 29, 31, 109; 49, 136.

6. Frederick L. Gwynn and Joseph L. Blotner, eds., *Faulkner in the University: Class Conferences at the University of Virginia, 1957–1958* (1959; reprint ed., New York: Vintage-Random, 1965), p. 110.

7. *As I Lay Dying,* pp. 62–63.

8. Gwynn and Blotner, eds., *Faulkner in the University,* pp. 113–14.

9. *As I Lay Dying,* p. 19.

10. Ibid., p. 42.

11. Ibid., p. 58.

12. William Gass, "The Concept of Character in Fiction," in *Fiction and the Figures of Life* (New York: Alfred A. Knopf, 1970), p. 37.

13. *As I Lay Dying,* p. 52.

14. Ibid., pp. 204–05, 119.

15. See Gwynn and Blotner, eds., *Faulkner in the University,* p. 113: "Who can say how much of the good poetry in the world has come out of madness, and who can say just how much of super-perceptivity the — a mad person might not have?" Faulkner even appeared to have apprehended an unconscious power in the character of Darl that, instead of leading to a fuller identification between author and character, rather disengaged them. "You can't make [a character] do things once he comes alive and stands up and casts his own shadow," Faulkner claimed. "I couldn't always undestand why [Darl] did things, and when we would quarrel about it, he always won, because at that time he was alive, he was under his own power" (Ibid., pp. 263–64).

16. *As I Lay Dying,* pp. 198, 26, 68.

17. In one of the best essays on the novel, Calvin Bedient speaks quite rightly of Darl's "vacuum of identity" and notes that, "although Darl is invaded by others as the mystic is innundated by God and the novelist possessed by his characters, those who occupy Darl do not replenish him." See "Pride and Nakedness in *As I Lay Dying,*" *Modern Language Quarterly* 29, no. 1 (March 1978): 67. For further theoretical consideration of the problems of voice and identity, see Stephen M. Ross, "'Voice' in Narrative Texts: The Example of *As I Lay Dying,*" *PMLA* 94, no. 2 (March 1979): 300–310.

18. *As I Lay Dying,* pp. 163–64.

19. Ibid., pp. 163–66.

20. John K. Simon, "The Scene and Imagery of Metamorphosis in *As I Lay Dying,*" *Criticism* 7, no. 1 (Winter 1965): 14.

21. *As I Lay Dying,* p. 59.

22. Ibid., pp. 115, 41.

23. André Bleikasten suggests an interesting approach to the fish analogy by noting that "it is perhaps not going too far to consider it also as a regressive image of the child. Is a fetus not physiologically a fish in its mother's womb?" If so, "the image should then be read as an expression of prenatal nostalgia, an emblem of the primal union of child and mother Vardaman is unconsciously yearning for." This seems perfectly plausible, though there is no reason to insist that the wish for union is wholly unconscious: on the contrary, the desire to be reunited with Addie, whether as pre- or post-natal mother, is what so much of the book's rhetorical power depends on. See *Faulkner's "As I Lay Dying,"* trans. Roger Little (Bloomington: Indiana University Press, 1973), p. 97.

24. *As I Lay Dying,* p. 86.

25. Stein, "William Faulkner: An Interview," p. 82.

26. Bleikasten, *Faulkner's "As I Lay Dying,"* p. 39.

27. Wright Morris, *The Territory Ahead* (1957; reprint ed., Lincoln: University of Nebraska Press, 1978), p. 177.

28. Stein, "William Faulkner: An Interview," p. 72.

29. *As I Lay Dying,* pp. 50, 91, 75.

30. Ibid., pp. 228, 206, 63.

31. Olga Vickery, *The Novels of William Faulkner: A Critical Interpretation* (Baton Rouge: Louisiana State University Press, 1959), p. 53.

32. *As I Lay Dying*, pp. 73–74.

33. Gwynn and Blotner, eds., *Faulkner in the University*, p. 39.

CHAPTER 3

1. Clifton Fadiman, *Party of One* (New York: World Publishing Co., 1955), p. 106.

2. *Chains: Lesser Novels and Stories* (New York: Boni & Liveright, 1927), pp. 9–42. Boni & Liveright had published *Soldier's Pay* and *Mosquitoes* but rejected *Flags in the Dust*.

3. Albert Camus, *The Rebel*, trans. Anthony Bower (New York: Vintage-Random, 1956), pp. 265–66.

4. *The Literary Criticism of Frank Norris*, ed. Donald Pizer (Austin: University of Texas Press, 1964), pp. 75–78. The most cogent argument concerning naturalism's incorporation of elements of the gothic romance and their convergence in Faulkner is Richard Chase, *The American Novel and Its Tradition* (1957; reprint ed., Baltimore: Johns Hopkins University Press, 1980), pp. 185–241, passim.

5. 1932 Modern Library edition, pp. v–vi.

6. *Sanctuary: The Original Text*, ed. Noel Polk (New York: Random House, 1981). In addition to Polk's discussion of Faulkner's revisions, see Gerald Langford, *Faulkner's Revisions of "Sanctuary"* (Austin: University of Texas Press, 1972).

7. *Sanctuary: The Original Text*, p. 142.

8. André Malraux, "A Preface for Faulkner's *Sanctuary*" (1933), translated and reprinted in *Yale French Studies* 10 (1953): 92.

9. *The Portable Faulkner*, ed. Malcolm Cowley, rev. ed. (New York: Viking, 1967), p. xxii.

10. Ibid. When Faulkner was later asked if Popeye is "emblematic of evil in materialistic society," he replied that Popeye is just "another lost human being" who "became a symbol of evil in modern society only by coincidence" (Frederick Gwynn and Joseph L. Blotner, eds., *Faulkner in the University: Class Conferences at the University of Virginia, 1957–1958* [1959; reprint ed., New York: Vintage-Random, 1965], p. 74). On another occasion he denied that Popeye had "any human prototype" and said he was "merely symbolical of evil. I just gave him two eyes, a nose, a mouth and a black suit. It was all allegory. . . . I was probably wrong in my portrayal because it was impossible for me to use anything like a scientific approach" (James B. Meriwether and Michael Millgate, eds., *Lion in the Garden: Interviews with William Faulkner, 1926–1962* [1968; reprint ed., Lincoln: University of Nebraska Press, 1980], p. 53). On probable real-life prototypes of Popeye—a Memphis gangster named Popeye Pumphrey—and other characters and events in *Sanctuary*, see Joseph Blotner, *Faulkner: A Biography*, 2 vols. (New York: Random House, 1974), 1:492–93, 607–8. The most notorious reading of the novel as blunt allegory is that of George Marion O'Donnell, who identifies Temple as "Southern Womanhood Corrupted but Undefiled," Popeye as "amoral Modernism," Horace as "Formalized Tradition," and so on. See "Faulkner's Mythology," in Frederick J. Hoffman and Olga W. Vickery, eds., *William Faulkner: Three Decades of Criticism* (New York: Harcourt, Brace & World), pp. 88–89.

11. Stephen Marcus, "Dashiell Hammett and the Continental Op," in *Representations: Essays on Literature and Society* (New York: Random House, 1975), pp. 324–25. Cf. Wyndham Lewis's claim that the essence of *Sanctuary* "is to be sought for in the pessimism engendered in any American of intelligence by the spectacle of child-corruption conjoined and coeval with the fantastic lawlessness which came in with Prohibition, culminating in the notorious case of the Lindberg Baby, and which gave Popeye and his kind (the violent little gutter-Caesars of the Underworld) their chance." See "William Faulkner: The Moralist with the Corncob," in *Men without Art* (London: Cassell, 1934), p. 60. Of Temple, Lewis observes: "She is the little sensational robot pupped by the American million-dollar-drugged capitalist system" (p. 63).

12. *Sanctuary* (New York: Vintage-Random, 1958), pp. 127, 115, 214.

13. See, for example, D. A. Miller, "The Novel and the Police," in *Glyph 8: Johns Hopkins Tex-*

tual Studies (Baltimore: Johns Hopkins University Press, 1981), pp. 127–47; and Mark Seltzer, "*The Princess Casamassima:* Realism and the Fantasy of Surveillance," *Nineteenth-Century Fiction* 35, no. 4 (March 1981): 506–34.

14. Marcus, *Representations,* pp. 322–24.

15. Dashiell Hammett, *The Dain Curse* (New York: Vintage-Random, 1972), p. 32.

16. *Sanctuary,* pp. 215–16, 125.

17. Ibid., pp. 251, 248, 28, 47.

18. See the following passages in *Sanctuary: The Original Text:* "Horace could see broughams and victorias, French or English-made, perhaps, with delicate wheels behind sleek flicking pasterns in the mild dust, bearing women in flowered muslin and chip bonnets, their bodies rising pliant to the motion of deep springs, flanked by riders in broadcloth and wide hats, telling the month-old news of Chapultepec or Sumter across the glittering wheels" (p. 26); and, "As though whatever women had ever dwelled there had been no more than part of the vanished pageantry of a dream; in their hoops and crinoline but the lost puppets of someone's pomp and pride, moldering peacefully now in a closet somewhere, surrounded by a faint shattering of dried and odorless petals, leaving not so much as the print of a slipper on the dusty stage" (p. 51). Similar passages would later appear in *The Hamlet.*

19. "The Fiction of William Faulkner," in *Selected Essays of Delmore Schwartz,* ed. Donald A. Dike and David H. Zucker (Chicago: University of Chicago Press, 1970), pp. 284–85.

20. *Sanctuary,* p. 151; cf. *Light in August* (New York: Modern Library, 1968), p. 264.

21. *Absalom, Absalom!* (New York: Vintage-Random, 1972), pp. 144–45.

22. *Sanctuary,* pp. 146–47.

23. D. H. Lawrence, *Studies in Classic American Literature* (1923; reprint ed., New York: Viking Press, 1964), p. 85.

24. Joseph Reed, *Faulkner's Narrative* (New Haven: Yale University Press, 1973), p. 59. Reed offers an intriguing approach to the older allegorical forms that *Sanctuary* draws on when he suggests that the novel be read in the context of American captivity narratives (pp. 61–63).

25. Leslie Fiedler, *Love and Death in the American Novel,* rev. ed. (New York: Dell, 1966), p. 323.

26. See Blotner, *Faulkner: A Biography,* 1:764–65; *Selected Letters,* p. 65. The 1932 letter to Ben Wasson that contains Faulkner's humorous advice indicates, moreover, that *Light in August* presented similar problems and possibilities: "About Light in August. [Samuel] Marx asked me about it before I left. I told him I didn't think they [MGM] could use it. It would make a good Mickey Mouse picture, though Popeye is the part for Mickey Mouse. The frog could play Clarence Snopes. I hope to hell Paramount takes Sanctuary."

27. Jean Stein, "William Faulkner: An Interview," *Paris Review* (Spring 1956), reprinted in Hoffman and Vickery, eds., *William Faulkner: Three Decades of Criticism,* p. 68. Cf. Wright Morris's remarks on this statement: "It is a parody, in terms of clichés, of Mr. Faulkner's romantic agony, and a pitiless example of the impotence of his rage. In this fantasy the flight is shrouded in Yellow Book *décor:* the island of peace that once lay in the territory ahead, in the dark fields of the republic, is now at the very heart of urban corruption, the police-sanctioned whorehouse. Through this door the artist escapes from Aunt Sally into the world of art." See *The Territory Ahead* (1957; reprint ed., Lincoln: University of Nebraska Press, 1978), pp. 171–72.

28. *Sanctuary,* p. 289.

29. The best known is Lawrence S. Kubie's 1934 essay "William Faulkner's *Sanctuary*" in *Faulkner: A Collection of Critical Essays,* ed. Robert Penn Warren (Englewood Cliffs, N.J.: Prentice-Hall, 1966), pp. 137–46.

30. Fiedler, *Love and Death in the American Novel,* pp. 346–47. Fiedler rightly places *Sanctuary* in the tradition of the popular western as it evolves into the detective novel, where violence extends sexual aggression and often sublimates a suggested lack of restraint of sexual virility. The best reading of *Sanctuary* in the larger context of Faulkner's misogyny is Albert J. Guerard, *The Triumph of the Novel: Dickens, Dostoevsky, Faulkner* (New York: Oxford University Press, 1976), pp. 109–35.

31. Joseph L. Fant III and Robert Ashley, eds., *Faulkner at West Point* (New York: Random House, 1964), p. 83.

32. *Sanctuary,* pp. 47, 105, 5–7.

33. *Sanctuary: The Original Text,* p. 9.

34. *Sanctuary,* pp. 212–13, 229. Cf. *Light in August,* p. 245. In his hallucination about Little Belle that follows from Temple's account of her fantasy, Horace imagines her watching "something black and furious go roaring out of her pale body" (p. 216); in the original version Little Belle merges with his mother, who is turn merges with Popeye, in a nightmare of childhood: "He saw her mouth open; a thick, black liquid welled in a bursting bubble that splayed out upon her fading chin and the sun was shining on his face and he was thinking He smells black. He smells like that black stuff that ran out of Bovary's mouth when they raised her head" (p. 60).

35. Claude-Edmond Magny, "Faulkner or Theological Inversion," in Warren, ed., *Faulkner: A Collection of Critical Essays,* p. 71.

36. Allen Tate, "Remarks on the Southern Religion," in *I'll Take My Stand* (New York: Harper & Row, 1962), p. 174.

37. Malraux, "A Preface for Faulkner's *Sanctuary,*" p. 94.

CHAPTER 4

1. Ralph Ellison, *Invisible Man* (New York: Random House, 1952), p. 3.

2. Frederick L. Gwynn and Joseph L. Blotner, eds., *Faulkner in the University: Class Conferences at the University of Virginia, 1957–1958* (1959; reprint ed., New York: Vintage-Random, 1965), p. 72.

3. James B. Meriwether and Michael Millgate, eds., *Lion in the Garden: Interviews with William Faulkner, 1926–1962* (1968; reprint ed., Lincoln: University of Nebraska Press, 1980), p. 185. In 1945 Faulkner had complimented Wright on *Black Boy,* but noted his preference for *Native Son:* "I think you will agree that the good lasting stuff comes out of one individual's imagination and sensitivity to and comprehension of the suffering of Everyman, Anyman, not out of the memory of his own grief." See *Selected Letters,* p. 201.

4. Meriwether and Millgate, eds., *Lion in the Garden,* p. 260.

5. Ibid., pp. 90, 258. For Faulkner's further remarks and public stands on race and desegregation, see Gwynn and Blotner, eds., *Faulkner in the University,* pp. 258–65, passim; Meriwether and Millgate, eds., *Lion in the Garden,* pp. 209–27, passim; *Essays, Speeches, and Public Letters,* ed. James B. Meriwether (New York: Random House, 1965), pp. 86–112, 148–51, 155–59, 214–31; Joseph Blotner, *Faulkner: A Biography,* 2 vols. (New York: Random House, 1974), 2:1582–92; and Charles D. Peavy, *Go Slow Now: Faulkner and the Race Question* (Eugene: University of Oregon Press, 1971).

6. Meriwether and Millgate, eds., *Lion in the Garden,* p. 117.

7. C. Vann Woodward, *The Strange Career of Jim Crow,* 2nd ed. rev. (New York: Oxford University Press, 1966), pp. 174–75. On Mississippi's preeminence in the history of segregation, see also pp. 83, 152, 155, 173, 185–86; and James W. Silver, *Mississippi: The Closed Society* (New York: Harcourt, Brace & World, 1966).

8. Blotner, *Faulkner: A Biography,* 2:1833.

9. Faulkner, *Essays, Speeches, and Public Letters,* p. 88.

10. Ralph Ellison, "Twentieth-Century Fiction and the Black Mask of Humanity," in *Shadow and Act* (1964; reprint ed., New York: Vintage-Random, 1972), p. 42. For more extended considerations of this problem in a larger context, see Frantz Fanon, "The Negro and Psychopathology," in *Black Skin, White Masks,* trans. Charles Markmann (1952; reprint ed., New York: Grove Press, 1967), pp. 141–209; and Joel Kovel, *White Racism: A Psychohistory* (New York: Random House, 1970), pp. 51–92.

11. Daniel Aaron, *The Unwritten War: American Writers and the Civil War* (New York: Oxford University Press, 1973), pp. xviii, 333. For discussions of black or mulatto characters in American literature since the Civil War from various points of view, see Nancy M. Tischler, *Black Masks: Negro Characters in Modern Southern Fiction* (University Park: Pennsylvania State University Press, 1969); Judith R. Berzon, *Neither White Nor Black: The Mulatto Character in*

American Fiction (New York: New York University Press, 1978); and John G. Mencke, *Mulattoes and Race Mixture: American Attitudes and Images, 1865–1918* (Ann Arbor, Mich.: UMI Research Press, 1979), pp. 141–232.

12. *The Sound and the Fury,* p. 106.

13. Gwynn and Blotner, eds., *Faulkner in the University,* p. 72.

14. Ralph Ellison, "Change the Joke and Slip the Yoke," in *Shadow and Act,* pp. 55–56.

15. Kenneth M. Stampp, *The Peculiar Institution: Slavery in the Ante-Bellum South* (New York: Vintage-Random, 1956), p. vii.

16. Gwynn and Blotner, eds., *Faulkner in the University,* p. 211.

17. For an account of the case and context of *Plessy* v. *Ferguson,* which was carefully engineered by Albion Tourgée and Homer Plessy to test the constitutionality of Jim Crow laws, see C. Vann Woodward, "The National Decision Against Equality," in *American Counterpoint: Slavery and Racism in the North-South Dialogue* (Boston: Little, Brown, 1971), pp. 212–33. The best general study of the transformation in both white and black attitudes toward mulattoes between the Civil War and the Jim Crow era is Joel Williamson's *New People: Miscegenation and Mulattoes in the United States* (New York: The Free Press, 1980). Williamson argues that "essentially, what happened in the changeover was that the dominant white society moved from semiacceptance of free mulattoes, especially in the lower South, to outright rejection. As mulatto communities in the 1850s confronted an increasingly hostile white world implementing increasingly stringent rules against them in the form either of laws or of social pressures, they themselves moved from a position of basic sympathy with the white world to one of guarded antagonism. In the movement the mulatto elite gave up white alliances and picked up black alliances. The change accelerated in the Civil War, took its set during the critical year 1865, and continued through Reconstruction, post-Reconstruction, and into the twentieth century. By the end of the period, roughly in the two decades between 1905 and 1925, mulattoes led by the mulatto elite had allied themselves rather totally with the black world. Meanwhile the white world had arrived at an almost total commitment to the one-drop rule. In white eyes, all Negroes came to look alike" (pp. 61–186; quote at p. 62).

18. Gwynn and Blotner, eds., *Faulkner in the University,* pp. 209–10; e.g., Meriwether and Millgate, eds., *Lion in the Garden,* p. 143.

19. Mark Twain, *Pudd'nhead Wilson* and *Those Extraordinary Twins* (Baltimore: Penguin Books, 1969), pp. 56, 208, 59.

20. Ibid., pp. 229, 157–58. Myra Jehlen has also noted the resemblances between *Light in August* and *Pudd'nhead Wilson,* and here, as elsewhere in her revealing discussions of Faulkner's racism, speaks pointedly to the issue. Twain, Faulkner, and others "who have written about mulattoes who pass for white only to have their black selves emerge in the end," she remarks, betray an aversion to true equality such "that even when blacks look equal, i.e., white, they are really black, meaning other, different, and inferior. Finally the mulatto theme does not speak to the problem of individual identity in a racially divided society, but, quite the contrary, implicitly denies the individualism of its black protagonists." The question Jehlen rightly begs in raising is one that Twain and Faulkner had no clear answer to. See *Class and Character in Faulkner's South* (New York: Columbia University Press, 1976), pp. 81–84.

21. *Light in August* (New York: Modern Library, 1968), pp. 424–25. Faulkner would later call Stevens's theory "an assumption, a rationalization." See Gwynn and Blotner, eds., *Faulkner in the University,* p. 72.

22. Twain, *Pudd'nhead Wilson,* p. 64.

23. *Light in August,* pp. 184, 241, 195 — second ellipsis Faulkner's.

24. James Weldon Johnson, *The Autobiography of an Ex-Coloured Man* (New York: Alfred A. Knopf, 1927), p. 21.

25. Kenneth Burke, *A Rhetoric of Motives,* quoted in Joseph Skerrett, "Irony and Symbolic Action in James Weldon Johnson's *The Autobiography of an Ex-Coloured Man,*" *American Quarterly* 32, no. 5 (Winter 1980): 558. On Johnson's incest novel, see Skerrett, p. 550. On Dixon's novel, also published in 1912, see pp. 143–44 below.

26. Irving Howe, *William Faulkner: A Critical Study*, 2nd ed. rev. (New York: Vintage-Random, 1960), p. 65.

27. *Light in August*, pp. 321, 326, 331.

28. The best considerations of the novel's form along these lines are Donald M. Kartiganer, *The Fragile Thread: The Meaning of Form in Faulkner's Novels* (Amherst: University of Massachusetts Press, 1979), pp. 37–68; and Alfred Kazin, "The Stillness of *Light in August*," in Frederick J. Hoffman and Olga W. Vickery, eds., *William Faulkner: Three Decades of Criticism* (New York: Harcourt, Brace & World, 1963), pp. 247–65.

29. *Selected Letters*, p. 66.

30. Malcolm Cowley, *The Faulkner-Cowley File: Letters and Memories, 1944–1962* (1966; reprint ed., Baltimore: Viking-Penguin, 1978), pp. 28–29.

31. Cleanth Brooks, *William Faulkner: The Yoknapatawpha Country* (New Haven: Yale University Press, 1963), p. 54.

32. *Light in August*, pp. 376, 388 — ellipsis Faulkner's.

33. Walter White, *Rope and Faggot: A Biography of Judge Lynch* (New York: Alfred A. Knopf, 1929), pp. 69–75. This would seem far-fetched if the official United States census for 1930 had not itself carried the following instructions: "A person of mixed white and Negro blood should be returned as a Negro, no matter how small the percentage of Negro blood." See Woodward, *American Counterpoint*, p. 86.

34. Howe, *William Faulkner: A Critical Study*, p. 129.

35. Brooks, *William Faulkner: The Yoknapatawpha Country*, pp. 51–52, 60–62.

36. White, *Rope and Faggot*, pp. 54–55.

37. *Light in August*, p. 439.

38. For the best discussion of this problem, see Carolyn Porter, "The Problem of Time in *Light in August*," *Rice University Studies* 61, no. 1 (Winter 1975): 107–25.

39. In this regard Wright Morris is correct to point out that, although she is "the great mother, the abiding earth, the patient and enduring force of life," it is the reciprocally "surrounding tension and incipient violence that give Lena Grove such serenity, and *Light in August* a ballast, an emotional stability, almost unique in the works of Faulkner." See *The Territory Ahead*, p. 181.

40. *Light in August*, pp. 330, 6.

41. Gwynn and Blotner, eds., *Faulkner in the University*, p. 77.

42. W. J. Cash, *The Mind of the South* (1941; reprint ed., New York: Vintage-Random, 1960), p. 51.

43. Charles Carroll further maintained, for example, that at the time of the Flood, Noah and his wife were the only pure whites left on the earth; unfortunately, there was a pair of Negroes among the beasts on the Ark, and amalgamation began again soon after the Flood. Christ was then sent to "redeem man from atheism, amalgamation, and idolatry" and "to rebuild the barriers which God erected in the Creation between man and the ape." Miscegenation, Carroll argued (and here he was more in line with some more rational antebellum abolitionists), was the reason for God's destruction of slavery; but he concluded from this that the "cursed" and "degenerate" mulattoes descended from these and more recent couplings had no right to live. See I. A. Newby, *Jim Crow's Defense: Anti-Negro Thought in America, 1900–1930* (Baton Rouge: Louisiana State University Press, 1965), pp. 92–98; and George M. Fredrickson, *The Black Image in the White Mind: The Debate on Afro-American Character and Destiny, 1817–1914* (New York: Harper & Row, 1971), p. 277.

44. *Light in August*, pp. 120, 159, 189, 173–74, 146–47.

45. René Girard, *Violence and the Sacred*, trans. Patrick Gregory (Baltimore: Johns Hopkins University Press, 1977), pp. 34–36.

46. *Light in August*, pp. 32, 271–72.

47. On this problem in particular and the attitudes and theories that produced it, see Cash, *Mind of the South*, pp. 85–89, 117–20; White, *Rope and Faggot*, pp. 54–81; Newby, *Jim Crow's Defense*, pp. 122–40; Claude H. Nolen, *The Negro's Image in the South: The Anatomy of White Supremacy* (Lexington: University of Kentucky Press, 1967), pp. 29–39; Forrest G. Wood, *Black Scare: The*

Racist Response to Emancipation and Reconstruction (Berkeley and Los Angeles: University of California Press, 1967), pp. 143–53; Lawrence J. Friedman, *The White Savage: Racial Fantasies in the Postbellum South* (Englewood Cliffs, N.J.: Prentice-Hall, 1970), pp. 140–68; and Fredrickson, *The Black Image in the White Mind*, pp. 256–88.

48. Thomas Dixon, *The Clansman: An Historical Romance of the Ku Klux Klan* (Ridgewood, N.J.: Gregg Press, 1967), pp. 304–8. Throughout his life Faulkner owned a copy of the novel that had been presented to him by his first-grade teacher in 1905. See Blotner, *Faulkner: A Biography,* 1:94.

49. William Hannibal Thomas, *The American Negro: What He Was, What He Is, What He May Become* (New York: Macmillan, 1901), pp. v, 180, 182.

50. Thomas Nelson Page, *The Negro: The Southerner's Problem* (New York: Charles Scribner's Sons, 1904), pp. 80–85, 99–100, 112–13.

51. Thomas, *American Negro,* pp. 407, 411.

52. James D. Sayers, *Can the White Race Survive?* (Washington, D.C.: Independent Publishing Co., 1929), pp. 11, 171.

53. See Arthur F. Raper, *The Tragedy of Lynching* (Chapel Hill: University of North Carolina Press, 1933), p. 20.

54. Frederick Douglass, "The Color Line" (1881), in *The Life and Writings of Frederick Douglass,* ed. Philip S. Foner, 4 vols. (New York: International Publishers, 1955), 4:343. In "Why Is the Negro Lynched?" (1894), Douglass noted that from Reconstruction through the early 1890s, the South employed on behalf of lynching an "orderly arrangement" of excuses that "show design, plan, purpose and invention." As the old lies of insurrection and Negro supremacy lost their ability to deceive, Douglass wrote, the "heart-rending cry of the white women and little white children" took their place. See pp. 491–523.

55. Thomas Dixon, *The Leopard's Spots: A Romance of the White Man's Burden, 1865–1900* (Ridgewood, N.J.: Gregg Press, 1967), pp. x, 336, 463–64, 5.

56. *Light in August,* pp. 107, 245.

57. See *Collected Stories of William Faulkner* (New York: Random House, 1950), pp. 169–83. Unlike *Light in August,* the crisp power of "Dry September" derives from Faulkner's not depicting the "attack" or the lynching but dwelling instead on the surrounding actions. The last image we get of Minnie Cooper, who had attended a motion picture while her accused attacker is being beaten or killed, is particularly revealing: "They removed the pink voile and the sheer underthings and the stockings, and put her to bed, and cracked ice for her temples, and sent for the doctor. He was hard to locate, so they ministered to her with hushed ejaculations, renewing the ice and fanning her. While the ice was fresh and cold she stopped laughing and lay still for a time, moaning only a little. But soon the laughing welled again and her voice rose screaming. . . . 'Do you suppose anything really happened?' [they said,] their eyes darkly aglitter, secret and passionate. 'Shhhhhhh! Poor girl! Poor Minnie!'" As Walter White remarked, "the Southern white woman's proneness to hysteria where Negroes are concerned . . . needs investigation by a competent psychologist" (*Rope and Faggot,* p. 57).

58. Johnson, *Autobiography of an Ex-Coloured Man,* p. 75.

59. *Light in August,* p. 212.

60. Howe, *William Faulkner: A Critical Study,* p. 69.

61. *Light in August,* pp. 99, 242, 246, 248, 255, 313, 440, 264, 251.

62. Maxwell Geismar, *Writers in Crisis: The American Novel, 1925–40* (1947; reprint ed., New York: E. P. Dutton, 1971), pp. 164–68. The same half twist of logic that makes Geismar's argument useful also betrays him in his further insistence that Christmas is "the 'emancipated' new negro, who must be punished with all the devices of Faulkner's hatred." Because the pair "symbolize for Faulkner all the evils which have befallen his land," Geismar remarks, "what better expression of his scorn can the southern writer produce than to have the sterile female accept the emancipated negro as her sexual partner, to have her humiliated by the negro, and to have her murdered by the negro" (p. 174).

63. *The Portable Thomas Jefferson,* ed. Merrill D. Peterson (New York: Viking Press, 1975), pp. 193, 186–87.

64. Winthrop Jordan, *White over Black: American Attitudes Toward the Negro, 1550–1812* (1968;

reprint ed., New York: W. W. Norton, 1977), pp. 458–59. On this aspect of Jefferson's thought and life in general, see pp. 457–99; and John C. Miller, *The Wolf by the Ears: Thomas Jefferson and Slavery* (New York: The Free Press, 1977). The evidence for Jefferson's fathering of mulatto children has been widely disputed and is not conclusive.

65. *Portable Thomas Jefferson*, p. 187.

66. Richard Wright, *Native Son* (New York: Harper & Row, 1966), pp. 260, 261, 123, 376, 214.

67. Ibid., pp. 376, 23. Cf. *Light in August*, pp. 97, 110, 256, 261.

68. *Light in August*, p. 85.

69. Overshadowed by *The Narrative of A. Gordon Pym*, the peculiarly Southern dimensions of several of Poe's stories is often overlooked. The most relevant passage in "The Murders in the Rue Morgue" runs as follows:

> As the sailor looked in, the gigantic animal had seized Madame L'Espanaye by the hair (which was loose, as she had been combing it), and was flourishing the razor about her face, in imitation of the motions of a barber. The daughter lay prostrate and motionless; she had swooned. The screams and struggles of the old lady (during which the hair was torn from her head) had the effect of changing the probably pacific purposes of the Ourang-Outang into those of wrath. With one determined sweep of its muscular arm it nearly severed her head from her body. The sight of blood inflamed its anger into phrensy. Gnashing its teeth, and flashing fire from its eyes, it flew upon the body of the girl, and imbedded its fearful talons in her throat, retaining its grasp until she expired. Its wandering and wild glances fell at this moment upon the head of the bed, over which the face of its master, rigid with horror, was just discernible. The fury of the beast, who no doubt still bore in mind the dreaded whip, was instantly converted into fear. Conscious of having deserved punishment, it seemed desirous of concealing its bloody deeds, and skipped about the chamber in an agony of nervous agitation; throwing down and breaking the furniture as it moved, and dragging the bed from the bedstead. In conclusion, it seized first the corpse of the daughter, and thrust it up the chimney, as it was found; then that of the old lady, which it immediately hurled through the window headlong.

See *The Complete Tales and Poems of Edgar Allan Poe* (New York: Modern Library, 1938), p. 167. Poe's representation of the murderous ape, as well as Dupin's procedure of capturing him by placing an ad in the newspaper, is reenforced by the perhaps typical example of an ad for a runaway slave placed in the *South-Carolina Gazette* of 1734: "Whereas a stately *Baboon* hath lately slipp'd his Colar and run away; He is big-bon'd full of flesh, and has learn'd to walk very erect on his two Hind-Legs, he grins and chatters much, but will not bite, he plays Tricks impudently well, and is mightily given to clambering, whereby he often shews his A — — —. If any one finds him. . . ." Quoted in Jordan, *White over Black*, p. 238.

70. Blotner, *Faulkner: A Biography*, 1:113–14.

71. Olga Vickery remarks that the razor and revolver are "phantom weapons directed at phantom opponents. For each sees embodied in the other that racial myth which has dominated their lives and which they must destroy if they are to be free." There remains, of course, some question about the degree of freedom achieved. See *The Novels of William Faulkner: A Critical Interpretation* (Baton Rouge: Louisiana State University Press), p. 72.

72. *Light in August*, pp. 173, 239. Joanna reports moreover that her father had told her that "the curse of the black race is God's curse. But the curse of the white race is the black man who will be forever God's chosen own because He once cursed Him" (p. 240), a passage that only makes sense if we think ahead to *Go Down, Moses* and read "Ham" (the supposed biblical progenitor of the African races) for "Him." See *Selected Letters*, p. 374.

73. "The Confessions of Nat Turner," reprinted in Herbert Aptheker, *Nat Turner's Slave Rebellion* (New York: Humanities Press, 1966), pp. 136–38.

74. William Styron, *The Confessions of Nat Turner* (New York: Signet-Random, 1968), pp. 349, 255–56.

75. James Baldwin, "Many Thousands Gone," in *Notes of a Native Son* (1955; reprint ed., New York: Bantam, 1964), p. 29.

76. Meriwether and Millgate, eds., *Lion in the Garden*, pp. 206–7.

77. Richard Chase, *The American Novel and Its Tradition* (1957; reprint ed., Baltimore: Johns

Hopkins University Press), p. 214; Geismar, *Writers in Crisis,* p. 144; Alfred Kazin, "The Stillness of *Light in August,"* in *William Faulkner: Three Decades of Criticism,* p. 253.

78. W.E.B. Du Bois, *The Souls of Black Folk* (New York: Fawcett World, 1967), p. 23.

79. Kartiganer, *Fragile Thread,* pp. 37, 68.

80. *Light in August,* pp. 419, 438, 425, 439–40.

81. Gwynn and Blotner, eds., *Faulkner in the University,* p. 117.

82. Harriet Beecher Stowe, *Uncle Tom's Cabin* (New York: Collier Books, 1962), pp. 506, 325.

83. James Baldwin, "Everybody's Protest Novel," in *Notes of a Native Son,* pp. 10, 13, 17. Faulkner's opinion of Stowe's novel was more generously mixed: "I would say that *Uncle Tom's Cabin* was written out of violent and misdirected compassion and ignorance of the author toward a situation which she knew only by hearsay. But it was not an intellectual process, it was hotter than that; it was out of her heart." See Joseph L. Fant III and Robert Ashley, eds., *Faulkner at West Point* (New York: Random House, 1964), p. 104. On the intellectual climate of which Stowe was a part see Fredrickson, "Uncle Tom and the Anglo-Saxons: Romantic Racialism in the North," *The Black Image in the White Mind,* pp. 97–129.

84. White, *Rope and Faggot,* p. 57. Twain had reached a similar conclusion when he wrote in "The United States of Lyncherdom" (1901) that, because "communities as well as individuals are imitators," lynchers are themselves the worst enemies of their women. As each Negro crime begets others, Twain believed, so each lynching begets other crimes and other lynchings, eventually breeding "a mania . . . a fashion which will spread wider and wider, year by year, covering state after state, as with an advancing disease." See *The Portable Mark Twain,* ed. Bernard DeVoto (New York: Viking Press, 1968), p. 586.

85. Cowley, *Faulkner-Cowley File,* p. 32.

86. The most important and debated is that of Stanley M. Elkins, *Slavery: A Problem in American Institutional and Intellectual Life,* 3rd ed. rev. (Chicago: University of Chicago Press, 1976), pp. 103–39, 242–53. Geismar (*Writers in Crisis,* pp. 181–82) invokes the analogy and extends his attack on Faulkner's Negro-Female obsession by asserting, strangely enough, that Faulkner's "infantile preoccupation with scapegoats" diverts attention away from the "genuine ills" of society. But compare Fanon's claim that "the scapegoat for white society — which is based on myths of progress, civilization, liberalism, education, enlightenment, refinement — will be precisely the force that opposes the expansion and the triumph of those myths. This brutal opposing force is supplied by the Negro" (*Black Skin, White Masks,* p. 194).

87. Girard, *Violence and the Sacred,* pp. 81, 271. Cf. Girard's observation that masks, because they do not efface differences but rather "incorporate and rearrange them," are "another aspect of the monstrous double" and thus stand "at that equivocal frontier between the human and the 'divine,' between a differentiated order in the process of disintegration and its final undifferentiated state — the point where all differences, all monstrosities are concentrated, and from which a new order will emerge" (pp. 167–68).

88. Blotner, *Faulkner: A Biography,* 1:113–14, 189–90, 301, 601, 880; 2:1246.

89. *Light in August,* pp. 421, 437, 280.

90. Twain, *Pudd'nhead Wilson,* pp. 103, 303, 117.

CHAPTER 5

1. Harriet Beecher Stowe, *Dred: A Tale of the Great Dismal Swamp* (London: Sampson Low, Son, 1856), p. 30.

2. Ibid., pp. 124, 54. For a reading of Stowe's novels and others dealing with black characters before the Civil War, see Jean Fagan Yellin, *The Intricate Knot: Black Figures in American Literature, 1776–1863* (New York: New York University Press, 1972).

3. For accounts of slaveholding miscegenation see Kenneth M. Stampp, *The Peculiar Institution: Slavery in the Ante-Bellum South* (New York: Vintage-Random, 1956), pp. 350–61; Winthrop Jordan, *White over Black: American Attitudes Toward the Negro, 1550–1812* (1968; reprint ed., New

York: W. W. Norton, 1977), pp. 136–78, 578–82; Eugene D. Genovese, *Roll, Jordan, Roll: The World the Slaves Made* (New York: Random House, 1974), pp. 413–31; and Joel Williamson, *New People: Miscegenation and Mulattoes in the United States* (New York: The Free Press, 1980), pp. 42–91.

4. Legree, it was claimed, was not a "father" to his slaves; as Mary Chesnut put it in her diary, however, "Mrs. Stowe did not hit the sorest spot. She makes Legree a bachelor." See C. Vann Woodward, ed., *Mary Chesnut's Civil War* (New Haven: Yale University Press, 1981), p. 168.

5. George B. Forgie, *Patricide in the House Divided: A Psychological Interpretation of Lincoln and His Age* (New York: W. W. Norton, 1979), pp. 184–85. Forgie's general argument that the American Revolution issued in fraternal rivalries between individuals and groups that were both devoted to, and recoiled from, the paternal authority of the founding fathers is continually relevant at different levels to the familial-social conflicts engaged by *Absalom, Absalom!*

6. *Absalom, Absalom!* (New York: Vintage-Random, 1972), pp. 267, 271, 274.

7. W. J. Cash, *The Mind of the South* (1941; reprint ed., Vintage-Random, 1960), p. 71.

8. Eugene D. Genovese, *The World the Slaveholders Made: Two Essays in Interpretation* (1969; reprint ed., New York: Vintage-Random, 1971), p. 140. As Genovese goes on to point out, Cash "identifies as aristocracies only those classes exhibiting the grace and *noblesse oblige* of fourth- or fifth-generation gentlemen. There is some advantage to this viewpoint, which Cash uses to devastating effect against attempts to romanticize the antebellum planters, but for the most part it represents a secondary line of criticism. All ruling classes have been, by definition, acquisitive, and therefore their origins have been violent and ugly; the first and second generations have naturally borne the marks of their origin, and in a frontier country so may have later generations. The juxtaposition of elegance and vulgarity existed in [Southern slaveholding] society as a whole and could easily have been reflected within any given family" (p. 141). See also Woodward, "The Southern Ethic in a Puritan World," *American Counterpoint: Slavery and Racism in the North-South Dialogue* (Boston: Little, Brown, 1971), pp. 13–46. For extended considerations of Sutpen as a typical planter, see Melvin Backman, *Faulkner: The Major Years* (Bloomington: Indiana University Press, 1977), pp. 88–112; Cleanth Brooks, *William Faulkner: Toward Yoknapatawpha and Beyond* (New Haven: Yale University Press, 1978), pp. 283–300; and particularly the fine discussion by Carolyn Porter, *Seeing and Being: The Plight of the Participant Observer in Emerson, James, Adams, and Faulkner* (Middletown, Conn.: Wesleyan University Press, 1981), pp. 207–40.

9. Cash, *Mind of the South*, p. 127.

10. *Absalom, Absalom!*, pp. 250–51.

11. Philip Van Doren Stern, ed., *The Life and Writings of Abraham Lincoln* (New York: Modern Library, 1940), pp. 421–22, 425. An excellent account of ambivalent abolitionist views of the South as an arena of sexual dissipation may be found in Ronald G. Walters, *The Antislavery Appeal: American Abolitionism after 1830* (Baltimore: Johns Hopkins University Press, 1976), pp. 70–87; cf. George M. Fredrickson, *The Black Image in the White Mind: The Debate on Afro-American Character and Destiny, 1817–1914* (New York: Harper & Row, 1971), pp. 97–129. Lincoln's own ambivalence even made it possible years later for Thomas Dixon, ironically enough, to represent him in *The Clansman* as the true friend of the defeated South: "I have urged the colonisation of the negroes, and I shall continue until it is accomplished. My emancipation proclamation was linked with this plan. . . . I can conceive of no greater calamity than the assimilation of the Negro into our social and political life as our equal. A mulatto citizenship would be too dear a price to pay even for emancipation. . . . It was the fear of the black tragedy behind emancipation that led the South into the insanity of secession. We can never attain the ideal Union our fathers dreamed, with millions of an alien, inferior race among us, whose assimilation is neither possible nor desirable. The Nation cannot now exist half white and half black, any more than it could exist half slave and half free" (pp. 46–47). The further irony, of course, is that Dixon's Lincoln is not far from the real one.

12. Stern, ed., *Life and Writings of Abraham Lincoln*, pp. 425–27.

13. Forgie, *Patricide in the House Divided*, pp. 123–58, 243–81.

14. Stern, ed., *Life and Writings of Abraham Lincoln*, pp. 654, 657, 684.

15. Ibid., pp. 429, 439. For a detailed reading of the House Divided speech, see Don E.

Fehrenbacher, *Prelude to Greatness: Lincoln in the 1850s* (Stanford: Stanford University Press, 1962), pp. 70–95.

16. Forgie, *Patricide in the House Divided,* pp. 268, 280. On Lincoln's self-conscious role as savior of the House, see also Michael Paul Rogin, "The King's Two Bodies: Lincoln, Wilson, Nixon, and Presidential Self-Sacrifice," in J. David Greenstone, ed., *Public Values and Private Power in American Politics* (Chicago: University of Chicago Press, 1982), pp. 71–107.

17. C. Vann Woodward, "The Northern Crusade Against Slavery," in *American Counterpoint,* pp. 140–62; quote on p. 162. See also Fredrickson, *Black Image in the White Mind,* pp. 130–64, and, on Lincoln in particular, Don E. Fehrenbacher, "Only His Stepchildren: Lincoln and the Negro," in George M. Fredrickson, ed., *A Nation Divided: Problems and Issues of the Civil War and Reconstruction* (Minneapolis, Minn.: Burgess, 1975), pp. 35–55, and Kenneth Stampp, "Race, Slavery, and the Republican Party of the 1850s," in *The Imperiled Union: Essays on the Background of the Civil War* (New York: Oxford University Press, 1980), pp. 105–35.

18. Frederick L. Gwynn and Joseph L. Blotner, eds., *Faulkner in the University: Class Conferences at the University of Virginia, 1957–1958* (1959; reprint ed., New York: Vintage-Random, 1965), pp. 216, 210, 209.

19. *Absalom, Absalom!,* p. 220.

20. C. Vann Woodward, *The Burden of Southern History,* rev. ed. (Baton Rouge: Louisiana State University Press, 1968), pp. 20–21.

21. *Absalom, Absalom!,* p. 145.

22. On "Miscegenation" and the aspects of the 1864 campaign that follow, see Forrest G. Wood, *Black Scare: The Racist Response to Emancipation and Reconstruction* (Berkeley and Los Angeles: University of California Press, 1970), pp. 53–79 and plates 1–5.

23. J. H. van Evrie, *White Supremacy and Negro Subordination* (New York: Van Evrie, Horton, 1868), pp. 151, 157, 167.

24. Margaret Mitchell, *Gone with the Wind* (New York: Avon Books, 1973), pp. 647, 640.

25. Woodward, ed., *Mary Chesnut's Civil War,* p. 29.

26. van Evrie, *White Supremacy and Negro Subordination,* pp. 152, 201.

27. Ibid., pp. 144–45, 153–55. For Sherwood Anderson's assertion that Faulkner himself once claimed miscegenation would lead, in human beings as in mules, to sterility, see Joseph Blotner, *Faulkner: A Biography,* 2 vols. (New York: Random House, 1974), 1:498–99. There is less doubt, however, that Faulkner considered miscegenation part of the South's doom and curse for its sins.

28. *Absalom, Absalom!,* p. 378.

29. van Evrie, *White Supremacy and Negro Subordination,* pp. 233–44.

30. For an interesting account of the critical and popular receptions of both novels, see James W. Mathews, "The Civil War of 1936: *Gone with the Wind* and *Absalom, Absalom!,*" *Georgia Review* 21, no. 4 (Winter 1967): 462–69.

31. Henry Hughes, *Treatise on Sociology, Theoretical and Practical* (Philadelphia: Lippincott, Grambo, and Co., 1854), p. 31.

32. James B. Meriwether and Michael Millgate, eds., *Lion in the Garden: Interviews with William Faulkner, 1926–1962* (1968; reprint ed., Lincoln: University of Nebraska Press, 1980), p. 34; Gwynn and Blotner, eds., *Faulkner in the University,* p. 249. Faulkner articulated his point more clearly in *Requiem for a Nun* (New York: Vintage-Random, 1975) when he spoke of "the spinsters, maiden and childless out of a time when there were too many women because too many of the young men were maimed or dead: the indomitable and undefeated, maiden progenistresses of spinster and childless descendants still capable of rising up and stalking out in the middle of *Gone with the Wind*" (p. 220).

33. *Absalom, Absalom!,* pp. 7, 61, 171, 180.

34. Ibid., pp. 146–48, 350. It is not entirely clear whether Rosa's monologue (chapter five) is delivered in the afternoon, and thus continues from chapter one, or at night when she and Quentin ride out to Sutpen's Hundred. In any event, it is clear that Quentin's conversations with his father are divided by the visit to Sutpen's Hundred (and his purported discovery of the crucial information about Bon) and that the chronology of the first five chapters is thus, more or less,

one, two, four, five, three. With respect to the later chapters, it should also be recalled, from *The Sound and the Fury,* that Quentin goes home at Christmas, 1909, and for Caddy's wedding in April 1910. Among the numerous investigations of the novel's narrative confusions, the most useful are the two by Cleanth Brooks, *William Faulkner: The Yoknapatawpha Country* (New Haven: Yale University Press, 1963), pp. 295–324, 429–41; and *William Faulkner: Toward Yoknapatawpha and Beyond,* pp. 301–28.

35. *Absalom, Absalom!,* pp. 137–40, 155–56.

36. Jordan, *White over Black,* pp. 178, 149. Cf. Oscar Handlin, *Race and Nationality in American Life* (Boston: Little, Brown, 1957), pp. 155: "And the ladies in crinoline, for whom love was a tender, ethereal moment, with what pain they closed their thoughts to the fears of temptation that encompassed their husbands. And what slow, burning resentment they attached to the sources of that temptation, and to the 'mongrels' of every shade who were evidence of a yielding."

37. *Absalom, Absalom!,* pp. 145, 142, 136, 143.

38. Ibid., pp. 149, 77, 80.

39. Frederick Douglass, *Narrative of the Life of Frederick Douglass* (New York: Signet Books, 1968), p. 23.

40. Gwynn and Blotner, eds., *Faulkner in the University,* p. 73.

41. Cash, *Mind of the South,* pp. 386–87.

42. Irwin's interpretation of the relationship between the two novels and their characters is essentially an Oedipal one; rather than make my debt to it cumbersome by constant reference, let me quote at length several passages that seem to contain the crucial points of his reading:

> That Quentin identifies with both Henry, the brother as protector, and with Bon, the brother as seducer, is not extraordinary, for in Quentin's narrative they are not so much two separate figures as two aspects of the same figure. Quentin projects onto the characters of Bon and Henry opposing elements in his own personality — Bon represents Quentin's unconsciously motivated desire for his sister Candace, while Henry represents the conscious repression or punishment of that desire.

> The brother avenger and the brother seducer are [moreover] substitutes for the father and the son in the Oedipal triangle. . . . Thus, when Henry kills Bon he is the father-surrogate killing the son, but since Henry, like Bon, is also in love with their sister Judith, he is as well the younger brother (son) killing the older brother who symbolizes the father, the father who is the rival for the mother and who punishes incest between brother and sister, son and mother.

> Since the relationship between the brother avenger and the brother seducer is a substitute for the father-son relationship in the Oedipal triangle, it is not surprising that when Quentin and Shreve identify with Henry and Bon, the narration turns into a father-son dialogue. . . . This basic interchangeability of the roles of father and son is present in both the [fantasy of a reversal of generations] and the incest complex, and it is internalized in the father-son relationship of the roles of the superego and the ego within the self.

See *Doubling and Incest, Repetition and Revenge: A Speculative Reading of Faulkner* (Baltimore: Johns Hopkins University Press), pp. 28, 118, 77. As indicated in chapter one, note 26, a treatment of this theme that expands upon Irwin's account may be found in Richard H. King, *A Southern Renaissance: The Cultural Awakening of the American South, 1930–1955* (New York: Oxford University Press, 1980), pp. 112–29.

43. *Absalom, Absalom!,* pp. 36, 13, 263, 77, 107.

44. Hyatt H. Waggoner, *William Faulkner: From Jefferson to the World* (Lexington: University of Kentucky Press, 1959), p. 150.

45. *Absalom, Absalom!,* p. 96.

46. Ibid., pp. 104, 100–101, 117–18. On the New Orleans *plaçage,* see John W. Blassingame, *Black New Orleans, 1860–1880* (Chicago: University of Chicago Press, 1973), pp. 17–20, 210–19.

47. *Absalom, Absalom!,* pp. 294, 316.

48. Ibid., p. 316. For an important and innovative reading of this scene and the marriage figure as it defines the articulation of desire and consecration throughout Faulkner's narrative,

see John T. Matthews, "The Marriage of Speaking and Hearing in *Absalom, Absalom!*" *ELH* 47, no. 3 (Fall 1980): 575-94.

49. *Absalom, Absalom!*, p. 336. Given the "monstrous" nature of miscegenation, deriving to such an extent from prevailing views of the Negro as simian "beast," the pun on "ape" is ironically to the point.

50. Leslie Fiedler, *Love and Death in the American Novel*, rev. ed. (New York: Dell, 1966), p. 414.

51. *Absalom, Absalom!*, p. 358.

52. Gwynn and Blotner, eds., *Faulkner in the University*, p. 275; *Absalom, Absalom!*, p. 11.

53. *Absalom, Absalom!*, p. 163.

54. Faulkner, "An Introduction for *The Sound and the Fury*," pp. 708-9. For another reading of the introduction in the context of the problem of repetition, see Irwin, *Doubling and Incest, Repetition and Revenge*, pp. 169-72. Readings of the novel that variously emphasize the convergence of Faulkner's design and that of Sutpen include James Guetti, *The Limits of Metaphor: A Study of Melville, Conrad, and Faulkner* (Ithaca: Cornell University Press, 1967), pp. 82-107; David L. Minter, *The Interpreted Design as a Structural Principle in American Prose* (New Haven: Yale University Press, 1969), pp. 191-219, and *William Faulkner: His Life and Work* (Baltimore: Johns Hopkins University Press, 1980), pp. 153-60; Gary Lee Stonum, *Faulkner's Career: An Internal Literary History* (Ithaca: Cornell University Press, 1979), pp. 123-52; and Donald M. Kartiganer, *The Fragile Thread: The Meaning of Form in Faulkner's Novels* (Amherst: University of Massachusetts Press, 1979), pp. 96-102.

55. Faulkner, "An Introduction for *The Sound and the Fury*," p. 709; *Absalom, Absalom!*, p. 150.

56. Gwynn and Blotner, eds., *Faulkner in the University*, p. 35. Although the Oedipus cycle and *Agamemnon* contain readily obvious analogues to Faulkner's drama, a full explication of revenge and reciprocal action, and particularly the motifs of incest and twinship, require reference to the rest of the Oresteian trilogy (*The Choepheri* and *The Eumenides*) and to Euripides' *Iphigenia in Tauris*.

57. René Girard, *Violence and the Sacred*, trans. Patrick Gregory (Baltimore: Johns Hopkins University Press, 1977), pp. 47, 49, 64, 75. Cf. pp. 50-67, 159-63.

58. Genovese, *The World the Slaveholders Made*, pp. 6-7. For a further elaboration of this ambivalence and the crisis it can produce, see Stanley M. Elkins, *Slavery: A Problem in American Institutional and Intellectual Life*, 3rd ed. rev. (Chicago: University of Chicago Press, 1976), pp. 115-33.

59. *Absalom, Absalom!*, p. 62; *The Sound and the Fury*, p. 145.

60. *Great Short Works of Herman Melville*, ed. Warner Berthoff (New York: Harper Perennial, 1969), p. 442.

61. "The Art of Authorship," in *Selected Shorter Writings of Mark Twain*, ed. Walter Blair (Boston: Houghton, Mifflin, 1962), p. 226.

62. *Absalom, Absalom!*, pp. 373, 139, 328, 286, 348, 15.

63. Ibid., pp. 127-28, 348.

64. Cowley, *Faulkner-Cowley File*, p. 79.

65. Kartiganer, *Fragile Thread*, p. 103.

66. *Absalom, Absalom!*, p. 378. Shreve appears to have read *Pudd'nhead Wilson*.

67. George Washington Cable, *The Silent South* (New York: Scribner's, 1885), p. 6.

68. Gwynn and Blotner, eds., *Faulkner in the University*, p. 94.

CHAPTER 6

1. Joseph Blotner, *Faulkner: A Biography*, 2 vols. (New York: Random House, 1974), 2:1055. The story also included a black Ellen Sutpen, a midwife who had delivered Gavin Stevens.

2. On Faulkner's composition of the book, entitled *"Go Down, Moses" and Other Stories* upon first publication, see Blotner, *Faulkner: A Biography*, 2:1040-95, passim; James Early, *The Making of "Go Down, Moses"* (Dallas: Southern Methodist University Press, 1972); and Karl Zender, "Faulkner at Forty: The Artist at Home," *Southern Review* 17, no. 2 (Spring 1981): 288-302. Malcolm Cowley once remarked to Faulkner that, while many authors issued collections of

stories thinly disguised as novels, *Go Down, Moses* was "the only instance on record of a novel that masqueraded as a collection of stories." When he asked about the relationship of "Pantaloon in Black" to the rest of the stories, Faulkner replied that "Rider was one of the McCaslin Negroes." As Cowley adds, "It was no use asking, 'Why didn't you say so?' " See *The Faulkner-Cowley File: Letters and Memories, 1944–1962* (New York: Viking Press, 1966), p. 113. Although my argument will often suggest the contrary, I take the liberty of referring to *Go Down, Moses* as a novel.

3. Herman Melville, *Moby-Dick* (New York: W. W. Norton, 1967), p. 406.

4. James B. Meriwether and Michael Millgate, eds., *Lion in the Garden: Interviews with William Faulkner, 1926–1962* (1968; reprint ed., Lincoln: University of Nebraska Press, 1980), p. 48. Although he named different books at different times, Faulkner remarked on several occasions that his favorite novels were *Moby-Dick* and *The Nigger of the Narcissus* (e.g., Ibid., pp. 17, 21, 60). *Go Down, Moses* seems indeed to fuse their respective themes and powers.

5. *Go Down, Moses* (New York: Modern Library, 1955), pp. 337, 22, 282, 154, 55.

6. Karl E. Zink, "William Faulkner: Form as Experience," *South Atlantic Quarterly* 53 (July 1954): 387.

7. *Go Down, Moses,* pp. 6, 388, 361–62.

8. Michael Millgate, *The Achievement of William Faulkner* (1966; reprint ed., Lincoln: University of Nebrasks Press, 1978), p. 211.

9. *Go Down, Moses,* p. 351; cf. p. 315.

10. Ibid., pp. 257, 259, 300, 168.

11. Ibid., pp. 112, 268, 271, 297.

12. Here and following the quotations from "Ode on a Grecian Urn" refer to Keats, *Selected Poems and Letters,* ed. Douglas Bush (Boston: Houghton, Mifflin, 1959), pp. 207–8.

13. *Go Down, Moses,* pp. 269–70.

14. Ibid., p. 44.

15. Ibid., pp. 297, 240–41.

16. Ibid., pp. 266, 354, 361.

17. On the figure and status of the Negro during the prehistory and early history of America, see Winthrop Jordan, *White over Black: American Attitudes Toward the Negro, 1550–1812* (1968; reprint ed., New York: W. W. Norton, 1977), especially pp. 136–265, 482–582; and David Brion Davis, *The Problem of Slavery in Western Culture* (Ithaca: Cornell University Press, 1966), especially pp. 165–96, 262–88, 446–82. The curse of the sons of Ham — reputedly the African races — derived from Gen. 9:18-27, where Ham, the father of Canaan, looks upon the nakedness of Noah, his father: "Cursed be Canaan; a servant of servants shall he be unto his brethren."

18. *Go Down, Moses,* pp. 181, 164–65, 178.

19. José Ortega y Gasset, *Meditations on Hunting,* trans. Howard B. Wescott (New York: Scribners, 1972), pp. 110–11. See also Ortega's relevant remarks about the mediating function of dogs (p. 92), the mirroring actions of hunter and beast (pp. 59, 111), and the mystical union of their points of view: "The pursuer cannot pursue if he does not integrate his vision with that of the pursued. That is to say, *hunting is an imitation of the animal*" (p. 142).

20. *Go Down, Moses,* pp. 326, 198, 210, 204.

21. Ortega, *Meditations on Hunting,* p. 105.

22. Jordan, *White over Black,* p. 579.

23. Frederick L. Gwynn and Joseph L. Blotner, eds., *Faulkner in the University: Class Conferences at the University of Virginia, 1957–1958* (1959; reprint ed., New York: Vintage-Random, 1965), pp. 39–40.

24. Thomas Dixon, *The Sins of the Father: A Romance of the South* (New York: Grosset & Dunlap, 1912), pp. 25, 37, 43, 137. A further point, which bears on *Absalom, Absalom!* as well as *Go Down, Moses,* is made by Norton's mother-in-law when she explains to her daughter the cursed passions of Southern gentlemen: "And this is one of the reasons, my child, why slavery was doomed. The war was a wicked and awful tragedy. The white motherhood of the South would have crushed slavery. Before the war began we had six hundred thousand mulattoes — six hundred thousand reasons why slavery had to die" (p. 136).

25. *Go Down, Moses,* pp. 171, 256.

26. D. H. Lawrence, *Studies in Classic American Literature* (1923; reprint ed., New York: Viking Press, 1964), pp. 62, 51. For an extended consideration of this theme and the ritual of the hunt in the context of captivity narratives in early American history and mythology, see Richard Slotkin, *Regeneration through Violence: The Mythology of the American Frontier, 1600–1860* (Middletown, Conn.: Wesleyan University Press, 1973), especially pp. 25–179, and the brief sections on slave narratives and racist literature, pp. 440–44, 561–62.

27. R.W.B. Lewis, "William Faulkner: The Hero in the New World," in *Faulkner: A Collection of Critical Essays,* ed. Robert Penn Warren (Englewood Cliffs, N.J.: Prentice-Hall, 1966), p. 209.

28. Jonathan Edwards, *The Injustice and Impolicy of the Slave-Trade and of the Slavery of the Africans,* quoted in Jordan, *White over Black,* pp. 543–44. As Jordan remarks, "a blackened posterity would mean that the basest of energies had guided the direction of the American experiment and that civilized man had turned beast in the forest" and betrayed the very purpose and sanction of his errand into the New World. "Here was the brutally real dilemma: the sin of slavery required the wholesale abandonment of America or loss of original identity; either way it was a failure of mission. Edwards's intense Puritan conception of this mission led him to pose superficially ridiculous alternatives which were actually in the very long run probably the only ones possible."

29. *Go Down, Moses,* p. 259.

30. Ortega, *Meditations on Hunting,* p. 131.

31. William Pratt, ed., *The Fugitive Poets* (New York: E. P. Dutton, 1965), p. 98.

32. See, for example, Cowley, *Faulkner-Cowley File,* p. 98, for Faulkner's 1946 letter: "I missed a beautiful stag last fall. . . . He broke out of a thicket at full speed; I just heard a stick crack and looked around and there he was, running flat like a horse, not jumping at all, about 30 mph, about 100 yards away. He ran in full sight for 50 yards. I think perhaps the first bullet (it was a .270) hit a twig and blew up. But the second shot I missed him clean. He was running too fast for me. He was a beautiful sight. Now it's done, I'm glad his head is still in the woods instead of on a plank on the wall." (In the same letter Faulkner went on to say that he had "become the slave of [a] vast and growing mass of inanimate junk, possessions" that he could not escape.) On the same day, apparently, Faulkner repeated the story of his hunt in a letter to Robert Haas but concluded, "I'm glad now he got away from me though I would have liked his head." See *Selected Letters,* p. 244.

33. *Intruder in the Dust* (New York: Vintage-Random, 1972), p. 154.

34. Mark Twain, *Adventures of Huckleberry Finn* (New York: W. W. Norton, 1977), p. 227.

35. *Intruder in the Dust,* pp. 15, 199.

36. *Go Down, Moses,* pp. 263–65.

37. *Selected Letters,* pp. 122, 124.

38. Elizabeth Hardwick, "Faulkner and the South Today," in Warren, ed., *Faulkner: A Collection of Critical Essays,* p. 230. The most valuable defense of *Intruder in the Dust* against such charges is Cleanth Brooks, *William Faulkner: The Yoknapatawpha Country* (New Haven: Yale University Press, 1963), pp. 279–94.

39. *Go Down, Moses,* p. 371.

40. Ibid., pp. 293, 371.

41. *Intruder in the Dust;* e.g., pp. 26, 27, 28, 30, 31, 34, 38.

42. Irving Howe, *William Faulkner: A Critical Study,* 2nd ed. rev. (New York: Vintage-Random, 1960), p. 95. For a brief reading that deals very capably with this transposition and points at the same time to the "costs of creation" demanded of Faulkner, see Richard H. King, *A Southern Renaissance: The Cultural Awakening of the American South, 1930–1955* (New York: Oxford University Press, 1980), pp. 130–45.

43. *Go Down, Moses,* p. 328.

44. James Weldon Johnson, *The Autobiography of an Ex-Coloured Man* (New York: Alfred A. Knopf, 1927), p. 168.

45. *Requiem for a Nun* (New York: Vintage-Random, 1975), p. 198.

46. *Go Down, Moses,* pp. 87, 47, 55–57.

47. Ibid., pp. 58–59.
48. Ibid., pp. 71, 118, 108, 118.
49. Ibid., p. 281.
50. Minter, *William Faulkner: His Life and Work,* pp. 189–90.
51. *Go Down, Moses,* pp. 111, 115.
52. Ibid., pp. 110, 115.
53. Ibid., p. 363.

Index

The Johns Hopkins University Press

FAULKNER
The House Divided

This book was composed in Baskerville text and Americana
Classic display type by Capitol Communication Systems, Inc.
from a design by Lisa S. Mirski. It was printed on 50-lb.
Glatfelter Offset paper and bound in G.S.B. Natural Finish
cloth by Thomson-Shore, Inc.

DATE DUE

PRINTED IN U.S.A.